SME Policy Index

The Mediterranean Middle East and North Africa 2018

INTERIM ASSESSMENT OF KEY SME REFORMS

This work is published under the responsibility of the Secretary-General of the OECD. The opinions expressed and arguments employed herein do not necessarily reflect the official views of the OECD member countries, the European Commission or the European Training Foundation.

This document, as well as any data and any map included herein, are without prejudice to the status of or sovereignty over any territory, to the delimitation of international frontiers and boundaries and to the name of any territory, city or area.

Please cite this publication as:
OECD/EU/ETF (2018), *The Mediterranean Middle East and North Africa 2018: Interim Assessment of Key SME Reforms*, SME Policy Index, OECD Publishing, Paris.
https://doi.org/10.1787/9789264304161-en

ISBN 978-92-64-30415-4 (print)
ISBN 978-92-64-30416-1 (pdf)
ISBN 978-92-64-30665-3 (HTML)
ISBN 978-92-64-30664-6 (epub)

Series: SME Policy Index
ISSN 2413-6875 (print)
ISSN 2413-6883 (online)

European Union: Catalogue number
EZ-01-18-716-EN-C (Print)
EZ-01-18-716-EN-N (PDF)

ISBN 978-92-79-89117-5 (Print)
ISBN 978-92-79-89114-4 (PDF)

Revised version, November 2018
Details of revisions available at: *http://www.oecd.org/about/publishing/Corrigendum_MediterraneanMiddleEastNorthAfrica2018.pdf*

The statistical data for Israel are supplied by and under the responsibility of the relevant Israeli authorities. The use of such data by the OECD is without prejudice to the status of the Golan Heights, East Jerusalem and Israeli settlements in the West Bank under the terms of international law.

Photo credits: Cover © Andrew Esson/Baseline Arts Ltd.

Corrigenda to OECD publications may be found on line at: *www.oecd.org/publishing/corrigenda*.

Foreword

During the past decades, countries in the Middle East and North Africa have introduced a number of measures and reforms to promote the development of the private sector as a driver of jobs and development. Those reforms have varied in depth and form and have included opening up to trade and investment; improving the regulatory environment for businesses; promoting the development of financial markets; and the enactment of enterprise development policies. MENA countries have also implemented policies to promote the development of entrepreneurship and small businesses in recognition of the significant role those actors can play in the economy.

This report constitutes an interim assessment of the main policy reforms for micro, small and medium-sized enterprises (SMEs) undertaken by Algeria, Egypt, Israel, Jordan, Lebanon, Morocco, the Palestinian Authority (PA) and Tunisia (the MED economies or the MED region), since the publication of the *SME Policy Index for the Mediterranean Middle East and North Africa 2014: Implementation of the Small Business Act for Europe*.

The objective of the report is to inform governments, private sector organisations, social partners, civic interest groups, donors and other stakeholders of the progress in the implementation of the key actions of, and the level of convergence with, the Small Business Act for Europe (SBA). It also aims to sustain the process of regional dialogue among MED economies and the co-operation between the region, the European Union (EU) and the Organisation for Economic Co-operation and Development (OECD).

For the OECD, *PA* is an abbreviation of "Palestinian Authority" and defines either the territories in the West Bank and Gaza under the administration of the Palestinian Authority, or the Palestinian Authority itself, according to the context. For the European Commission and the EU institutions contributing to the report, *PA* stands for "Palestine and its institutions". This designation shall not be construed as recognition of a State of Palestine and is without prejudice to the individual positions of the EU Member States on this issue.

Acknowledgements

This project was funded by the European Commission and supported by the network of Experts on Industrial Co-operation of the Union for the Mediterranean. The project was undertaken in the context of the MENA-OECD Competitiveness Programme, which is supported financially by the Swedish International Development Co-operation Agency (SIDA).

The assessment leading to this report was based on a collaborative and consultative process involving MED governments and public institutions, private sector organisations and civil society. Each of the participating MED economies contributed to the collection of data and information on SME policies under the supervision of a national co-ordinator. The Delegations of the European Union in each MED economy also provided important information.

National co-ordinators were: Abdellah Telailia (Ministry of Industrial Development and Investment Promotion, Algeria); Amr Taha (Industrial Modernisation Centre, Egypt); Nir Ben-Aharon (Ministry of Economy, Israel); Mira Hussein (Jordan Enterprise Development Corporation); Manal Yassine (Ministry of Industry, Lebanon); Abderraouf Aissaoui (Morocco SME, Morocco); Manal Farhan Ibrahim/Shkoukani and Haytham Wahidi (Palestinian Ministry of National Economy and Palestinian Investment Promotion Agency); and Mr Wajdi Neffati (Agency of Industrial Promotion and Innovation, Tunisia).

Useful comments were provided by the EU Delegations in Algeria, Egypt, Israel, Jordan, Lebanon, Morocco, PA and Tunisia. The report was also peer reviewed by Ludovica Agrò (Italian Agency for Territorial Development) and Sadok Bejja (Tunisian Ministry of Industry) in their role as co-chairs of the MENA-OECD Working Group on SME and Entrepreneurship Policy, under the MENA-OECD Competitiveness Programme.

This report was prepared by the Middle East and Africa (MEA) Division of the OECD Global Relations Secretariat and the European Training Foundation (ETF). The OECD team involved in preparing the report included Jorge Galvez Mendez, Pilar Sánchez-Bella, Roger Fores Carrion, Elise Jelsma, Chema Triki and Lucie Kirstein, under the supervision of Carlos Conde, Head of the MEA Division. The ETF team preparing the sections on human capital development included Mariavittoria Garlappi, Anthony Gribben, Olena Bekh, Kristien Van den Eynde and Alice Zanasi. Bill Tompson and Antonio Fanelli from the Global Relations Secretariat provided important comments on the report. Miriam Allam, Kenza Kachani and other colleagues at the Public Governance Directorate of the OECD also provided useful comments.

Table of contents

Foreword ... 3

Acknowledgments ... 5

Scope of the report ... 11

1. The foundations of SME policy: definitions, statistics and institutions ... 12
2. Improving business environments for SMEs and entrepreneurs ... 12
3. Fostering access to finance ... 12
4. Nurturing start-ups and SME growth ... 13
5. Entrepreneurial human capital development ... 13

Notes ... 14

List of Acronyms ... 15

Executive Summary ... 19

Part I. Regional Trends by Policy Area ... 23

Chapter 1. The foundations of SME policy: definitions, statistics, and institutions ... 25

There is plenty of scope for developing clear and consistent SME definitions enshrined in legislation ... 26
Efforts are ongoing to develop comprehensive and accurate statistics, but work is still preliminary. ... 29
Decisive action is still needed to make SME and entrepreneurship policy more coherent and strategic. ... 32
Some public-private dialogue initiatives in the region could be of inspiration for MED peers, yet the voice of SMEs and entrepreneurs through business associations could be enhanced. ... 36
The way forward ... 38
Notes ... 40
Bibliography ... 40

Chapter 2. Improving the business environment for SMEs and entrepreneurs ... 43

Most MED economies have progressed in the implementation of regulatory impact analysis, but the implementation of the SME test is preliminary at best. ... 44
There has been progress in online registration and single identification numbers, but little development of one-stop shops. ... 47
Many MED economies have updated their bankruptcy laws, but the impact will depend on their implementation. ... 49
The way forward ... 51
Notes ... 52
Bibliography ... 53

Chapter 3. Fostering access to finance ... 55

Most MED economies have undertaken important initiatives in the past few years to improve the regulatory framework for access to finance. 57
Many initiatives have been introduced to increase the sources of external finance; however, the state continues to be the main actor – especially in terms of credit guarantee schemes, but also in equity investments. 61
The way forward 63
Bibliography 64

Chapter 4. Nurturing start-ups and SME growth 65

SMEs and entrepreneurs could be better informed on the large and expanding availability of business development services. 68
E-procurement could be further promoted to facilitate the participation of SMEs. 70
Some efforts have been made to promote exports and access to markets, but the links to SME policy remain weak in most cases. 71
The way forward 73
Notes 73
Bibliography 73

Chapter 5. Entrepreneurial human capital development 75

Building entrepreneurship as a key competence is the next challenge for policy makers and schools. 76
Momentum is growing in women's entrepreneurship and requires a comprehensive policy response. 78
Moving SMEs forward in international trade – the case for improved training 80
The way forward 82
Notes 83
Bibliography 83

Part II. Mediterranean Middle East and North Africa Economy Profiles 85

Chapter 6. Algeria 87

The foundations of SME policy: definitions, statistics and institutions 87
Improving business environments for SMEs and entrepreneurs 89
Fostering access to finance 91
Nurturing entrepreneurship and SME growth 92
Investing in entrepreneurial human capital 93
The way forward 94
Notes 95

Chapter 7. Egypt 97

The foundations of SME policy: definitions, statistics and institutions 97
Improving business environments for SMEs and entrepreneurs 100
Fostering access to finance 102
Nurturing entrepreneurship and SME growth 103
Investing in entrepreneurial human capital 105
The way forward 106
Notes 107

Chapter 8. Israel 109

The foundations of SME policy: definitions, statistics and institutions 109
Improving the business environment for SMEs and entrepreneurs 111

Fostering access to finance 113
Nurturing entrepreneurship and SME growth 115
Investing in entrepreneurial human capital 117
The way forward 118
Notes 119

Chapter 9. Jordan 121

The foundations of SME policy: definitions, statistics and institutions 121
Improving the business environment for SMEs and entrepreneurs 123
Fostering access to finance 124
Nurturing entrepreneurship and SME growth 125
Investing in entrepreneurial human capital 127
The way forward 128
Notes 129

Chapter 10. Lebanon 131

The foundations of SME policy: definitions, statistics and institutions 131
Improving business environments for SMEs and entrepreneurs 133
Fostering access to finance 134
Nurturing entrepreneurship and SME growth 135
Investing in entrepreneurial human capital 136
The way forward 138
Notes 139

Chapter 11. Morocco 141

The foundations of SME policy: definitions, statistics and institutions 141
Improving business environments for SMEs and entrepreneurs 142
Fostering access to finance 144
Nurturing entrepreneurship and SME growth 145
Investing in entrepreneurial human capital 147
The way forward 148
Notes 149

Chapter 12. Palestinian Authority 151

The foundations of SME policy: definitions, statistics and institutions 151
Improving business environments for SMEs and entrepreneurs 152
Fostering access to finance 153
Nurturing start-ups and SME growth 154
Investing in entrepreneurial human capital 155
The way forward 157
Notes 158

Chapter 13. Tunisia 159

The foundations of SME policy: definitions, statistics and institutions 159
Improving business environments for SMEs and entrepreneurs 160
Fostering access to finance 161
Nurturing entrepreneurship and SME growth 163
Investing in entrepreneurial human capital 165
The way forward 166
Notes 167

Tables

Table 1.1. Overview of existence and use of SME definitions across the MED region 27
Table 1.2. SME definitions 28
Table 1.3. Enterprise and business environment indicators 31
Table 1.4. Institutional frameworks for SME policy 34

Boxes

Box 1. Overview of the SME Policy Index for the Mediterranean Middle East and North Africa 2014: Implementation of the Small Business Act for Europe 11
Box 1.1. EU guidance to apply the SME definition 29

Scope of the report

This interim assessment *is not* a full update of the 2014 SME Policy Index, which includes ten policy areas and more than 100 policy indicators (see Box 1).[1] Rather, it consists of an overview of the progress made by MED economies with respect to the implementation of key reforms identified in 2014.

The report covers five policy domains: 1) the foundations of SME policy – definitions, statistics and institutions; 2) improving business environments for SMEs and entrepreneurs; 3) fostering access to finance; 4) nurturing start-ups and SME growth; and 5) entrepreneurial human capital development. The following sections briefly describe the rationale and the specific policy aspects analysed in this report.

Box 1. Overview of the SME Policy Index for the Mediterranean Middle East and North Africa 2014: Implementation of the Small Business Act for Europe

The *SME Policy Index for the Mediterranean Middle East and North Africa 2014* was co-ordinated by the OECD, the European Commission and the European Training Foundation (ETF), in consultation with the European Investment Bank (EIB). The assessment measured SME policy convergence between the European Union and the MED region. It also included an overview of SME policy in Libya.

The SME Policy Index is an analytical tool developed by the OECD, in co-operation with international partners including the European Commission and the ETF, to assess and compare SME policy across economies and time. It was developed within the framework of regional programmes conducted by the OECD with non-member emerging economies. It has been implemented in Eastern Europe and Central Asia, the Western Balkans and Turkey, Latin America, and Southeast Asia.

The SME Policy Index has been adapted for the MED region building on the Small Business Act for Europe (SBA),[1] an SME policy framework adopted by the EU in 2008, which is becoming the reference for Euro-Mediterranean co-operation for enterprise development. It was first carried out in 2007-2008, leading to the publication of the *Report on the Implementation of the Euro-Mediterranean Charter for Enterprise*.[2] The 2014 assessment updated the previous 2007-2008 exercise to show progress made over the period covered.

The exercise was structured around the ten policy principles of the SBA:

a) Education and training for entrepreneurship, including women's entrepreneurship.

b) Efficient bankruptcy procedures and "second chance" for entrepreneurs.

c) Institutional and regulatory framework for SME policy making.

d) Operational environment for business creation.

e) Support services for SMEs and public procurement.

f) Access to finance for SMEs.

g) Supporting SMEs to benefit from Euro-MED networks and partnerships.

h) Enterprise skills and innovation.

i) SMEs in a green economy.

j) Internationalisation of SMEs.

1. https://ec.europa.eu/growth/smes/business-friendly-environment/small-business-act_en.
2. http://www.oecd.org/global-relations/41779100.pdf.

1. The foundations of SME policy: definitions, statistics and institutions

SME and entrepreneurship policies involve a wide range of institutions and actors. Establishing the right co-ordination and consultation mechanisms is essential for effective policy implementation.[2] This interim assessment analyses the progress made in the MED economies concerning:

1. The existence of official SME definitions and the availability of SME statistics;
2. The institutional framework for SME policies (sub-dimension 3.1 in the SME Policy Index 2014), particularly the development and implementation of SME strategies and improved institutional or multi-stakeholder co-ordination; and
3. Public-private consultations (sub-dimension 3.3 in the SME Policy Index 2014). This area assesses whether multi-stakeholder committees (public and private) have been created/improved.

2. Improving business environments for SMEs and entrepreneurs

The business environment can significantly affect SME and entrepreneurship performance. Most MED economies are implementing measures to enhance their business environments. The interim assessment attempts to assess these reform efforts by focusing on:

1. Better legislation and administrative simplification (sub-dimension 3.2 in the SME Policy Index 2014), in particular the introduction/improvement of regulatory impact analysis (RIA) and the implementation of the SME test of the "think small first" SBA principle;
2. The operational environment for business creation (dimension 4 in the SME Policy Index 2014), assessing reforms related to the ease of company registration and notification and compliance (e.g. progress in the implementation of single company identification numbers, online registration and one-stop shops);[3] and
3. Bankruptcy procedures (sub-dimension 2.1 in the SME Policy Index 2014), capturing reforms and implementation of bankruptcy laws.[4]

3. Fostering access to finance

Facilitating access to finance is one of the most essential areas for the promotion of SMEs and entrepreneurship.[5] The interim assessment looks at:

1. The legal and regulatory environment for access to finance (sub-dimension 6.2 in the SME Policy Index 2014), analysing in particular progress in the implementation of credit information systems and registries of movable assets; and

2. Sources of external finance (sub-dimension 6.1 in the SME Policy Index 2014), focusing on progress made on access to credit and other sources of finance.

4. Nurturing start-ups and SME growth

Beyond measures to improve the business environment, SMEs face specific needs and therefore require tailored policies that support their creation and growth.[6] The interim assessment captures progress made in the following areas:

1. The availability of business support services, including business incubators and the ease of access to information about these services (sub-dimensions 5.1 and 5.2 in the SME Policy Index 2014);
2. Measures to promote SME access to public procurement opportunities (sub-dimension 5.3 in the SME Policy Index 2014), in particular the ease of access to information on procurement opportunities and e-procurement; and
3. Measures to increase SME access to international trade (sub-dimension 10.2 in the SME Policy Index 2014).

5. Entrepreneurial human capital development

This report also includes an assessment of human capital development initiatives related to entrepreneurship and SME growth.[7] This assessment was undertaken by the European Training Foundation (ETF) and looks at:

1. Entrepreneurial learning in upper secondary education (both general and vocational), addressing both policy and practice – with particular attention given to entrepreneurship as a key competence as well as entrepreneurship skills;
2. Women's entrepreneurship, in particular how policies and training support for women's entrepreneurship are addressed; and
3. SME skills, particularly training to help SMEs internationalise.

The report was undertaken jointly by the OECD, which focused on policy areas 1 to 4, and the ETF, which covered policy area 5. The information for policy areas 1 to 4 was collected through questionnaires completed by different stakeholders in co-operation with national co-ordinators. The information from the questionnaires was also discussed during fact-finding missions and focus groups in each MED economy. These meetings provided the opportunity to obtain more information on the policy reform efforts implemented.

The human capital dimension (policy area 5) was assessed by ETF through multi-stakeholder focus groups in each MED economy. This covered three policy indicators:

- Indicator 1 assessed the extent to which upper secondary education promotes entrepreneurship as a key competence, and entrepreneurship skills for young people.
- Indicator 2 assessed the extent to which training for women's entrepreneurship is supported by mutually-reinforcing policies and implementation measures.
- Indicator 3 assessed the extent to which economies dispose of training provisions for SME trading, or with potential to trade, based on knowledge of international standards and markets

Notes

[1] OECD, European Commission, ETF. 2014. *SME Policy Index for The Mediterranean Middle East and North Africa 2014: Implementation of the Small Business Act for Europe* (Paris: OECD Publishing). http://www.etf.europa.eu/web.nsf/pages/SME_Policy_Index_MENA_2014.

[2] These policy areas correspond to SBA principle 3, "Design rules according to the 'think small first' principle", which requires public authorities to consider SMEs' interests early in the policy-making process. For all 10 principles, see http://publications.europa.eu/resource/cellar/4a5a13ba-4411-4602-a903-6d3b85005624.0005.02/DOC_5.

[3] This area corresponds to SBA principle 4, "Make public administrations responsive to SME needs".

[4] This area corresponds to SBA principle 2, "Ensure that honest entrepreneurs who have faced bankruptcy quickly get a second chance".

[5] These policy areas correspond to SBA principle 6, "Facilitate SME access to finance and develop a legal and business environment supportive to timely payments and commercial transactions".

[6] These policy areas correspond to SBA principles 5 ("Adapt public policy tools to SME needs") and 10 ("Encourage and support SMEs to benefit from the growth of markets").

[7] This section covers SBA principles 1 ("Create an environment in which entrepreneurs and family business can thrive and entrepreneurship is rewarded") and 8 ("Promote the upgrading of skills in SMEs and all forms of innovation").

List of Acronyms

AfDB	African Development Bank
ALGEX	Algerian Agency for the Promotion of Foreign Trade
AMDIE	Agency for the Development of Investment and Exports (Morocco)
ANDI	National Agency for Investment Development (Algeria)
ANDPME	National Agency for SME Development (Algeria)
ANGEM	National Microcredit Agency (Algeria)
ANSEJ	National Agency for the Support of Youth Employment (Algeria)
APII	Agency for the Promotion of Industry and Innovation (Tunisia)
BAM	Bank Al-Maghrib (the Moroccan Central Bank)
BDC	Business Development Centre (Jordan)
BDL	Central Bank of Lebanon
BDS	business development services
BFPME	Tunisian SME Bank
CACI	Chamber of Commerce and Industry (Algeria)
CAGEX	Company of Export Guarantees (Algeria)
CAPMAS	Central Agency for Public Mobilisation and Statistics (Egypt)
CASNOS	Institute for Social Security for the Self-Employed and Independent Professionals (Algeria)
CAWTAR	Centre of Arab Women for Training and Research
CBE	Central Bank of Egypt
CCG	Credit Guarantee Agency (Morocco)
CGC	Credit Guarantee Company (Egypt)
CGEM	National Confederation of Moroccan Enterprises
CGGI	Fund of Guarantees for Credit Investment (Algeria)
CIP	Capital Investment Programme (Lebanon)
CNAS	National Social Security Institute (Algeria)
CNC	National Consultation Council for SME Development (Algeria)
CNRC	National Centre of the Commercial Register (Algeria)
CNEA	National Committee of the Business Climate (Morocco)

CREOL	Online System for Enterprise Creation (Morocco)
DGI	General Directorate for Taxes (Morocco)
DGPME	General Directorate for SMEs (Tunisia)
DGRA	General Directorate for Reform and Administrative Outlook (Tunisia)
DOS	Department of Statistics (Jordan)
EASME	Executive Agency for Small & Medium Enterprises (EU)
EBESM	Enhancement of the Business Environment in the Southern Mediterranean Project
EBI	Egyptian Banking Institute
EBRD	European Bank for Reconstruction and Development
EEN	European Enterprise Network
EEWC	Economic Empowerment of Women Centre Israel
EFSA	Egyptian Financial Supervisory Authority
EIB	European Investment Bank
EIP	Entrepreneurship Indicators Programme (OECD-Eurostat)
ELCIM	Euro-Lebanese Centre for Industrial Modernisation
ENTRECOMP	European Entrepreneurship Key Competence Framework
EPCGF	European-Palestinian Credit Guarantee Fund
ERRADA	Egyptian Regulatory Reform and Development Activity
ETF	European Training Foundation
EU	European Union
FGAR	Algerian Credit Guarantee Fund for SMEs
FICC	Federation of Israeli Chambers of Commerce
FTA	Foreign Trade Administration (Israel)
GAFI	General Authority for Investment and Free Zones (Egypt)
GDF	Governorate Development Fund (Jordan)
GEM	Global Entrepreneurship Monitor
GIZ	German development agency
GPA	General Procurement Authority (Israel)
HCP	National Statistics Office (Morocco)
IBEL	Improving the Business Environment in Lebanon
ICE	single identification number (Morocco)

ICRAM	Concerted Initiative for Strengthening Moroccan Achievements (*Initiative Concerée pour le renforcement des Acquis des Marocaines*)
IDA	Industrial Development Authority (Egypt)
IDAL	Investment Development Agency (Lebanon)
IEICI	Israel Export and International Co-operation Institute
IFC	International Finance Corporation
ILO	International Labour Organization
IMC	Industrial Modernisation Centre (Egypt)
IMF	International Monetary Fund
ISO	International Organisation for Standards
ITC	Industrial Training Centre (Egypt chapter only)
ITC	International Trade Centre
JEDCO	Jordan Enterprise Development Corporation
JEGP	Jordan Economic Growth Plan for 2018-2022
JLGC	Jordan Loan Guarantee Corporation
LENS	Local Enterprise Support Project Jordan
LLWB	Lebanese League for Women in Business
MAOF	Small Business Development Centres (Israel)
MED	Mediterranean Middle East and North Africa
MSME	micro, small and medium-sized enterprises
MSMEDA	MSME Development Agency (Egypt)
M&E	monitoring and evaluation
NBA	National Business Agenda (Tunisia)
NCLW	National Commission for Lebanese Women
NEET	not in education, employment or training
OECD	Organisation for Economic Co-operation and Development
OMPIC	National Office for Intellectual and Commercial Property (Morocco)
OMSAR	Office of the Minister of State for Administrative Reform (Lebanon)
ONS	National Statistics Office (Algeria)
P2P	peer-to-peer (lending)
PAD-PME	Project for the Support of SME Development (Algeria)
PIPA	Palestinian Investment Promotion Agency

PMA	Palestinian Monetary Authority
PPD	public-private dialogue
PROMEX	Office of Promotion of Foreign Trade (Algeria)
RIA	regulatory impact analysis
SBA	Small Business Act for Europe
SFD	Social Fund for Development (Egypt)
SMBA	Small and Medium Business Agency (Israel)
SMBF	Small and Medium Business Fund (Israel)
SMEs	micro, small and medium-sized enterprises
TAIEX	Technical Assistance and Information Exchange instrument (European Union)
TVET	technical and vocational education and training
UGTA	General Union of Algerian Workers
UNCITRAL	United Nations Commission on International Trade Law
UNIDO	United Nations Industrial Development Organisation
USAID	United States Agency for International Development
UTICA	Union of Industry, Commerce and Crafts (Tunisia)
VC	venture capital
VET	vocational education and training
WB	World Bank
WTO	World Trade Organisation

Executive Summary

Micro, small and medium-sized enterprises (SMEs) come in all different flavours and forms, from traditional artisans and retailers with few or no paid employees, to mid-sized manufacturing firms and high-growth firms offering innovative goods, services or business models. Entrepreneurs are also driven by different motivations, broadly ranging from those who aim to seize an opportunity to those who lack alternatives to earn an income.

MED economies increasingly recognise the social and economic role of SMEs and entrepreneurs, and devise actions to support them. The SME Policy Index for the MED region has documented these actions in 2008 and 2014. This interim assessment constitutes an update of major reforms implemented between 2014 and 2018 and identifies pending areas for action. Its conclusions are intended to inform MED governments and their partners of the priorities ahead. The report is also an effort to continue and strengthen the co-operation among MED partners, the Organisation for Economic Co-operation and Development (OECD) and the European Union (EU).

Major takeaways from this report, corresponding to each of the policy areas covered, are as follows:

1. MED economies continue putting into place the **building blocks of SME and entrepreneurship policy** (definitions, statistics and institutions), although with very different levels of advancement. For example, Morocco has had for several years a legal and strategic framework for SME policy benefiting from a relatively effective system of consultation and coordination mechanisms. Tunisia, to mention another case, is building such a system based on the strong dialogue ethos build over the past few years through its political and economic transition.

    a. MED economies could in general do more to maximise the resources already devoted to SME and entrepreneurship support by enhancing co-ordination among the many policy actors. This could include mechanisms comprising co-ordination at the highest political level, technical collaboration among national and sub-national agencies, and inclusive public-private dialogue platforms that are representative of the diversity of SMEs and entrepreneurs.

    b. MED economies can also improve SME definitions and statistics by adopting international practices (e.g. definitions officially recognised and uniformly used) and increasing efforts to disseminate data and information. The SME Observatories being established across the region are a useful initial effort in that respect.

2. Whereas most MED economies have undertaken efforts to improve the **business environment** by simplifying business start-up and bankruptcy procedures, more can be done to simplify the regulatory environment.

    a. Regulatory impact analyses (RIAs) exist, to varying degrees, in Egypt, Israel, Jordan and Tunisia. However, no economy yet implements the "SME test" (a system for assessing the impact of laws and regulations on SMEs). The introduction and expansion of RIA and the SME test remain a priority.

b. There are also varying levels of effort to facilitate procedures for enterprise creation, particularly through the introduction of single identification numbers and online registration, in five MED economies (Algeria, Egypt, Israel, Morocco and Tunisia). However, more work is needed to establish and expand one-stop-shops for business creation.

c. Egypt, Jordan, Israel, Morocco and Tunisia have adopted new bankruptcy laws. However, the *Doing Business* indicators on Resolving Insolvency indicate that this is one of the most difficult areas in the business environment across the region. Hence, the full implementation of the new regulatory frameworks will be critical.

3. Major reforms have been undertaken to improve the legal and regulatory framework for **access to finance** in most MED economies. The most notable example is that of the recent reforms by PA, which has established a registry of moveable assets and passed a secured transactions law. Because of these reforms, PA now performs at a higher level than its regional peers in this area in *Doing Business*. Furthermore, initiatives to increase the availability of equity finance were introduced, especially in Lebanon and PA.

   a. In this area, the region could in general continue bridging information asymmetries by creating and expanding credit bureaus and registries of moveable assets so that SMEs and entrepreneurs can access credit more easily.

   b. MED economies could also work towards a greater diversity and reach of different sources of finance (credit, equity and hybrid instruments). This could include encouraging private sector participants to take on a greater role in the financing of SMEs and entrepreneurship. Indeed, the state continues to be the main actor, especially in terms of credit guarantee schemes but also in equity investments.

4. A number of measures have been introduced to foster **SME growth and entrepreneurship**. These include the expansion of business development services in Lebanon and PA and the introduction of a comprehensive programme for entrepreneurship in Morocco. They also include several actions in almost all MED economies to facilitate SME access to public procurement and to promote exports.

   a. MED economies could further ease access to information on all the different support services and programmes by consolidating that information and disseminating it. This can be done in many ways, including the publication of leaflets and the establishment of consolidated web portals. SME Observatories could play an important role in this regard.

   b. More could be done to implement e-procurement systems and track the extent to which specific measures have actually benefited SMEs. Procurement observatories could be a useful tool in order to assess the effectiveness of these measures.

5. All MED economies have progressed well in developing policy frameworks to develop **entrepreneurial human capital**. However, challenges remain, including 1) the implementation of policies by partnerships including all relevant

stakeholders and 2) data collection and analysis on training provision and its effectiveness.

a. Building entrepreneurship as a key competence is the next challenge for policy makers and schools. It is about cultivating an entrepreneurial attitude characterised by a sense of initiative and agency, and proactivity in achieving projects. MED economies need also to move from project-based initiatives to a systemic approach by inserting entrepreneurial learning into the national curricula at all levels of education.

b. Momentum is growing in women's entrepreneurship. MED economies need to develop comprehensive policy responses in the economic context (beyond the social, gender-equality agenda) and to move beyond individual policy measures and actions. Development measures to build skills and competence should go beyond general SME training courses and include mentorship, coaching, network support – and the creation of enabling systems for women's entrepreneurship that foster growth and innovation of women-led and women-owned enterprises.

c. More developed data on SME training, particularly in terms of export potential, is required in all countries. Further, trade and SME policies require alignment to ensure training meets external trade interest, to include a closer interface with the vocational training environment, and particularly to address quality improvements in sectors with improved export potential.

Part I. Regional Trends by Policy Area

Chapter 1. The foundations of SME policy: definitions, statistics, and institutions

This chapter analyses the main reforms undertaken by MED economies since 2014 in terms of the building blocks of SME policy: the adoption of official definitions of micro, small and medium-sized enterprises; the collection and dissemination of business statistics; and the establishment of effective institutional co-ordination and public-private dialogue mechanisms.

Overall, the assessment finds that MED economies are stepping up their efforts in these areas. Nevertheless, more could be done to:

1. Adopt official SME definitions that combine various criteria – notably employment, turnover and balance sheet considerations. Doing so would help to better reflect the diverse nature of SMEs operating in different sectors and with different levels of productivity. SME definitions could also have a clear legal or official status – reflected, for example, in SME laws and bills.

2. Collect SME data from administrative sources of information (such as business registries, tax administrations, social security administrations) and also from business associations. Apart from reducing the administrative burden on enterprises, this could help to cut data collection costs and increase the availability of statistics.

3. Strengthen co-ordination among SME policy actors (public and private), including at the high level (e.g. ministerial), technical level (e.g. agency) and sub-national level. Such co-ordination could be guided by the implementation of multiannual SME and entrepreneurship strategies and the designation of a specialised secretariat (e.g. a SME agency or unit) to execute the strategy.

4. Establish public-private dialogue platforms that are representative of the various types of SMEs and entrepreneurs operating throughout each country and in different economic activities.

The statistical data for Israel are supplied by and under the responsibility of the relevant Israeli authorities. The use of such data by the OECD is without prejudice to the status of the Golan Heights, East Jerusalem and Israeli settlements in the West Bank under the terms of international law.

The promotion of entrepreneurship and SME growth is a complex endeavour given the number of policy levers and actors on the one hand, and the diversity of firms on the other. SME performance is determined by a wide range of policy dimensions, including horizontal (e.g. infrastructure, public governance, quality of legal framework) and targeted factors (e.g. credit guarantee schemes for women and young people, grants for R&D activities in SMEs). Therefore, in order to be effective, an SME policy requires a well-structured institutional framework and strong mechanisms of policy co-ordination and consultation.

As seen in the previous editions of the SME Policy Index and in this interim assessment, the level of institutional development in the region tends to drive results across a number of SME policy dimensions, including those related to the promotion of entrepreneurship, the provision of services to SMEs, access to finance, and improving business licensing and regulations. Hence, the MED economies with the most developed institutional frameworks tend to perform consistently better across policy dimensions than those with less developed or more fragmented frameworks.

This chapter focuses on key reforms and actions since the SME Policy Index 2014 in adopting SME definitions, improving SME statistics, strengthening inter-governmental co-ordination for SME policy and the strategic framework for SMEs, and fostering public-private dialogue.

There is plenty of scope for developing clear and consistent SME definitions enshrined in legislation

Having a clear definition of *micro, small and medium-sized enterprises* is important when identifying the firms that are eligible for targeted support programmes, to collect data on the state of the enterprise population, and to have clear parameters for policy monitoring and evaluation. Official SME definitions are also important for SME policy co-ordination and multi-level governance of policies.

Ideally, a single definition of *micro, small and medium-sized enterprises* should be used across different policy areas and regulations in order to improve the consistency and effectiveness of SME support measures. Clear distinctions between the various types of SMEs (e.g. micro-enterprises and medium-sized businesses) are also needed so that policy measures can be tailored to the needs of each type. Furthermore, SME definitions should not be considered static and should be revised every few years to ensure they are still relevant to the economic context.

Progress since 2014

There has been limited progress at the regional level regarding the adoption of official SME definitions that are 1) enshrined in legislation; 2) consistently used across different policy areas, and therefore recognised by different institutions; and 3) combine employment, turnover and assets criteria. Table 1.1 summarises the results of the interim assessment in this area. Table 1.2 includes summary of all definitions in the MED region.

Table 1.1. Overview of existence and use of SME definitions across the MED region

	Criteria	AL	EG	IS	JO	LE	MO	PA	TU
SME definition	Is it enshrined in legislation?	Yes	No[1]	No	No[1]	No	No	Yes	Yes[2]
	Is it consistently used across institutions and policy areas?	Not clear	No	No	No	No	Not clear	No	No
	Does it combine different criteria?	Yes	Yes	Yes	Yes	Yes	No employment criteria	Yes	Yes

1. There are ongoing initiatives in Egypt and Jordan to enshrine the SME definition in law.
2. The SME definition in Tunisia is enshrined in the Investment Law, not in the SME Law.

In terms of adopting an official definition enshrined in law:

- **Algeria,** in its new SME Law 1702 of 2017, revised the SME definition, and it is now close to the EU's in terms of employment criteria. However, it is not clear whether that definition is consistently used across different institutions.
- **Tunisia** adopted a new SME definition in the context of a new Investment Law, but it is mainly based on financial criteria, with no distinction between micro, small and medium-sized firms. Furthermore, although the definition is used by the Agency for the Promotion of Industry and Innovation (APII – one of the institutions in charge of enterprise policy) to delimit its field of action, there are other definitions used by other actors (e.g. the SME bank [BFPME] and the statistics office [INS]).
- Three other MED economies report they are working on the adoption of an SME definition to be enshrined in law and to be used by all SME parties. These are **Egypt,** which is redesigning its entire SME policy and developing an SME law; and **Jordan** and **Lebanon**, which are in the process of adopting SME strategies and SME laws. However, there is no clear indication of when these strategies and laws will be officially endorsed; for example, in the case of Jordan, the SME strategy has been due for adoption since 2015.

Other economies have made revisions to pre-existing definitions:

- **Israel** has two definitions, one established by Government Decision 2190 and the other used by the Small and Medium Business Agency (SMBA). The SMBA definition has been revised in alignment with the strategic plan of the agency. However, there is no intent to unify the both definitions.
- The 2014 report noted that the **Moroccan** SME Agency[1] had established a definition of SMEs. The definition was revised in 2015 in the context of the "Contractual Framework" between the State and SME Morocco for 2015-2020. Nonetheless, the definition refers only to financial criteria and contains no headcount criterion.
- In the case of **PA**, an SME definition established by cabinet decree has existed since the SME Policy Index in 2014. This definition has not changed since then, and it is

not consistently applied by different agencies supporting SMEs directly or indirectly.

Table 1.2. SME definitions

Economy	Criterion	Micro	Small	Medium	Notes and source
EU	Employment	1-9 employees	10-49 employees	50-249 employees	EU Recommendation 2003/361.
	Financial	Annual turnover *or* annual balance sheet ≤ EUR 2 m	Annual turnover *or* annual balance sheet ≤ EUR 10 m	Annual turnover ≤ EUR 50 m *or* annual balance sheet ≤ EUR 43 m	
Algeria	Employment	1-9 employees	10-49 employees	50-250 employees	SME Law 1702 of 2017.
	Financial	Annual turnover < DZD 40 m Year-end statement < DZD 20 m	Annual turnover < DZD 400 m Year-end statement < DZD 200 m	Annual turnover < DZD 4 bn Year-end statement < DZD 1 bn	
Egypt	Employment	<10	<200	None	Central Bank definition issued on 17 December 2015. The Ministry of Trade and Industry is developing a new definition, to be adopted in 2018.
	Financial	Annual turnover for existing firms: < EGP 1 m Paid-up capital for new firms < EGP 50 000	Annual turnover for existing firms: EGP 1–50 m Paid-up capital for new firms[1] EGP 50 000–500 000	Annual turnover for existing firms: EGP 50–200 m Paid-up capital for new firms[1] EGP 5–10 m	
Israel	Employment	≤ 4 employees	≤ 20 employees	≤ 100 employees	Definition by the Small and Medium Business Agency. A Government Decision no. 2190 definition also exists.
	Financial	Annual turnover of ≤ NIS 2 m	Annual turnover of ≤ NIS 20 m	Annual turnover of ≤ NIS 100 m	
Jordan	Employment	1–4 employees	5-19 employees	20–99 employees	Definition in the SME Strategy, not yet adopted.
	Financial	Annual turnover ≤ JOD 100 000	Annual turnover ≤ JOD 1 m	Annual turnover ≤ JOD 5 m	
Lebanon	Employment	< 10 employees	< 50 employees	< 100 employees	SME definition adopted by the Ministry of Economy and Trade.
	Financial	Annual turnover of < LBP 500 m	Annual turnover of < LBP 5 bn	Annual turnover of < LBP 25 bn	
Morocco	Employment	None	None	None	Contractual Framework between the State and Morocco SME for 2015-2020.
	Financial	Annual turnover ≤ MAD 10 m	Annual turnover[2] ≤ MAD 200 m		
PA	Employment	1-4 employees	5-9 employees	10-19 employees	SME Definition by the Palestinian Authority.
	Financial	Annual turnover ≤ USD 20 000 Paid-up capital ≤ USD 5 000	Annual turnover ≤ USD 200 000 Paid-up capital ≤ USD 50 000	Annual turnover ≤ USD 500 000 Paid-up capital ≤ USD 100 000	
Tunisia	Employment	< 6 employees	< 49 employees	< 199 employees	Statistical definition by the National Statistics Institute for employment criteria; and financial definition contained in the new Investment Law.
	Financial		Paid-up capital*** < TND 15 m		

Notes: Figures in euros are shown in the MED economy chapters. For Tunisia there is a statistical definition by the National Institute of Statistics; and a separate definition in the new Investment Law relative to financial incentives for SMEs with a total investment of less than TND 15 million, with no distinction between micro, small or medium-sized firms.

1. Refers to industrial firms only.

2. Small and medium enterprises form a single category of firms; Morocco also clearly distinguishes the status of "auto-entrepreneur" or roughly "self-employed" as a separate category of economic unit.

Most SME definitions combine different criteria, but few include financial criteria:

- Only **Algeria** and **PA** distinguish between micro, small and medium-sized firms using a combination of employment, turnover and balance sheet criteria along the lines of the European Union's (EU) definition (see Box 1.1). However, it is not clear that SME definitions are consistently applied across different institutions and programmes in these economies.

Box 1.1. EU guidance to apply the SME definition

The European Commission has published a *User Guide to the SME Definition*[1] aimed at helping entrepreneurs, SME managers and government officials (at the EU, national and local level) to understand the criteria and cases when an enterprise qualifies as a micro, small or medium-sized enterprise and is eligible, for example, to receive specific SME support measures. The user guide details with clear and specific examples how to apply the headcount (employment), turnover and financial criteria. The guide also explains in detail other important factors such as:

1. What qualifies as an *enterprise*, i.e. an entity engaged in economic activity, irrespective of the legal form (e.g. self-employed, family firm, limited liability).
2. The level of independence or autonomy of a firm (e.g. whether it is a standalone business or belongs to or owns another firm or group of firms, partly or fully).
3. In which cases a firm is considered to have transited from one size-type to the other (micro to small, small to medium, medium to small, etc.).

1. European Union (2015), *User guide to the SME Definition*, available at https://ec.europa.eu/growth/content/revised-user-guide-sme-definition-0_en.

For further action

Overall, the interim assessment shows that there is ample scope for the MED region to adopt legal definitions of micro, small and medium-sized firms that are officially accepted by the various agencies in charge of different policy areas. It is also noted that, compared to other regions covered by the EU Neighbourhood Policy (Eastern Partner countries and the Western Balkans and Turkey), there are no evident efforts towards convergence with the EU definition.

Efforts are ongoing to develop comprehensive and accurate statistics, but work is still preliminary.

Structural and demographic business statistics are essential for analysing the structure and dynamism of an economy. These statistics include indicators such as the number of firms; the shares of micro, small and medium-sized businesses; the economic activities in which they operate; and their contribution to the economy (employment, value added, imports and exports, productivity, etc.). They also include indicators on business dynamics and job creation including business entries, growth and exits, and high-growth enterprises. Other indicators look at the characteristics of the entrepreneurs and their firms in terms of gender, age, education, motivation, etc.

Other indicators measure aspects of the business environment such as the regulatory burden and access to resources like skills and finance, innovation, etc. The sources of these data include economic censuses and surveys by national statistics offices; administrative sources, such as business registries, tax authorities and social security institutes; and other surveys and research by academics, think tanks and international organisations.

Progress since 2014

Although comprehensive and internationally comparable SME and entrepreneurship statistics are still lacking in the region, progress has been done in this area over the past few years. This includes the establishment of SME Observatories to disseminate SME and entrepreneurship-related information and statistics.

- **Jordan** has launched an SME Observatory run by a unit of the Jordan Enterprise Development Corporation (JEDCO), the SME agency. Its objective is to strengthen SME data collection, analysis and dissemination. The SME Observatory has already published comprehensive statistical reports based on official data and other sources such as the *Global Entrepreneurship Monitor* (*GEM*).[2] It is also planning to launch a web portal to widely disseminate its information.
- One of the most important initiatives over the past few years has been the establishment by **Morocco** of an SME and Entrepreneurship Observatory tasked with producing and disseminating ample information. It is based on a collaborative approach between eleven founding agencies.[3] The SME Observatory is already operational and has started signing collaboration agreements with other agencies to establish an institutional and legal framework for consolidating information on private enterprises.

Furthermore, all MED economies except Lebanon have official data from statistical offices or other administrative sources, with descriptive SME structural statistics and information about their contribution to the economy (see Table 1.3).

- In **Algeria** the Ministry of Industry and Mines collects and publishes extensive and regular statistical bulletins with detailed information on SMEs based on the official definitions.[4] The 2017 SME Law mandates the National Agency for SME Development (ANDPME) to implement an SME information system to serve as a planning and decision-making tool, equivalent to an SME Observatory.[5] The system is being developed under the Project for the Support of SME Development (PAD-PME) with the African Development Bank (AfDB).
- In **Egypt** the Central Agency for Public Mobilisation and Statistics (CAPMAS) is the main source of SME statistics through the Establishment Census, which is conducted every few years. The results of the latest edition (2017) were published in December 2017. The Egyptian Banking Institute (EBI), the financial development arm of the Central Bank of Egypt and CAPMAS conducted a SME survey in 2010-2011. The EBI provided access to the full database to the banking sector and relevant governmental agencies. For the first time, Egypt will participate in the OECD Scoreboard on Financing SMEs and Entrepreneurs, in the 2019 edition.
- **Israel** continues to participate in the main OECD statistical instruments on business indicators: the OECD-Eurostat Entrepreneurship Indicators Programme (EIP) and the OECD Scoreboard on Financing SMEs and Entrepreneurs. EIP provides

comprehensive internationally comparable statistics on SME and entrepreneurship performance based on official sources.[6] The Scoreboard on Financing SMEs and Entrepreneurs comprises an important set of indicators on debt, equity, asset-based finance and framework conditions for access to finance.

- In **Tunisia** the National Statistics Institute (INS) publishes an annual report on Statistics from the National Enterprise Compendium. This includes structural, demographic and business dynamics (firm entry and exit) indicators.

Table 1.3. Enterprise and business environment indicators

Economy	National sources of enterprise data	Participation in international data sources and indicators	New initiatives since 2014	Sources and links to national data
Algeria	2011 Economic Census and regular SME Bulletins (latest 2017)	Doing Business GEM (2013)	SME Law of 2017 mandates the establishment of an SME Observatory	http://www.ons.dz www.mdipi.gov.dz/?Bulletin-de-veille-statistique
Egypt	2017 Establishment Census and 2010-2011 SME Survey	Doing Business Enterprise Surveys (2016) GEM (2017)	OECD Scoreboard on Financing SMEs and Entrepreneurs (2019)	http://www.capmas.gov.eg/ http://sme.ebi.gov.eg/Pages/smedb.aspx
Israel	Central Bureau of Statistics *Yearly Statistical Abstract on Israel* includes data on enterprise size	OECD-Eurostat EIP Doing Business Enterprise Surveys (2013) GEM (2017)	None	http://www.cbs.gov.il/reader/shnatonenew_site.htm
Jordan	Establishments Census (latest 2011, new edition to be released first half 2018)	Doing Business Enterprise Surveys (2013) GEM (2016)	SME Observatory (publishes data but has not yet established a website)	http://dosweb.dos.gov.jo/censuses/economic-establishments-census/
Lebanon	Census of Buildings, Dwellings and Establishments (2004)	Doing Business Enterprise Surveys (2013) GEM (2016)	Planning to establish an SME Observatory	http://www.cas.gov.lb/index.php/census-of-building-cbde-en
Morocco	Haut-Commissariat au Plan (HCP)	Doing Business Enterprise Surveys (2013) CGEM (2017)	SME Observatory (working towards a system for the collection of administrative data)	https://www.hcp.ma/Enquetes_r10.html
PA	Population, Housing and Establishments Census 2017	Doing Business GEM (2012)	Population, Housing and Establishments Census	http://www.pcbs.gov.ps/Downloads/book2364-1.pdf
Tunisia	Tunisian Business Register (yearly)	Doing Business Enterprise Surveys (2013)	None	http://www.ins.tn/en/themes/entreprises#sub-318

For further action

There is extensive SME and entrepreneurship data collection across the region from official sources. All MED economies are also covered by most international business environment and entrepreneurship gauges such as the *Doing Business* indicators, the World Bank *Enterprise Surveys*, and the *Global Entrepreneurship Monitor*. MED economies could step up their efforts towards international data harmonisation and dissemination by participating in the OECD-Eurostat EIP and the OECD Scoreboard on Financing SMEs and Entrepreneurs. This would allow them to compare their SME performance internationally. Some of the required data are already collected through official sources such as economic or enterprise censuses. It could also represent an incentive to gather data that are still missing in the region (for example, timely indicators on enterprise entry, exit and growth).

MED economies could also work towards the development of institutional, legal and technical mechanisms to exploit administrative sources of information on enterprises from business registries, tax offices, social security, etc. These sources of information could complement the statistics obtained from economic or enterprise censuses undertaken every few years and could lead to more timely and accurate business statistics. Furthermore, such data- and information-sharing initiatives could reduce red tape for businesses since companies and entrepreneurs would not need to provide the same information to different agencies. Nonetheless, privacy and confidentiality issues would need to be addressed for such a system to be operational.

Decisive action is still needed to make SME and entrepreneurship policy more coherent and strategic.

There are five important elements to consider when developing and implementing an effective SME policy agenda. The first is to ponder *whether* a country has a wider **economic development strategy or agenda,** and how SME policy fits within it. Policy objectives might include fostering economic diversification, reducing unemployment, or promoting the development of specific economic activities or sectors.

A second element is the enactment of a medium-term **strategic framework** (i.e. SME strategy) defining the policy priorities, goals and responsibilities of different actors. Such strategies reflect the economic priorities and approaches in each economy. For example, "*laissez faire*-minded" economies could prioritise the removal of barriers to doing business, whereas others could focus on providing more direct incentives to enterprises in certain economic activities deemed as a priority.

The development of strategies can facilitate co-ordination among public authorities and provide a platform for dialogue with the private sector, and notably SMEs. Hence, SME strategies should be based on a clear diagnosis of the main constraints confronting SMEs and grounded in the country's broader socio-economic or development strategic framework. They should also include prioritised and sequenced reforms and initiatives, a clear division of responsibilities, and targets and performance indicators to monitor progress and evaluate final results. Their implementation is ideally guided by regular action plans.

SME and entrepreneurship strategies are especially useful in economies with an emerging or transitioning private sector, where co-ordination and communication among actors is still nascent. A number of economies have introduced or are introducing SME laws, which officialise SME policy by giving legal status to SME definitions, co-ordination mechanisms, policy responsibilities and leadership, and funds allocated to undertake an SME policy, among other things.

The third element is to set up a comprehensive and well-structured **inter-governmental co-ordination mechanism**. This is essential given the cross-cutting nature of SME development policies and the involvement of several government ministries, agencies and departments. Governments need to introduce formal co-ordination mechanisms to avoid policy fragmentation while ensuring effective communication and collaboration across institutions. This can be done through inter-ministerial committees or working groups, or through a specialised SME development department (typically in the ministry of economy or industry) with a co-ordination mandate.

The fourth element is the existence of an **SME agency, or a specialised department** within an appropriate ministry (e.g. economy or industry), that can act as secretariat or technical co-ordination body for the implementation of the strategic framework. Strong political support and adequate human, technical and financial resources are necessary for such entity to deliver its mandate. In some countries SME agencies provide services, whereas in others they act at the policy level, ensuring coherence across support initiatives implemented by others. What is important is that there is an entity in charge of co-ordination, regardless of whether it is an autonomous SME agency or a unit of a ministry, and whether it provides services or not.

The fifth element is the existence of **monitoring and evaluation** (M&E) mechanisms to assess the effectiveness in the execution of the individual measures identified in the action plans of the SME strategy as well as the overall impact of the strategy. Here the SME agency or unit can also play an important co-ordination and execution role.

Progress since 2014

The SME Policy Index 2014 noted a lack of cohesive approaches to SME policy making in the MED region. Only Israel and Morocco had put in place all the building blocks of a comprehensive and co-ordinated SME policy, while Jordan was making progress through the development of an SME strategy. The other MED economies did not have formal and effective institutional co-ordination mechanisms framed by an SME strategy.

The study recommended three actions: 1) developing a comprehensive medium-term strategy through a participatory process in those economies which did not already have one; 2) clarifying policy mandates and clearly defining the roles of the institutions responsible for policy development and implementation; and 3) introducing regular monitoring and evaluation mechanisms to assess accurately the effectiveness of SME policies and programmes. There has been relatively little progress in this area since the SME Policy Index 2014 (see Table 1.4).

- **Morocco** continues to have a relatively well-structured institutional framework for SME and entrepreneurship policies. The Ministry of Industry, Trade, Investment and Digital Economy is in charge of overseeing SME policy and developing and implementing industrial strategies, namely the Industrial Acceleration Plan for 2014-2020. Morocco SME adopted a new "Contractual Framework" for 2015-2020, which aims to increase SME competitiveness and to foster entrepreneurship, including high impact entrepreneurs.

Others have in recent years implemented major reforms to improve the policy framework:

- **Algeria** continues to put economic diversification and import substitution at the centre of its general policy agenda. As such, it gives SME policy an important orientation towards industrial development, notably as "sub-contracting" (*sous-traitance*) or finding local suppliers for imported goods. A significant development was the approval of SME Law 1702 of 2017, which 1) sets the basis for policy co-ordination and the development of a strategy and 2) creates a funding mechanism: the National Fund for the Upgrading of SMEs, Supporting Investment and Promoting Industrial Competitiveness.
- The Law designates the National Agency for the Development and Modernisation of SMEs (ANDPME) as the leading body to implement the "SME development strategy", which is yet to be developed. The AfDB PAD-PME project will support the development of a strategy and the reorganising of the ANDPME. The SME law also foresees the creation of a public-private consultation body, the National Consultation Council for SME Development (CNC), which should be formed by organisations and professional associations representing SMEs.

Table 1.4. Institutional frameworks for SME policy

	National economic agenda	Legal and strategic framework for SME policy	SME agency/unit	M&E
Algeria	Quinquennial Economic Development Plans	SME Law 2017 passed but no strategic framework in place	ADPME (under the Ministry of Industry)	No evidence
Egypt	Egypt Vision 2030 and structural reforms under IMF EFF	SME Law awaiting approval by Parliament and SME Strategy under preparation	MSMEDA (independent, non-profit organisation)	Performance Measurement Framework (PMF) being finalised by MSMEDA, not yet implemented
Israel	No formal national economic agenda	SME Bill awaiting approval; no SME strategy	SMBA (under the Ministry of Economy) but mostly in charge of co-ordinating BDS centres	Development services provided by SMBA are evaluated but no comprehensive mechanism for the overall SME policy
Jordan	Jordan Compact, Jordan 2025	SME Strategy drafted but not yet implemented	JEDCO (under Ministry of Industry)	Contemplated in SME Strategy but not yet implemented
Lebanon	Vision for Stabilisation, Growth and Employment	SME Strategy drafted but not yet implemented	SME unit (under Ministry of Economy)	No evidence
Morocco	Industrial Acceleration Plan	SME Charter of 2002	Morocco SME	Different structures have their monitoring mechanisms (CNEA, Morocco SME Programmes, *auto-entrepreneur* status)
PA	National Policy Agenda 2017-2022. Industrial strategy waiting for approval	No SME-specific framework	No SME unit	No evidence
Tunisia	National Development Plan 2016-2020	No SME-specific framework	General Directorate for SMEs (DGPME) and the Agency for the Promotion of Industry and Innovation (API)	No evidence

Note: Details on the national economic agendas are provided in Part II of this report.

- **Egypt** is taking important steps to address the fragmentation of its SME policy framework.[7] In April 2017, a Prime Ministerial Decree was issued to establish a new micro, small and medium-sized enterprises Development Agency (MSMEDA) under the directive of the Minister of Trade and Industry. The MSMEDA has absorbed the responsibilities of the Social Fund for Development (SFD) and the Industrial Training Centre (ITC) as well as responsibilities related to entrepreneurship and SME support of the Industrial Modernisation Centre (IMC). MSMEDA is in charge of strategic planning, implementing, co-ordinating and monitoring SME support initiatives and access to finance for SMEs. Its work will be guided by an institutional strategy, which is being developed with the support of the EU project "Support for the Implementation of Strategies to Foster MSME Development in Egypt" (MiSMESIS); the national SME and entrepreneurship strategy, also under development; and the National Strategy for Enhancing Industrial Development and Foreign Trade 2016-2020.

There has been little change in a few of the MED economies:

- In **Israel** the Ministry of Economy continues to oversee and implement SME policy through the Small and Medium Business Agency (SMBA). Over the past few years the SMBA has increased and improved the provision of support services to SMEs by reshuffling and extending its network of business development centres. However, although SMBA is in charge of the co-ordination of SME and entrepreneurship policy, there is no formal mechanism in place for this purpose (OECD, 2016). There is no inter-ministerial SME and entrepreneurship policy committee, and there are no focal points in government ministries and agencies.
- Furthermore, the SME Bill, which has been discussed since 2014 and is intended to strengthen the co-ordination role of the SMBA, is not yet approved by the Knesset (parliament). Finally, there is no integrated policy document setting out a strategic policy framework for SME and entrepreneurship development (OECD, 2016).
- In **Jordan** the institutional framework has not changed much during the past decade. The Ministry of Industry and Trade continues to be in charge of enterprise and SME policy development, with the support of JEDCO as the main SME agency. The Ministry of Planning and International Co-operation continues to be responsible for implementing the broader country development strategy and mobilising donor support, while SME policy implementation is delegated to a number of specialised agencies.
- The 2013-2020 SME and Entrepreneurship Development Strategy was finalised in 2014, but it has not been approved yet, and there appear to be difficulties related to funding its action plan. JEDCO and the OECD are currently working on operationalising the governance mechanisms foreseen in the SME Strategy, even if the document is still pending final approval.[8] The pending approval of the SME Strategy of Jordan means that institutional co-ordination is still very limited and that JEDCO does not have yet the convening power it should. Furthermore, the large influx of refugees into Jordan and the significant stress on public finances and donor priorities has meant that SME policy support budgets have been reduced in some cases. In this context, JEDCO has seen its budget and policy areas of intervention reduced.
- In **Tunisia**, as in 2014, the SME policy framework and institutional co-ordination continue to be fragmented. The Ministry of Industry is the main authority responsible for SME and entrepreneurship promotion, notably through the General Directorate for SMEs (DGPME) and the Agency for the Promotion of Industry and Innovation (API). A new Investment Law was approved in September 2016 and includes some provisions affecting SMEs. Although the Investment Law has created a specific governance structure for the investment regime, it is not a specific instrument or strategy for SME development. There is an unresolved issue with SME co-ordination. Each ministry or institution has some mandate to work with SMEs, typically by sector; for example, the Ministry of Agriculture supports SMEs in the agribusiness sector and the API focuses on the industrial sector. However, there is no strong co-ordination mechanism.
- Neither PA nor Lebanon have registered changes since the SME Policy Index 2014. In **PA** the Ministry of National Economy continues to be in charge of private sector development and the improvement of the business environment. In **Lebanon**, SME

policy continues to be fragmented: although the Ministry of Economy and the Ministry of Industry oversee various support activities, other agencies are also involved. The government developed an SME Strategy 2020 with the support of the United Nations Development Programme (UNDP), but the level of implementation is unclear. The SME unit at the Ministry of Economy is in charge of implementing the SME Strategy. There are also plans to develop an SME Law based on the strategy, but no concrete details or indications about what these plans are.

For further action

Overall, the MED region has advanced little in this area since the 2014 assessment. There are no new platforms established to improve the co-ordination among different SME actors. The Jordanian SME Strategy – which foresees a full co-ordination mechanism, including at the top political level and at the sub-national level – is not yet adopted. Egypt is starting to improve SME policy co-ordination and is deploying a new SME agency.

MED economies could do much more to improve the effectiveness of their SME policies. There are already many SME and entrepreneurship support actors – public, private, non-governmental, donor and other organisations – targeting different types of firms and profiles of entrepreneurs (SME agencies, ministries of economy, finance and industry, credit guarantee providers, etc.). There are also many other actors working to improve the business environment and whose actions can have direct or indirect effects on SMEs (central banks, business licensing and regulatory bodies, tax authorities, etc.).

Stronger political leadership is necessary for the creation of effective inter-ministerial committees and technical committees in different agencies, including at the subnational level. Furthermore, the development and effective implementation of SME strategies could provide a concrete framework for the operation of these high-level and technical committees, including through the identification of concrete goals, targets, actions and responsible parties. Nearly all MED economies lack operational or functioning SME development strategies, although several are in the process of developing them.

Finally, the existence of an SME agency or a specialised unit within a relevant ministry (e.g. ministry of economy or industry), with a clear but strong mandate and with sufficient financial, human and technical resources, could greatly facilitate policy co-ordination and effectiveness. These schemes could be further underpinned by relevant legislation such as SME or enterprise laws, which contain legal provisions that consider the importance and the needs of SMEs in all types of policy making. The "think small first" principle would be particularly relevant in this regard.

Some public-private dialogue initiatives in the region could be of inspiration for MED peers, yet the voice of SMEs and entrepreneurs through business associations could be enhanced.

Public-private dialogue (PPD) is an essential element for an articulate SME policy given the very heterogeneous nature of SMEs and the large number of policy areas affecting SME performance. Consultations with private-sector organisations that are truly representative of different types of SMEs are necessary throughout the policy cycle, including needs analysis, design, implementation, and monitoring and evaluation. PPD should follow a formal and transparent structure (e.g. regular meetings, electronic consultations). Participants should understand clearly the policy implications or results of the consultations. Furthermore, private sector organisations should effectively disseminate the information from PPD among their associates.

Progress since 2014

This interim assessment shows that although PPD is a common practice across all MED economies, the formality and regularity of the consultations differs from place to place. Furthermore, it is not clear how well different types of SMEs and entrepreneurs are represented in policy making.

Morocco and Israel already had strong PPD mechanisms, and there have been few advances in the past four years:

- **Morocco** continues to have a strong PPD mechanism through the National Committee for the Business Climate (CNEA), which provides a formal platform for various governmental and non-governmental actors, including from the private sector, to identify design and execute actions to improve the business environment. The most important organisation from the private sector is the General Confederation of Moroccan Enterprises (CGEM), with about 88 000 members representing different sectors and regions. The CGEM is formed by "commissions", one of which is devoted to representing the interests of SMEs. Since its creation in 2009, the CNEA has contributed to significant improvements of the business climate in Morocco, as reflected in the *Doing Business* and the Global Competitiveness Index rankings.
- **Israel** continues to have a well-developed system of PPD, especially around regulatory reform. The SMBA holds quarterly meetings with the SME community. Organisations such as the Independent Businesses Association (LAHAV), the Federation of Israeli Chambers of Commerce (FICC), the Manufacturers Association of Israel and the Enterprise Europe Network Partners have been very active in PPD processes.

New platforms for PPD have been created in Algeria and Tunisia, but they are at an early stage:

- **Tunisia's** transition has involved a complex process of political and economic dialogue among numerous actors in recent years. This has been reflected in important achievements such as the adoption of a new Constitution in 2014 and economic reforms such as the adoption of the new Investment Law. In 2014, building on the strong process of multipartite political and economic exchange of ideas, Tunisia launched the National Business Agenda (NBA) to create a public-private dialogue platform to advance business climate reforms. The NBA includes the government, the Tunisian Union of Industry, Commerce and Crafts (UTICA), the Tunisian Union of Agriculture and Fisheries (UTAP) and the Arab Institute of Business Leaders (IACE).
- In **Algeria**, broad economic issues continue to be tackled by a Tripartite Council (*la Tripartite*) comprising the government, the General Union of Algerian Workers (UGTA) and numerous private sector associations. Most recently, the National Consultation Council for SME development (CNC) was created as stipulated by the SME Law of 2017.

Less progress has been made in most of the other MED economies covered, although there are ongoing discussions to take action:

- **Egypt** continues to have a very fragmented landscape of business organisations representing SMEs.[9] Private sector organisations are considering establishing departments for SMEs, while the MSMEDA is expected to promote stronger PPD. Of the three boards in the MSMEDA – the Advisory Board, the Board of Directors, and the Board of Trustees – the first two include representatives from the private sector and from non-governmental organisations (NGOs).
- Public-private consultations were already a common practice in **Jordan**. The Economic and Social Council was the main conduit for public-private consultations, meeting at least twice a year. The preparation of the national SME Strategy in 2013-2014 involved extensive consultations with different participants. Yet the pending implementation of the SME Strategy means that the PPD mechanisms foreseen in that document, especially the creation of an SME Advisory Committee composed of private sector and non-governmental organisations, are not functioning. JEDCO and the OECD are currently working on making such mechanisms operational.
- In 2014 the main initiative promoting PPD in **Lebanon** was the multipartite platform Improving the Business Environment in Lebanon (IBEL). However, IBEL is no longer operational. The Ministry of Industry is developing an action plan to institutionalise PPD in the SME policy-making process through a ministerial decree.[10] The SME Strategy to 2020 and its action plan include provisions to foster PPD through regular roundtables, the establishment of a web portal and mobile application to facilitate the engagement of SMEs, and a yearly SME forum to gather stakeholders.
- Public-private dialogue was already a common practice in **PA**. The main PPD forum still is the Private Sector Coordinating Council, but it no longer holds regular consultations. Additionally, SMEs were often sidelined as SME associations did not play a significant role. The Palestinian Export Council was created to implement the National Export Strategy and works as an advisory council with the private sector. The Ministry of National Economy is also implementing a Clusters Development Project to promote five business agglomerations: leather and shoes, palm and dates, stone and marble, tourism, and furniture. The project builds on a strong PPD mechanism representing hundreds of SMEs.

For further action

Public-private dialogue is a common practice across the MED region. However, there is little or unclear information on what the modalities of PPD are: how formal PPD platforms are; how often the consultations are held; and, how satisfied different types of SMEs and entrepreneurs are with their representation in PPD.

There is ample scope in the region to improve public-private dialogue during the full policy cycle and to enhance the representation of SMEs in that dialogue, including also the sub-national and sectoral levels.

The way forward

Overall, MED economies continue to put into place and reinforce the building blocks of SME and entrepreneurship policy: establishing official SME definitions, collecting and disseminating SME and entrepreneurship statistics, strengthening institutional co-ordination and cohesive approaches in all SME policy areas, and further engaging SMEs in public-private dialogue. This interim assessment puts forward the following additional actions for MED economies:

- SME definitions could be revised to include a mix of criteria, especially employment, turnover and balance sheet considerations. Some MED definitions do not include employment criteria and some others do not even distinguish between micro, small and medium-sized firms. Furthermore, almost no definition seems to explicitly address the independence or autonomy of SMEs (i.e. whether they should be eligible for government support when a SME belongs to or has ownership over other company or companies). Doing so would help to better reflect the diverse nature of micro, small and medium-sized enterprises operating in different sectors and with different levels of efficiency and productivity. SME definitions could also have a clear legal or official status – reflected, for example, in SME laws. This should help to unify the many definitions used by different institutions.
- The adoption of official SME definitions, especially those including employment criteria, is important for the collection of more and better official statistics on SMEs and entrepreneurship. Economic and enterprise censuses could use these definitions to gather data and publish indicators. Efforts to gather SME data from official sources (e.g. business registries, tax administrations, and social security administrations) and business associations could ease the burden on enterprises and reduce data collection costs by making it unnecessary to conduct costly censuses every few years. The data collected directly from these administrative sources could also be useful to take the pulse of SMEs and entrepreneurship by producing timely indicators on enterprise entry, exit, growth and job creation and losses. In economies with significant informal sectors, the data could be complemented by surveys covering informal employment.
- MED economies could do much more to maximise resources devoted to SME and entrepreneurship development by enhancing co-ordination among the many policy actors active in this area. High-level co-ordination and leadership would provide strategic coherence at the national level and could also be invaluable as a source of SME policy advocacy. Technical-level co-operation and sub-national co-ordination would help to avoid policy overlaps and address policy gaps, including in less developed interior areas. Such co-ordination could be guided by the effective implementation of multiannual SME and entrepreneurship strategies identifying key objectives, key performance indicators, responsible parties, and budgets to be mobilised. The designation of an SME agency or unit as secretariat for the implementation and co-ordination of the SME strategy could be highly valuable as long as that agency has the appropriate political mandate and the necessary human, technical and financial resources.
- Comprehensive PPD platforms for the participation of private sector associations, non-governmental actors and, when relevant, donor agencies, are also important in ensuring that the co-ordination and implementation of strategies is coherent. To be effective, these PPD platforms have to be truly representative of the various SMEs and entrepreneurs operating across the territory and in different economic activities.

Notes

[1] Morocco's SME agency was called ANPME in 2014, and it has now been renamed Morocco SME.

[2] http://www.gemconsortium.org/.

[3] They include Morocco SME, the Central Bank (BAM), the Ministry of Industry, the National Confederation of Moroccan Enterprises (CGEM), the credit guarantee agency (CCG) and the statistics office (HCP).

[4] The bulletins include total SME population, SME entries and exits, employment, and exports and imports. They also comprise information on SMEs by economic activity and territorial distribution. The data is obtained from official sources such as the National Social Security Institute (CNAS) and its equivalent for the self-employed and independent professionals (CASNOS).

[5] The following institutions are involved: the National Statistics Office (ONS), the business registry, the CNAS and CASNOS, the tax administration, the customs administration, the chamber of commerce and industry, and the Association of Banks and Financial Institutions (ABEF).

[6] This includes extensive information on the structure and performance of the enterprise population (firm demographics, value added, employment, etc.), productivity, business dynamics (entry, exit, high growth firms, etc.), job creation, international trade and other indicators.

[7] The SME Policy Index 2014 noted a blurred separation between the functions of policy development and implementation. Policy development responsibilities were split between different ministries: Trade and Industry, Investment and Finance, and Planning. In terms of implementation, the Social Fund for Development (SFD) was in charge of micro and small enterprises, while the General Authority for Investment and Free Zones (GAFI) focused on small and medium-sized enterprises with high growth potential. The Ministry of Trade and Industry, through the Industrial Modernisation Centre (IMC) and other affiliated organisations, supported small-to-large enterprises operating in industrial sectors.

[8] The SME Strategy includes a complete policy framework covering six strategic pillars and a governance structure including: 1) a high-level committee (formed by relevant ministers, the governor of the Central Bank and private sector organisations); 2) a technical-level committee composed of focal points in relevant public sector institutions; 3) an SME Advisory Committee composed of private sector and non-governmental organisations (which are very active in providing SME and entrepreneurship support in Jordan); and 4) SME regional committees in each governorate. The SME Strategy also foresees designating JEDCO as the SME co-ordination agency and the secretariat to the high-level committee.

[9] Some of the most important private sector organisations are the Federation of Egyptian Chambers of Commerce, the Federation of Egyptian Industries, the Egyptian Business Association, the Egyptian Junior Business Association, the Egyptian Federation of Investors, the Alexandria Business Association, and the Women's Business Association.

[10] The government is working in collaboration with national and international experts, and receives support under the Enhancement of the Business Environment in the Southern Mediterranean (EBESM) project.

Bibliography

European Union (2015), *User guide to the SME Definition,* https://ec.europa.eu/growth/content/revised-user-guide-sme-definition-0_en.

OECD (forthcoming), SME and Entrepreneurship Outlook 2018.

OECD (2016), *SME and Entrepreneurship Policy in Israel 2016*, OECD Publishing, Paris, http://dx.doi.org/10.1787/9789264262324-en.

Chapter 2. Improving the business environment for SMEs and entrepreneurs

Business laws and regulations need to serve the public interest without placing undue burdens on private enterprise. This chapter focuses on key reforms and actions since 2014 in terms of administrative reform and simplification, the operational environment for business creation, and bankruptcy laws and procedures.

The interim assessment finds that several MED economies are working towards establishing formal mechanisms for regulatory impact analysis – although not yet through the implementation of an SME test. The interim assessment also notes increasing efforts to facilitate procedures for enterprise creation, particularly through the introduction of single identification numbers and online registration, to different degrees.

Key recommendations from the chapter are as follows:

1. MED economies could step up their efforts to introduce ex ante and ex post regulatory impact analysis (RIA) – especially those that have not yet established a comprehensive committee and strategy to improve the business environment. Governments could also introduce the SME test, which is still absent in the MED region.

2. There are laudable efforts to facilitate the creation of new firms by introducing online portals and single identification numbers when dealing with different organisations. These efforts could be taken a step further by reinforcing the role of one-stop shops in the facilitation of business registration.

3. Those economies that have reformed their insolvency legislation could support the implementation phase closely, particularly through training programmes supporting professionals working in the judiciary and related occupations.

The statistical data for Israel are supplied by and under the responsibility of the relevant Israeli authorities. The use of such data by the OECD is without prejudice to the status of the Golan Heights, East Jerusalem and Israeli settlements in the West Bank under the terms of international law.

Enterprises constantly interact with the public administration throughout their life cycles. This interaction starts with registration procedures, including applications for the licenses and permits needed to launch a business. Enterprises have to comply with a wide range of regulations (either horizontal or sector-specific) related to taxation, the use of production factors (such as labour and energy), protection of consumers and the environment, supervision of market activity, and restriction of anti-competitive practices. In addition, enterprises are asked to report regularly on their activities and respond to data and information requests from public bodies. On top of this, businesses must comply with requirements set by different levels of government: national, regional and local.

If it is not efficiently organised, this interaction with the public administration may lead to an unnecessary administrative burden that can weigh heavily on company resources, particularly for smaller enterprises. In the case of micro enterprises, it is often the entrepreneur who takes on the obligation to deal with administrative requirements, diverting time and resources from the core business activity. A more responsive public administration, with the capacity to interact efficiently with all classes of enterprises, provides a better environment for the productivity and growth of the enterprise sector.

This chapter focuses on key reforms and actions carried out since 2014 in terms of administrative reform and simplification, the operational environment for business creation, and bankruptcy laws and procedures. The interim assessment finds progress in almost all the economies and policy areas assessed, as summarised in Table 2.1.

Table 2.1. Overview of improving business environments for SMEs and entrepreneurs

	RIA and SME test	Single ID number	Online registration	OSS for enterprise creation	New bankruptcy law
Algeria	No	No	Yes, through a notary at www.jecreemonentreprise.dz. Implementation is limited due to the non-recognition of e-signature and e-payment.	No	No
Egypt	Yes, under ERRADA but for the revision of some laws. No SME test.	No	Yes, although documents have to be signed in person.	Yes	Yes
Israel	Yes, under Government Resolution 2118. No SME test.	Yes	Yes, no lawyer or notary needs to be involved if the company has an e-certificate.	Yes	Yes
Jordan	Yes, under MENA Transition Fund project *Jordan Economic Legislation Reform 2016-2018.* No SME test.	Yes	No	No	Yes
Lebanon	No	No	No, but there is an e-government project for business regulations at OMSAR.	No	No
Morocco	No RIA. CNEA is working towards an SME test.	Yes	CREOL is in progress; the pilot phase has been completed.	Yes	Yes
PA	No	No	No	No	No
Tunisia	A regulatory guillotine exists. No SME test.	Yes	Yes	Yes	No

Most MED economies have progressed in the implementation of regulatory impact analysis, but the implementation of the SME test is preliminary at best.

Regulatory impact analysis (RIA) is a systemic approach to critically assessing the positive and negative effects of proposed and existing regulations and non-regulatory alternatives. In other words, RIA helps to ensure that regulation is produced efficiently and effectively and that regulatory decisions have considered issues such as costs, benefits, distributional effects and administrative requirements.[1] RIA mechanisms can help to systematically improve the current stock of business regulations (*ex post* regulatory stock-taking/evaluation) by reviewing or eliminating redundant, burdensome or outdated procedures and rules, or by adapting existing regulations to changes in the economy and society. RIA can also improve future regulations (*ex ante*) by providing mechanisms to assess the merits, costs and benefits of new procedures and rules.

Beyond analysing the impact on the general businesses, RIA mechanisms can also explicitly consider the impact of SME legislation through the introduction of the "SME test", which is a fundamental part of the "think small first" principle.[2] The SME test may lead to the exclusion of SMEs (often micro enterprises) from the scope of regulations or to the introduction of exemptions, transition periods or tailor-made provisions for SMEs.

Progress since 2014

The SME Policy Index 2014 pointed to the increasing awareness among MED economies of the importance of improving the quality of the regulatory environment and launching legislative simplification and regulatory reform programmes. Of the eight economies, however, only Egypt and Morocco had implemented systematic regulatory reform programmes, co-ordinated by an inter-ministerial body and organised around a multi-year strategy complemented by short-term action plans. Furthermore, none of the MED economies had applied RIA formally and consistently, with the exception of pilot projects in Egypt, Israel and Jordan.

This interim assessment registers progress on RIA in the following economies:

- In **Israel**, the October 2014 Resolution 2118 includes provisions for RIA *ex ante* and *ex post* (OECD, 2015). The Resolution is applied by a special unit at the Prime Minister's Office, in collaboration with contact points in each ministry or government agency involved in matters related to regulations. Nonetheless, the implementation of Resolution 2118 started in January 2017 and there are no published results. As part of the wider RIA efforts, the SMBA has published guidance for the implementation of an SME test; however, the guidance is not yet part of the RIA process.
- In **Jordan** a pilot regulatory guillotine initially launched before the 2014 assessment has been continued and significantly expanded under a MENA Transition Fund project, Jordan Economic Legislation Reform Project (2016-2018). The project is developing a roadmap for regulatory reform and building implementation capacity. Its ultimate goal is to establish a regulatory impact analysis mechanism to ensure the quality of new laws and regulations and the quality of regulatory delivery. There is no reference to the development of an SME test, though.
- In **Tunisia**, the General Directorate for Reform and Administrative Outlook (DGRA), within the Office of the Head of Government, continues to co-ordinate the implementation of a regulatory guillotine. Furthermore, a new initiative called "SOS *Ijraat*" was created in 2016 to receive information from businesses on difficulties with administrative matters. The initiative is framed by a public-private consultation platform called the National Business Agenda (NBA). There is no reference to the development of an SME test.

The assessment also notes efforts to improve the business environment in the following economies:

- In **Egypt**, the Egyptian Regulatory Reform and Development Activity (ERRADA) has been reactivated and is currently participating in the revision of a number of laws and the implementation of a comprehensive inventory of business regulations (these are being published in an e-registry for public consultation). ERRADA is one of the most advanced initiatives in this area in the region. However, there is no evidence of the *consistent* application of RIA to business regulations. The SME Strategy under preparation is expected to fully reflect the SME test and the "think small first" principle.
- The National Committee of the Business Climate (CNEA) continues to be the main driver of regulatory reform and administrative simplification in **Morocco**, but it is not an RIA initiative. There is an RIA requirement in the Law on the Functioning of Government Bodies and the Status of their Members. According to it, every new law proposal should be accompanied by an impact assessment. In compliance with this, the Secretary General of the Government (SGG) and SME Morocco are studying the possibility of introducing the SME test.

There has been little progress in other MED economies:

- There is no evidence of concrete efforts in **Algeria** or **Lebanon** to develop and implement RIA and introduce an SME test.
- In **PA** there is no practice of RIA or the SME test and there are no plans for their introduction. Gathering evidence for RIA requires consultation mechanisms which are essential to fill the democratic vacuum created by the non-functioning of the Palestinian Parliament. Laws are not approved by the parliament but issued by the President under a state of emergency. A strong public-private dialogue could provide a platform for such consultation mechanisms.

It is worth noting that Jordan, Morocco and Tunisia systematically publish draft laws online and in a centralised manner for consultation. In Jordan and Tunisia, the online consultation is part of their open government commitments.[3]

For further action

This interim assessment notes progress in the implementation of RIA, in particular through the creation of formal mechanisms in Israel and Tunisia and the continuation of pilot projects in Jordan. It also notes the continuation of efforts to improve business environments through comprehensive initiatives (although not through RIA, strictly speaking) in Egypt and Morocco. None of the MED economies applies the SME test, although there are ongoing efforts in that direction in Israel and Morocco with the technical support of the EU's Enhancement of the Business Environment in the Southern Mediterranean (EBESM) project.

All MED economies have public-private dialogue platforms that could advocate the implementation of formal *ex ante* and *ex post* RIA mechanisms and the introduction of an SME test. Such efforts would go beyond targeting very specific regulatory aspects (for example, those reflected in *Doing Business*) and would involve improving the business environment for SMEs in a systematic and comprehensive way.

There has been progress in online registration and single identification numbers, but little development of one-stop shops.

Firms have to comply with a wide range of laws and regulations throughout their life cycles. This section focuses on a one-off procedure: business registration. Other legal requirements and administrative procedures also have a great impact on enterprise performance, such as those concerning taxation and labour. However, business registration may be viewed as a proxy for the overall level of efficiency of the public administration. Furthermore, it is often the entrepreneur who takes on the obligation to deal with administrative requirements, diverting time and resources from the core business activity. This is very often the case for start-ups.

Both the level of entrepreneurial activity and the rate of formal business start-ups in the MED region are usually lower than in other emerging markets. More efficient business registration procedures may help reduce barriers to business creation and provide an incentive for the formal registration of ongoing business activities. Inefficient business registration and burdensome licence application procedures are one of the many factors pushing a large number of private enterprises to operate informally.

This interim assessment looks at three specific issues related to the formalities for enterprise creation:

- The availability of *single identification numbers* used by different administrations involved in company registration (business registry, social security, tax administration, business associations, etc.). Single identification numbers help reduce the costs of, and time required for, registration by making it simple for different agencies to share administrative information on a specific firm. They can also provide an important source of administrative information for the development of more timely, extensive and accurate statistics.
- The ability to *register a company using online platforms*. This results in a faster and smoother registration process for entrepreneurs.
- The availability of *one-stop shops* that allow firms and entrepreneurs to deal with different administrations from a single space.

Progress since 2014

The SME Policy Index 2014 noted some efforts by MED economies to facilitate enterprise creation through single identification numbers, online registration and one-stop shops. Algeria had extended its network of one-stop shops to facilitate company registration, and Egypt had established three one-stop-shop networks. Jordan and Tunisia had introduced single identification numbers, and Morocco had eliminated minimum capital requirements. Company registration processes in Israel and Lebanon were still relatively costly, whereas in PA the process was quite lengthy. The provision of e-government services, including online registration, remained limited.

This interim assessment finds that MED economies have generally progressed in these policy areas. However, looking at the *Doing Business* "Starting a business" indicators reveals that the region has plenty of room to improve – with the exception of Israel and Morocco, which perform relatively well in this area (see Table 2.2).

Table 2.2. *Doing Business* indicators for 'Starting a business'

Economy	Starting a Business DTF[1]	Starting a Business rank	Procedure – Men (number)	Time – Men (days)	Cost – Men (% of income per capita)	Procedure – Women (number)	Time – Women (days)	Cost – Women (% of income per capita)	Paid-in min. capital (% of income per capita)
Algeria	77.54	145	12	20	11.1	12	20	11.1	0
Egypt	84.53	103	8	14	7.4	9	15	7.4	0
Israel	92.3	37	4	12	3.2	4	12	3.2	0
Jordan	84.4	105	7	12	24.2	8	13	24.2	0.1
Lebanon	78.17	143	8	15	42	8	15	42	42.3
Morocco	92.46	35	4	9	8	4	9	8	0
Tunisia	85.02	100	9	11	4.6	9	11	4.6	0
PA	69.59	169	10	43	45.1	11	44	45.1	0
OECD	91.35	47	4.9	8.5	3.1	4.9	8.5	3.1	8.7

1 An economy's distance to frontier (DTF) is reflected on a scale from 0 to 100, where 0 represents the lowest performance and 100 represents the frontier. The distance to frontier score helps assess the absolute level of regulatory performance over time. It measures the distance of each economy to the "frontier", which represents the best performance observed on each of the indicators across all economies in the *Doing Business* sample since 2005.

Source: World Bank (2018), *Doing Business.*

A few economies have in place all three elements related to the formalities for enterprise creation analysed in this section (i.e. single identification numbers, online registration and one-stop-shops for enterprise creation).

- In **Egypt** a company's registration can now be initiated online and physically concluded in one window and one step at the facilities of the General Authority for Investment (GAFI). As reflected by *Doing Business*, in 2016 Egypt improved its one-stop shop for business registration by introducing a unit to liaise between the tax and labour authorities on one the hand, and the firm on the other.[4] However, there is no evidence of the implementation of a single identification number for companies, although such stipulation is reflected in the new Investment Law of 2017.
- In **Israel,** business registration has become easier through the adoption of 1) a single identification number to deal with different government agencies and 2) the establishment of an online registration platform that, according to reports, handles 75% of all applications and provides registration between two and four days.
- As part of the *Doing Business* reforms driven by CNEA, **Morocco** has streamlined the process of starting a company by eliminating the minimum capital requirement, reducing registration costs, simplifying documentation requirements and introducing an online platform to reserve the company name. Morocco is also revamping a project to create an online system for enterprise creation, and it has created a single identification number (*identifiant commun de l'entreprise,* or ICE) for natural and legal persons to register more easily.

Other economies have different degrees of advancement towards that direction:

- In May 2017, **Algeria** created a new electronic portal for enterprise registration, which provides useful information on the different requirements to create a firm. However, the procedure has to be accompanied by a notary registered with the National Centre of the Commercial Register (CNRC). The notary is in charge of transferring the information and the documents necessary to the agencies concerned by the procedure. The portal has registered 80 new enterprises and around 276 notaries have been trained to use the platform.

- In **Jordan** a Local Enterprise Support (LENS) project has been established by the United States Agency for International Development (USAID) to, among other things, improve business registration by strengthening the IT capacity of the business registry (Companies Control Department) and developing a business registration manual to help entrepreneurs learn the registration process for different types of businesses. Nonetheless, there is no evidence of concrete results for these initiatives in new enterprise registration – nor is there evidence of progress with regard to online registration services and one-stop shops for companies' registration.

More progress could be made by Lebanon and PA:

- **Lebanon** has initiated an e-government initiative led by the Office of the Minister of State for Administrative Reform (OMSAR) and in co-operation with relevant ministries involved in business regulations. However, as yet there is no evidence of improved regulations and procedures for enterprise creation.
- In **PA,** *Doing Business* reports the elimination of the paid-in minimum capital requirement for starting a business. The consultations for this interim assessment, however, noted no other important reforms to facilitate enterprise creation.

For further action

All MED economies, except Lebanon and PA, have progressed in the introduction of single identification numbers for company registration and online registration. However, there is still much to do in terms of one-stop shops, which have not expanded over the past few years.

Many MED economies have updated their bankruptcy laws, but the impact will depend on their implementation.

Efficient bankruptcy procedures allow the reorganisation of ailing but viable firms and the fast and inexpensive liquidation of unviable businesses. By providing an equitable and predictable framework, they also promote risk-taking by entrepreneurs and financers. This section analyses two themes: "bankruptcy procedures", which encompass the laws and procedures dealing with distressed companies, receivership and bankruptcy; and "resolving insolvency", which looks at the relevant indicators from *Doing Business.*

Progress since 2014

The SME Policy Index 2014 and this interim assessment show that all MED economies have in place laws and procedures to deal with enterprise insolvency and bankruptcy. In recent years Egypt, Israel, Jordan, Morocco and Tunisia have updated their bankruptcy legislation as follows:

- In **Egypt**, a new law was approved by parliament on 28 January 2018. The law decriminalises bankruptcy by abolishing prison sentences and allows companies more time and options for restructuring by introducing mechanisms to help settle commercial disputes outside the courtroom and simplify bankruptcy proceedings.

- In **Israel**, an Insolvency and Economic Rehabilitation Law was approved by the Knesset (the national legislature) in March 2018. This is reported to be a comprehensive law covering all procedures for individuals (bankruptcy) and for companies (liquidation, receivership, stay of proceedings and restructuring). Its goals are to advance the debtor's financial rehabilitation; to maximise the return to creditors; to increase the certainty and stability of the law; to shorten procedures; and to reduce the bureaucratic burden.
- **Jordan** in April 2018 approved a new Reorganisation, Bankruptcy and Liquidation Law establishing a legal framework for distressed companies.
- **Morocco** adopted a new law on insolvency on April 2018. Tellingly, the objectives of the new law are reflected in the proposed change of name, from "Enterprise difficulties" to "Procedures for the prevention, rescue and treatment of the difficulties of enterprises."
- In **Tunisia**, the Collective Insolvency Proceedings Act (*loi 2016-36 du 29 avril 2016 relative aux procédures collectives*) was enacted in April 2016. Some observers see it as more concerned with the liquidation of companies than with their restructuring for an eventual redressing. Others point to its positive aspects such as 1) alert systems for auditors of enterprises that could be in difficulty or 2) new rules of conduct to be observed by the courts, judicial experts, and the various partners of the company during the phases of amicable settlement, judicial settlement and eventually, bankruptcy.

The rest of the MED economies have less extensive initiatives related to improving the legal framework:

- **Algeria**'s Code of Commerce (order 75-79) of 1975 establishes bankruptcy procedures. This interim assessment notes that although Algeria trains judges in this area, there is no tracking of results of this programme – for example, whether the training has resulted in fewer liquidations and business exits and more business restructurings.
- In 2014, the government of **Lebanon** was revising the legal framework for insolvency and drafting a modern bankruptcy law through the IBEL initiative. There have been no changes in this regard since then.
- In the case of **PA**, the cabinet is reported to be working on a Companies Law that will update old bankruptcy laws.

The World Bank's *Doing Business* indicators provide a glimpse of the cost and duration of resolving insolvency and the recovery rates for creditors of distressed firms. These indicators show that only Israel and Tunisia have relatively effective bankruptcy mechanisms by regional standards (Table 2.3). In terms of changes over time, the *Doing Business* indicators do not register any major reforms. It is yet to be seen what impact the recent legal reforms will have in future editions; measuring the impact on performance indicators (time, cost and recovery rate) will require time.

Table 2.3. *Doing Business* indicators for Resolving insolvency

Economy	Resolving Insolvency DTF[1]	Resolving Insolvency rank	Recovery rate (cents on the dollar)	Time (years)	Cost (% of estate)
Algeria	49.24	71	50.8	1.3	7
Egypt	38.89	115	25.8	2.5	22
Israel	72.74	29	62.6	2	23
Jordan	30.53	146	27.7	3	20
Lebanon	29.42	147	31.4	3	15
Morocco	34.03	134	28.4	3.5	18
Tunisia	54.53	63	52	1.3	7
West Bank and Gaza	0	168	0	No Practice	No Practice
OECD high income	76.12	24	71.2	1.7	9.1

1 An economy's distance to frontier (DTF) is reflected on a scale from 0 to 100, where 0 represents the lowest performance and 100 represents the frontier. The distance to frontier score helps assess the absolute level of regulatory performance over time. It measures the distance of each economy to the "frontier", which represents the best performance observed on each of the indicators across all economies in the *Doing Business* sample since 2005.

Source: World Bank (2018), Doing Business.

For further action

As in 2014, this interim assessment notes that although MED economies have put in place laws and procedures to deal with insolvency and bankruptcy, evidence on levels of implementation remains scarce. As in 2014, this may point to a preferred use of out-of-court mechanisms, high levels of economic informality, and the lack of a system to track the effectiveness of insolvency mechanisms. MED economies could therefore strengthen their monitoring of insolvency and bankruptcy cases in order to better assess the efficiency of the legal and procedural framework.

This interim assessment also notes recent legal reforms in several MED economies over the past few years. These reforms could be accompanied by training programmes supporting professionals working in the judiciary and related occupations.

The way forward

Business laws and regulations need to serve the public interest without placing undue burdens on private enterprise. That is, they need to be effective and efficient. This interim assessment notes that MED economies have stepped up their efforts to improve the business environment, including through RIA, although not yet through the implementation of a SME Test.

The interim assessment also notes increasing efforts to facilitate the procedures for enterprise creation, particularly by introducing single identification numbers, in at least four of the eight MED economies; and the introduction of online registration, to varying degrees, in four economies. This is important since easy and inexpensive start-up procedures facilitate entrepreneurship and ease the expansion of the formal economy.

In addition, efficient bankruptcy leads to a better allocation of resources, and makes it easier for companies to reorganise or wind up. Progress in this area is much less evident and the interim assessment notes that, as in 2014, this remains an issue to be tackled in most MED economies, particularly in Jordan, Lebanon, Morocco and PA. On the other hand, the assessment also notes the recent legal reforms in Egypt, Israel, Jordan, Morocco and Tunisia.

This interim assessment puts forward the following additional actions for MED economies:

- More could be done to introduce *ex ante* and *ex post* RIA, especially in those MED economies that have not yet established a comprehensive committee and strategy to improve the business environment (Algeria, Lebanon and PA). Such an endeavour could be part of the agenda of the active public-private dialogue platforms that exist across the region.
- Governments could introduce the SME test, which is still absent in the MED region.
- There have also been laudable efforts to facilitate the creation of new firms through the introduction of online portals and single identification numbers when dealing with different organisations (in all cases except Lebanon and PA). These efforts could be taken a step further by reinforcing the role of one-stop shops in facilitating business registration.
- Economies that have reformed their insolvency legislation could do more to support the implementation phase, particularly through training programmes aimed at professionals working in the judiciary and related occupations.

Notes

[1] See OECD (2012), *Recommendation of the Council on Regulatory Policy and Governance*, OECD Publishing, Paris, http://dx.doi.org/10.1787/9789264209022-en and The OECD Reference Checklist for Regulatory-Decision Making.

[2] http://europa.eu/rapid/press-release_IP-08-1003_en.htm.

[3] Consultation in draft laws is a key principle of the OECD's Regulatory Policy Recommendation and Open Government. See OECD (2013), *Regulatory Reform in the Middle East and North Africa: Implementing Regulatory Policy Principles to Foster Inclusive Growth*, OECD Reviews of Regulatory Reform, OECD Publishing, Paris, http://dx.doi.org/10.1787/9789264204553-en and http://www.oecd.org/gov/regulatory-policy/mena-2013-report.htm.

[4] World Bank, *Doing Business* (2018), "Business Reforms in Egypt, Arab Rep.", http://www.doingbusiness.org/Reforms/Overview/Economy/egypt.

Bibliography

OECD (2015), *OECD Regulatory Policy Outlook 2015*, OECD Publishing, Paris, http://dx.doi.org/10.1787/9789264238770-en.

OECD (2013), *Regulatory Reform in the Middle East and North Africa: Implementing Regulatory Policy Principles to Foster Inclusive Growth*, OECD Reviews of Regulatory Reform, OECD Publishing, Paris, http://dx.doi.org/10.1787/9789264204553-en.

OECD (2012), *Recommendation of the Council on Regulatory Policy and Governance*, OECD Publishing, Paris, http://dx.doi.org/10.1787/9789264209022-en.

World Bank (2018), *Doing Business 2018: Reforming to Create Jobs*. World Bank, Washington, DC, http://www.doingbusiness.org/~/media/WBG/DoingBusiness/Documents/Annual-Reports/English/DB2018-Full-Report.pdf.

Chapter 3. Fostering access to finance

Access to finance is an area where significant progress has been achieved in the MED region over the past few years. This is especially the case in terms of the legal and regulatory framework for access to finance, where a number of credit bureaus and registries of moveable assets have been established, and where secured transactions laws have been passed or are in the process of being passed.

There has also been progress in terms of the expansion of sources of finance for SMEs and entrepreneurs, although here it is less evident how this has resulted in increased funding and whether there will be a greater role for private actors in the future – namely privately-owned credit guarantee schemes, business angel investments and private equity vehicles.

This interim assessment puts forward the following actions for MED economies:

1. Continue bridging information asymmetries through the creation and expansion of credit registries and, more notably, credit bureaus. Credit bureaus are especially useful because 1) they are managed by private actors and 2) they draw on more diverse sources of information than credit registries (utilities, consumption credit, microfinance institutions, etc.).

2. Increase efforts to create registries of moveable assets. This is important for entrepreneurs and SMEs lacking real estate to pledge as collateral, and particularly relevant for potentially innovative firms which may rely on intangible assets such as trademarks, patents and intellectual property.

3. Continue expanding the diversity and reach of different sources of finance (credit, equity and hybrid instruments) and include strategies for developing competitive markets in this area so that the state eventually steps out in favour of private actors.

4. Improve the monitoring and evaluation of the impact of reforms for access to finance. Joining the OECD Scoreboard on Financing SMEs and Entrepreneurs, which contributes to filling the knowledge gap in SME finance trends and conditions, would be an important step in this direction.

The statistical data for Israel are supplied by and under the responsibility of the relevant Israeli authorities. The use of such data by the OECD is without prejudice to the status of the Golan Heights, East Jerusalem and Israeli settlements in the West Bank under the terms of international law.

Access to finance is one of the critical pillars of policy on SMEs and entrepreneurship. By facilitating access to external finance, governments can help businesses meet their capital needs, handle cash-flow cycles, expand their business capacity, and address many other needs.

As in other regions in the world, SMEs in MED economies experience bigger obstacles than large enterprises in accessing external sources of financing. Some of these obstacles are related to structural problems concerning SMEs' managerial capacities, such as unclear business planning, weak accounting practices and bookkeeping, low financial education and low integration in the formal economy. Other obstacles stem from information asymmetries between credit providers and SMEs, moral hazard and high transaction costs. Deficient regulatory and legal frameworks, underdeveloped financial and banking systems also limit the credit supply.

In MED economies, bank lending – the main source of formal finance – is constrained by the relatively poor quality of the legal and regulatory environment, the limited depth of financial markets, and lack of competition among banking and financial institutions. Alternative sources of finance – such as leasing, factoring, mezzanine financing or the provision of equity capital – remain underdeveloped.

Facilitating access to finance for SMEs requires a holistic and multi-dimensional approach that combines the efforts of public authorities, local and international financial institutions, banks and private firms. Addressing financial market inefficiencies can increase the potential of firms to be created, grow and survive. This chapter focuses on key reforms and actions taken since the SME Policy Index 2014 in terms of the legal and regulatory framework for access to finance, particularly the existence of two tools for addressing information asymmetries in access to bank credit: credit information systems (public credit registries or private credit bureaus) and registries of moveable assets. The chapter also looks into the availability of sources of external finance, notably credit but also equity investments.

Table 3.1 summarises the information in this chapter, which overall finds positive to very positive developments on access to finance in all MED economies.

Table 3.1. Overview of fostering access to finance

	Credit information systems (credit registries and bureaus)	Registries of moveable assets	Other measures to improve access to credit	Reforms to facilitate access to equity and other sources of finance
Algeria	Relative expansion of credit registry and no credit bureau yet	No registry of moveable assets	No	A *Wilaya* (governorate) Investment Fund continues to operate
Egypt	Credit registry and credit bureau function	New initiative for the creation of registry of moveable assets, building on the 2015 Moveable Security Law	Injection of funds by the Central Bank	Working towards the establishment of venture capital for early-stage firms and for distressed but viable SMEs
Israel	Credit registry and two credit bureaus	Registry of moveable assets operational	Creation of a committee to reinforce competition in the banking sector	Several reforms on easier IPOs, P2P lending and creation of two new equity funds for medium-sized firms
Jordan	Credit registry and a new credit bureau	Recent registry established but not yet fully functional	Expansion of credit guarantees by the JLGC	Some reforms ongoing but pending the approval of the Companies Law
Lebanon	Credit registry but no credit bureau	No registry of moveable assets	Injection of funds by the Central Bank	Several new initiatives focusing on start-ups and innovative firms
Morocco	Expansion of the services of credit bureau and opening of a new credit bureau	Draft proposal to reform the law on moveable assets	Several measures by banks and government	No evidence
PA	Fully functioning credit registry but no credit bureau	Registry of moveable assets operational	Introduction of a Secured Transactions Law	New VC funds, although there is no formal legal framework
Tunisia	New credit registry for microfinance; expected creation of a credit bureau	Ongoing reform of the registry of moveable assets	Administrative instruction to develop a credit rating scheme	Collective Investment Code pending approval

Most MED economies have undertaken important initiatives in the past few years to improve the regulatory framework for access to finance.

The regulatory framework for access to finance plays a crucial role in encouraging lenders and investors to provide the capital that SMEs and entrepreneurs need to start up, continue and expand their businesses. This entails 1) the development of adequate *systems* that facilitate the flow of information between lenders and borrowers, and that support the pledging of collateral other than immoveable assets such as buildings and land; and 2) the existence and application of *laws* that determine the rights and obligations of lenders and borrowers, investors and investees.

Credit information systems can help to tackle information asymmetries that are especially relevant for SMEs and entrepreneurs. Credit information systems can be divided into two general categories:

- Credit *registries*, which are held at central banks and whose main function is to track the health of the financial system, but which can also be useful to provide information on individual loans and borrowers, including households, individuals and firms.
- Credit *bureaus*, which are handled by private firms and which can provide detailed information on loans and borrowers (and also households, individuals and firms).

Credit bureaus can obtain their information from various sources including banks, microcredit institutions, consumer credit firms, utilities and service providers, among many others. They can also offer additional services based on the information they possess, such as credit scoring or credit ratings.

The use of moveable assets as collateral can be especially important for people and firms with no real estate – such as young people, women, or innovative firms and SMEs based on intangible businesses. Moveable assets can be patents, trademarks, merchandise, accounts receivable, etc. Registries of moveable assets allow firms and entrepreneurs to extend the diversity of collateral that can be pledged for loans. It is also necessary to have adequate secured-transactions legislation that allows the use of this type of asset as collateral while providing enough guarantees and clarity.

Finally, it is also necessary to have a regulatory framework for business angels and venture capital, crowdfunding, leasing, and others so that these markets can develop.

Progress since 2014

This interim assessment finds very positive developments in this area, notably in terms of the creation or expansion of credit bureaus and registries for moveable assets. However, except for PA and Israel, MED economies still do not perform well globally according to the *Doing Business* "Getting credit" indicators (Table 3.2).

Table 3.2. *Doing Business* indicators for Getting credit

Economy	Getting Credit DTF[1]	Getting Credit rank	Strength of legal rights index (0-12)	Depth of credit information index (0-8)	Credit registry coverage (% of adults)	Credit bureau coverage (% of adults)
Algeria	10	177	2	0	2.9	0
Egypt	50	90	2	8	7.8	25.3
Israel	65	55	6	7	0	71.4
Jordan	25	159	0	5	2.2	15.3
Lebanon	40	122	2	6	22.9	0
Morocco	45	105	2	7	0	25
Tunisia	45	105	3	6	26.9	0
PA	80	20	8	8	19	0
OECD	63.03	62	6	6.6	18.3	63.7

[1] DTF: An economy's distance to frontier (DTF) is reflected on a scale from 0 to 100, where 0 represents the lowest performance and 100 represents the frontier. The distance to frontier score helps assess the absolute level of regulatory performance over time. It measures the distance of each economy to the "frontier", which represents the best performance observed on each of the indicators across all economies in the *Doing Business* sample since 2005.

Source: World Bank (2018), *Doing Business.*

PA has significantly improved its regulatory framework for access to credit by undertaking major reforms such as approving a new secured transactions law, creating an online collateral registry and improving its credit registry. Jordan has also made improvements thanks to the creation of its first credit bureau:

- **PA** continues to perform much higher than the regional average in this area. The SME Policy Index 2014 noted that the Palestine Monetary Authority (PMA) had established one of the most effective credit registries in the region, involving all banks and other financial institutions, such as microfinance institutions. Although no credit bureau has been created over the past few years, the coverage and services of the credit registry have expanded. According to *Doing Business* the credit registry began to distribute credit data from retailers and utility companies, increasing the wealth of information and therefore providing more complete reports.

- Important progress has also been made through the introduction in June 2017 of an online collateral registry for moveable assets hosted by the Ministry of Economy. According to *Doing Business*, the collateral registry is operational, unified geographically, searchable by a debtor's unique identifier, modern, and notice-based. In addition, a Secured Transactions Law was issued by the end of 2016. According to *Doing Business*, the new law implements a functional secured transactions system by allowing a general description of single categories of assets and a general description of debts and obligations. The new law gives priority to secured creditors outside insolvency procedures and allows out-of-court enforcement, thereby addressing indirectly some of the shortcomings of the bankruptcy system.
- In **Jordan**, one of the main developments has been the creation of the country's first credit bureau in December 2015. The new credit bureau aims to centralise and aggregate credit information on individuals and businesses – information that will be provided by financial institutions, microfinance organisations, insurance companies, and eventually public agencies such as the Jordan Enterprise Development Corporation (JEDCO). Jordan has also established a collateral registry of moveable assets; after focusing on leasing contracts during its first phase, the registry is now in the processing of becoming a full-fledged collateral registry.
- In terms of laws and regulations for venture capital and private equity, a draft law was developed but sidelined by the government. Instead, the government has approved a new Companies Law containing provisions on venture capital, but this still needs to be enacted by parliament.

In Egypt, Morocco and Tunisia there are ongoing reforms both on the institutional and on the regulatory side:

- **Egypt** in 2014 was already performing well in this area, having established both a credit registry and a credit bureau. The credit bureau, I-Score, issues credit reports based on data provided by banks and by the credit registry of the Central Bank. I-Score has increased the coverage of the adult population since the last assessment from 19.6% to 25.3% and has introduced a credit rating system. In September 2017, the Financial Supervisory Authority (EFSA) awarded I-Score a contract to create a registry of moveable assets.
- The government of **Morocco** has undertaken several measures to increase access to information and credit transparency. In 2016 the credit bureau expanded its services to include the provision of credit scores and the monitoring of portfolios and alert systems. The opening-up of the market for private credit bureaus in 2016 has led to the opening of a second bureau. There are also plans to expand the sources of information provided to the credit bureaus to include utilities and other service suppliers.

- Concerning the registration system for moveable assets – an area where Morocco has been lagging behind the rest of the region – there is a draft proposal to reform the law on moveable assets. The proposal is the product of a number of consultations taking place since 2015 and is being presented as a high priority by the National Committee for the Business Climate (CNEA), together with the reform of Book V of the Code of Commerce (bankruptcy). Notably, the proposal seeks to extend the array of goods that can be pledged when accessing credit.
- In **Tunisia** the credit registry has improved its services by making historical information available to individuals, whereas before it had been limited to enterprises. A credit registry for microfinance (CRM) was also created in 2016 to facilitate credit assessments. Furthermore, a new law on private credit bureaus has been developed by the government and presented to the National Assembly. The law seeks to establish a legal framework to authorise the sharing of negative and positive information on credit; establish the rights and obligations of all parties involved (credit bureau, users, consumers, etc.); and protect the right of users and enterprises to confidentiality in their information. It is expected that the approval of the law will pave the way for the establishment of the first (private) credit bureau in Tunisia.
- Additionally, a reform of the registry of moveable assets is ongoing in order to extend the array of assets that can be pledged as collateral, to allow the non-possessory security over moveable assets and rights, and to establish a general registry of moveable assets. Finally, a draft code for collective investment bodies has been developed to improve the regulatory framework for venture capital and promote these sources of funding (this draft code is currently being examined by the parliament).

Less progress has been made in the other MED economies, although they range from Algeria, which lacks the basic credit information institutions and has no regulatory framework for secured transactions, to Israel, which already had a well-developed system:

- **Algeria** has achieved limited progress compared to the rest of the region. The main development was the modernisation, in September 2015, of the Credit Registry (*Centrale de risques*) to include information about households and consumer credit. Algeria continues to have the weakest regional performance in terms of the *Doing Business* "getting credit" indicators.
- **Israel** continues to have a functioning credit registry, two credit bureaus, and a registry of moveable assets. Authorities are working to reinforce bank competition, which is seen as one of the major hurdles for access to finance for both firms and households. Other reforms are also intended to foster SME access to alternative sources of finance. For example, in October 2016 the Tel Aviv Stock Exchange relaxed its listing requirements to facilitate initial public offerings by R&D-intensive companies (thus facilitating their access to capital) in their early stages. Israel is also promoting access to crowdfunding and peer-to-peer (P2P) lending by allowing these transactions when they are ILS 1 million (about EUR 233 000) or less. Loans above that amount are supervised by the Israel Securities Authority.
- **Lebanon** is making the provision of information from its credit registry decentralised and faster by allowing legal and physical persons to request a credit information report from any Central Bank branch and not only from the

headquarters. There is an ongoing project to develop a law on secured transactions, which would be eventually followed by the creation of a collateral registry.

For further action

Improving the legal and regulatory environment for access to finance is one of the policy areas measured in this interim assessment where good progress has been achieved regionally. This is very positive and highlights the high priority that MED economies are giving to this vital issue. It also signals the potential for peer learning since governments that have already completed some reforms could share their lessons learned to others.

Algeria and Lebanon, the economies that show a comparatively low performance in this area, could step up their efforts to enhance the availability of credit information and create a registry of moveable assets. And despite recent reforms in Jordan, Morocco and Egypt, *Doing Business* indicates that these economies have plenty to do to enhance their performance in the "getting credit" indicators (Table 3.2).

Many initiatives have been introduced to increase the sources of external finance; however, the state continues to be the main actor – especially in terms of credit guarantee schemes, but also in equity investments.

Businesses have different needs and funding constraints depending on a large number of factors such as the profile of the entrepreneur (age, gender, experience, etc.), the assets available to the firm (real estate, machinery, patents, intangible assets, etc.), the stage in the lifecycle of the firm (start-up, expansion, consolidation, maturity, etc.), or the risk and potential profitability of the company (traditional business, highly innovative firm, internationally oriented business, etc.). This diversity means that for a vibrant private sector to thrive, an economy has to incentivise the development of a wide array of sources of finance, including those summarised in Table 3.3.

Table 3.3. External sources of finance for SMEs

	Debt			Hybrid instruments	Equity instruments
	Traditional debt	Asset-based finance	Alternative debt		
Products	Bank loans Credit lines Credit cards	Factoring Leasing Purchase order Warehouse receipts	Corporate bonds Securitised debt Private placements Crowdfunding (debt)	Mezzanine finance Subordinated loans/bonds Convertible bonds	Private equity (venture capital, business angels) Specialised platforms for public listing of SMEs Crowdfunding (equity)
Risk/return profile	Low	Low	Low	Medium	High
Characteristics	Finance regular operations, stable companies with access to collateral	Faster and more flexible terms; factoring used for trade finance	Does not dilute ownership	Turning point in business life cycle	Long-term corporate investment

Source: OECD (2017).

Progress since 2014

A large number of public and private initiatives to foster access to finance have been launched over the past few years across the region. However, there is almost no evidence on their impact, which suggests that the MED economies should dedicate more resources to monitor policy effectiveness. It is also unclear whether the introduction or expansion of sources of finance corresponds to a strategic approach in this area or whether the measures are disconnected.

- In **Algeria** the market for financial products continues to be dominated by public institutions, including two credit guarantees – the Credit Guarantee Fund for SMEs (FGAR) and the Fund of Guarantees for Credit Investment (CGGI) – and the *Wilaya*s (governorates) Investment Fund, which provides venture capital (up to 49% of equity) for new firms, growth capital and business restructuring to ensure the survival of firms and the jobs they sustain.
- **Egypt** has undertaken a large number of initiatives to facilitate lending to SMEs, including injecting money into the banking system – via the Central Bank of Egypt's micro, small and medium-sized enterprises (CBE MSME) lending initiative – and mandating public banks to devote at least 20% of their loans to SMEs. The authorities have also created a state-sponsored venture capital fund to invest in distressed SMEs.
- In **Israel** the market for credit guarantee schemes is dominated by a state actor: the Small and Medium Businesses Fund (SMBF), which is sponsored by the SME agency and the Ministry of Finance and managed by two private companies. Authorities track well the performance of this fund, which has high rejection rates in order to keep fees low and to ensure the sustainability of the fund. In terms of equity investments, two new funds have been created by the state but are managed by private companies to incentivise investments in high potential firms. This adds to an already vibrant venture capital (VC) market.
- In **Jordan** the credit guarantee market continues to be dominated by the state-sponsored Loan Guarantee Corporation (JLGC), which established two special funds in 2016 to provide guarantees for start-ups. The JLGC is a well-established organisation producing regular reports on its activities. Other developments regarding access to finance include the continued operation of the Governorate Development Fund (GDF), which has supported 96 projects between 2012 and 2018. However, the GDF staff has been reduced due to budget constraints. In addition, the JLGC made efforts to set up an Early Stage Venture Capital Fund, but due to funding issues it has not yet become operational.
- **Lebanon**'s Central Bank has given banks incentives to finance enterprises in different sectors and at very low interest rates (e.g. 1% from the Banque du Liban [BDL] to banks and up to 3% from banks to firms). First launched as a USD 1.47 billion stimulus package in 2013, this measure has been renewed for the fourth consecutive year, with an average of USD 1 billion per year. Kafalat, originally a credit guarantee scheme and now one of the most successful initiatives in the region and beyond, developed the iSME Programme to provide concept-development grants (of up to USD 15 000) for innovative projects and equity co-investments (between USD 100 000 and 1.2 million) provided alongside other capital investments by venture capital funds, holding companies, formal business angel groups and investment banks. These are just a few among many other initiatives.
- In 2016, the total activity of **Morocco**'s Central Guarantee Fund (CCG), both for businesses and individuals, totalled MAD 21 billion of mobilised loans (about EUR 1.9 billion), an increase of 23% compared to 2015. The CCG also created a dedicated Guarantee Fund for SMEs called "*Mouwakaba*." Overall, the credit

guarantee system in Morocco seems to be working well since almost 52% of firms in the *Enterprise Surveys* say they have a bank loan or line of credit (compared to 28.6% in the rest of the MENA region) and nearly 35% are using banks to finance investments, compared to 25.9% in MENA. On the other hand, there is no evidence of progress in terms of equity markets.

- **PA** has seen its market for credit guarantee schemes expand in recent years. The European-Palestinian Credit Guarantee Fund (EPCGF) and the Loan Guarantee Facility, already operational in 2014, continue to function. But two new vehicles have entered the market: the SIDA Guarantee Scheme Facility, launched in 2015 and managed by the Loan Guarantee Facility; and the Middle East Investment Initiative, focusing on SMEs and housing loans. New venture capital funds have also been established since 2014. However, no data are available on the reach and effectiveness of these measures.
- In **Tunisia** the main actors facilitating access to credit continue to be public institutions, notably the SME Bank (BFPME) for credit, the Guarantee Company (SOTUGAR) for credit guarantees, and the Solidarity Bank (BTS) for microcredit. Tunisian authorities are also developing a new programme, *Investir PME,* that aims to facilitate the introduction of SMEs to alternative markets through the stock market. As the cost of entering this market is normally high for SMEs, the new programme will focus on reducing entry barriers and helping SMEs diversify their sources of financing.

For further action

Overall, the state continues to be the main source, or at least facilitator, of access to finance for the MED region's SMEs – through state-sponsored credit guarantee schemes and, in many cases, venture capital funds. In most cases, however, there is little evidence to show how this activism has resulted in greater access to finance for SMEs and whether measures exist to eventually foster a greater participation of the private sector in funding the different categories of SMEs and entrepreneurs.

When the state creates vehicles for equity investment in SMEs (as in Algeria, Egypt, Israel and Jordan), it is not always clear how this will eventually lead to the development of a more dynamic venture capital and business angel market in the future. Given that globally governments only make good venture capitalists under certain conditions (OECD, 2018), governments in the region should carefully evaluate the impact of their activities in this domain.

The important reforms noted in the section on the legal and regulatory framework for access to finance should eventually lead to a greater participation by private actors in this market. But this is not yet explicitly or clearly described in the evidence and discussions for this interim assessment.

The way forward

Overall, access to finance is an area where significant progress has been achieved in the MED region over the past few years. This is especially the case in terms of the legal and regulatory framework for access to finance, where a number of credit bureaus and registries of moveable assets have entered into function, and where secured transactions laws have been passed or are in the process of being passed.

There has also been progress in terms of the expansion of sources of finance for SMEs and entrepreneurs, although in this case it is less evident how this has resulted in increased funding and whether there will be a greater role for private actors in the future – namely privately-owned credit guarantee schemes, business angel investments and private equity vehicles.

This interim assessment puts forward the following additional actions for MED economies:

- Continue bridging information asymmetries through the creation and expansion of credit registries and, more notably, credit bureaus. Credit bureaus are especially useful because they are managed by private actors and because they draw on more diverse sources of information than credit registries (utilities, consumption credit, microfinance institutions, etc.). However, the case of PA shows that registries can also be effective tools for facilitating the flow of information on debtors.
- Increase efforts to create registries of moveable assets – especially in Algeria and Lebanon, which have no ongoing work in this area. This is important for entrepreneurs and SMEs lacking real estate to pledge as collateral, and particularly relevant for potentially innovative firms which may rely on intangible assets such as trademarks, patents and intellectual property.
- Continue expanding the diversity and reach of different sources of finance (credit, equity and hybrid instruments) and include strategies for developing competitive markets in this area so that the state eventually steps out in favour of private actors.
- Improve the monitoring and evaluation of the impact of reforms for access to finance. Joining the OECD Scoreboard on Financing SMEs and Entrepreneurs, which contributes to filling the knowledge gap in SME finance trends and conditions, would be an important step in this direction.

Bibliography

OECD (2018), "Are governments good venture capitalists? New cross-country evidence from micro-data", working paper.

OECD (2017), *New Approaches to SME and Entrepreneurship Financing: Broadening the range of instruments*, OECD Publishing, Paris, http://www.oecd.org/publications/new-approaches-to-sme-and-entrepreneurship-financing-9789264240957-en.htm

World Bank (2018), *Doing Business 2018: Reforming to create jobs*, World Bank, Washington, DC, http://www.doingbusiness.org/~/media/WBG/DoingBusiness/Documents/Annual-Reports/English/DB2018-Full-Report.pdf.

Chapter 4. Nurturing start-ups and SME growth

This chapter focuses on three specific factors that can be significant drivers of private sector development in the context of MED economies: the availability and accessibility of business development services, the ease of access to public procurement opportunities for SMEs, and measures to promote SME internationalisation, notably through exports.

Overall, this interim assessment finds a large number of programmes and initiatives but very little evidence of their results. This could suggest 1) that these initiatives have effectively remained declarations of intent without clear strategies for SMEs to benefit; 2) that linking actions to results has been a weak exercise, with no evidence available on the extent to which SMEs have benefited from the many initiatives in these three policy areas; or 3) a combination of both.

This interim assessment puts forward the following actions for MED economies:

1. Consolidate and disseminate comprehensive information about SME and entrepreneurship support programmes provided by different institutions (government agencies, private sector providers, donors, etc.).

2. Publish the results of these inventories and make them easily available for their beneficiaries through simple means such as brochures and through comprehensive mechanisms such as SME Observatories.

3. Implement e-procurement systems and track the extent to which specific measures have actually benefited SMEs (e.g. splitting tenders into lots, easing procurement conditions, providing down payments, etc.). Procurement observatories could be a useful tool for assessing the effectiveness of these measures. They could be linked with SME Observatories.

4. Better link export promotion strategies with concrete measures for SMEs to benefit from these strategies, and better track whether exports or trade in general (exports and imports) actually increase, and to what extent these results end up benefitting SMEs (e.g. access to cheaper and better-quality inputs or greater access to markets).

The statistical data for Israel are supplied by and under the responsibility of the relevant Israeli authorities. The use of such data by the OECD is without prejudice to the status of the Golan Heights, East Jerusalem and Israeli settlements in the West Bank under the terms of international law.

Despite the differences in definitions applied across economies, SMEs constitute the overwhelming majority of enterprises, account for important shares of total employment and contribute to total value added and trade. However, to fully capture the role of SMEs as engines of wealth and job creation requires a dynamic perspective: what matters most for economic dynamism is not the number and size of firms *per se*, but the rates of firm creation, survival, growth and exit – that is to say, the *entrepreneurial performance* of economies (OECD, 2013).

Certainly, the entrepreneurial performance of an economy depends on many factors, ranging from macroeconomic stability to the quality of the education system and the competition framework. This chapter focuses on three factors that can be significant drivers of private sector development in the context of MED economies characterised by low levels of formal enterprise creation and the dominance of the state in the economy: 1) the availability and accessibility of business development services, 2) the ease of access to public procurement opportunities for SMEs, and 3) measures to promote SME internationalisation, notably through exports.

This interim assessment finds that a number of measures and initiatives have been undertaken in the three areas analysed in this chapter (see Table 4.1). However, although there are now several providers of business development services (BDS), little information on their offerings has been made available to SMEs. Similarly, although governments have made many efforts to facilitate access to public procurement for SMEs, concrete information on the results is scarce. Finally, despite ongoing initiatives to facilitate exports and access to new markets, the results in terms of SME creation and growth remain unclear.

Table 4.1. Overview of nurturing start-ups and SME growth

	Diversity and access to business development services	SME access to public procurement and e-procurement			Internationalisation of SMEs
		SME Quota	E-procurement	Other	
Algeria	Comparatively low diversity of BDS; mostly government-driven initiatives.	✓	X	Subcontracting possible	A national export strategy is being developed but no clear link to SMEs.
Egypt	Mostly donor- and publicly-sponsored BDS	✓	Ongoing	Reduced guarantee bond New procurement law 2016	Several internationalisation strategies including focus on SMEs.
Israel	Publicly funded, privately delivered BDS through Small Business Development Centres (MAOF).	X	Ongoing	Procurement law amended 2016	Several new measures, notably the Smart Money Initiative.
Jordan	Large diversity of services. The SME Observatory aims to facilitate access to information on BDS.	X	Ongoing	New procurement regulations	Some ongoing efforts, notably the relaxation of rules of origin for the EU market, but limited reported results.
Lebanon	Large diversity of services. New projects to reinforce BDS providers and access to information. Ministry of Economy prepared a manual to disseminate information on BDS.	X	X	Information published online	Several new measures but no concrete progress yet. A strategy on industrial exports will be developed.
Morocco	Diversity of BDS including publicly funded but privately delivered. Introduction of the *auto-entrepreneur* status.	✓	✓	Simplified procedures Proportionate qualification level	Important progress including digitalisation of trade procedures.
PA	Several BDS provided in the private sector; SMEs division in the MoNE provides information.	X	X	New procurement Law 2014 Preferential treatment for domestic products	New export strategy and public-private export council.
Tunisia	Public and private provision of BDS across the territory.	✓	✓	Unified provisions under Decree No. 1039, 2014 Penalties on late payments	Several initiatives exist, including participation in the Enterprise Europe Network (EEN).

SMEs and entrepreneurs could be better informed on the large and expanding availability of business development services.

Business development services (BDS) have the potential to improve the functioning and competitiveness of companies across a wide range of activities. BDS consist of the provision of specialised external advice and expertise on a temporary basis to supplement internal resources and capacities. The availability of a diverse and competitive market for BDS is a basic requirement for the development of a healthy entrepreneurial fabric, allowing firms to obtain guidance, engage in capacity building, and assess and improve their performance.

The BDS market is very diverse across the MED region, with public, private, and non-governmental organisations (NGOs) and other actors supplying services for women and young entrepreneurs; micro firms; and manufacturing, industrial and services firms, etc. Given this diversity, it is important to make information easily accessible for entrepreneurs and SMEs.

Progress since 2014

This interim assessment finds an expanding offer of BDS across the MED region, with the continuous active participation of government and private actors, as well as NGOs. Services are diverse and target many types of beneficiaries, from young and women entrepreneurs to industrial SMEs.

Overall, the region could improve the ease of access to information on these services, including from the simple creation and distribution of flyers or prospects to the establishment of comprehensive web portals:

- **Jordan** continues to have a diversified and extensive market for BDS. Some of the most important and active organisations in this regard include the Jordan Enterprise Development Corporation (JEDCO), the Business Development Centre, several NGOs and private service providers, and the Business Associations and Chambers of Industry and Commerce. Information about these support services is scattered across a large number of sources, but the SME Observatory has a mandate to centralise this information.
- **Lebanon** continues to have a rich market for BDS, with a diverse range of actors from the public and private sectors as well as civil society. New initiatives have also been introduced, such as the MSME TA Facility, which aims to expand BDS in such areas as product innovation, monitoring and evaluation of services. To increase the amount of information available on BDS and other support measures, the Ministry of Economy has published the guidebook *What's in Lebanon for SMEs 2017*.
- BDS providers in **PA** reflect a diversified and rich network of public, private and donor-funded institutions. The SME division under the Ministry of National Economy facilitates access to information on the multitude of business development services and providers available.

Morocco's SME agency has restructured the offer of BDS to target different types of SMEs and created a special programme for self-entrepreneurs:

- In **Morocco** BDS continue to be highly diversified, with a solid presence of both public and private providers. Morocco SME has restructured its support programmes in line with its strategic lines of work. Two main programmes, *Istitmar Croissance* and *Tahfiz,* support efforts by micro-enterprises to invest and modernise their systems. Support for SMEs is channelled through *Imtiaz Croissance*, which co-finances investment projects, and *Moussanada*, which funds technical assistance services. One of the most important improvements has been the introduction of the *statut de l'auto-entrepreneur* (*auto-entrepreneur* status), which creates incentives and support measures seeking to promote entrepreneurship. Launched in 2015, the system has a target of 20 000 beneficiaries per year and is seen as an innovative initiative to reduce Morocco's informal economy.

In Algeria and Egypt, most BDS providers are public institutions, whereas in Israel BDS centres are managed privately and in Tunisia there is a large presence of private organisations and NGOs:

- **Algeria** has a less diversified market for BDS compared to its regional peers. Through the National Upgrading Programme, managed by the SME Agency (ANDPME), the government continues to be the main actor providing support to industrial firms, in line with the general economic strategy in the country. Furthermore, the PME II programme, which provided assistance to SMEs with growth potential in 2014, is no longer operational.

- **Egypt** has a relatively diversified market for BDS, although the main actors continue to be governmental bodies such as the new micro, small and medium-sized enterprises agency (MSMEDA) and the Bedaya Centre for Entrepreneurship and SME Development. That said, recent donor-driven initiatives have focused on encouraging and facilitating SME access to BDS while supporting the expansion of these services across the country.

- **Israel**'s SMEs enjoy a broad and competitive BDS market, which has continued to improve over the last years. The Small Business Development Centres (MAOF) have expanded from 26 to 40 since 2014. These publicly funded, privately managed centres provide subsidised and tailor-made services while also acting as one-stop shops that give access to other government support schemes.

- **Tunisia** has a diverse source of BDS and players in this domain, including the Agency for the Promotion of Industry and Innovation, the Business Centres of the Ministry of Industry and a number of business incubators. Civil society organisations are also active in this field. For instance, the *Institut Tunisien pour la Démocratie et le Développement* (ITDD) supports young entrepreneurs develop business plans and reaching out to public institutions. Information on available services is available, although scattered in several websites.

For further action

The region could improve access to information on the variety of BDS on offer. This could be done through a number of measures ranging from leaflets (already available in Lebanon) to SME Observatories (not yet fully available but being developed in Jordan and Morocco).

E-procurement could be further promoted to facilitate the participation of SMEs.

On average, public procurement contracts account for about 18% of GDP in the MENA region (OECD, 2016). This represents a considerable source of revenue that, if used properly, could strongly contribute to the development of SMEs. Nevertheless, SMEs could be excluded from public procurement due to the unaffordable size of the average public contract, complex administrative processes and highly-selective prequalification requirements. In addition, SMEs face information gaps and lack the capacity to complete required documents, further reducing the firms' chances in public competitions. As a result, only major firms tend to compete for public contracts.

Progress since 2014

Several economies have introduced measures to facilitate SME access to public procurement, such as splitting tenders into lots, introducing penalties for late payments, eliminating participation fees for some procurement contracts, etc. These measures are positive, but the use of e-procurement is still limited. The establishment of electronic procedures for public procurement can significantly increase the participation of small firms.

Although there is much room to increase the use of e-procurement in the region, economies like Israel, Jordan, and Tunisia are working to improve already existing e-procurement systems or introduce new ones:

- **Israel** is developing with several pilot e-procurement platforms like Menorah or Zohar to consult and apply for tenders.
- **Jordan** is developing an e-procurement system in collaboration with the Korean International Co-operation Agency and will create a centralised system for procuring entities and bidders and suppliers. New procurement regulations have been adopted and an oversight structure for the public procurement system has been established.
- **Tunisia** already had an e-procurement system, but an ongoing project was launched in 2016 to reform electronic public procurement procedures. As a first step, Decree No. 1039, 2014, replaced all previous related legislation. Tunisia has also taken several measures to promote the participation of SMEs, such as making information on opportunities easily available, assessing penalties on late payments and mandating a period of at least 30 days for bid submission from the date a notice is published.

Several MED economies have reviewed the legal framework for public procurement:

- **Egypt** adopted a new Law on Public Procurement in 2016, further advancing transparency in public procurement (EBRD, 2017). The new law reduces by 50% the guarantee bond required from SMEs during the application to a public tender. An official portal is dedicated to public procurement at the national level, which allows all companies to access information on public tenders.[1] MSMEDA and the Authority for Government Services are expected to sign a protocol to facilitate SME access to public procurement.
- **Israel** in 2016 amended the Mandatory Tender Law and the Mandatory Tender Regulations to prevent the exclusion of SMEs from public contracts. The Government Procurement Administration (GPA) of the Ministry of Finance

publishes centralised tenders and disseminates codes and regulations on public procurement. Local authorities, however, have their own rules and their regulations and do not need to abide by the GPA, although there are ongoing efforts to align local and central processes (procurement by schools, for example, is under municipal responsibility).

- **PA** approved a Procurement Law of 2014. According to the consultations for this interim assessment, the Law is open and transparent and has a website with information.

Other countries have introduced various measures to encourage SME participation in public procurement opportunities:

- In **Algeria** a special decree of 2015 foresees subcontracting for firms winning contracts, increasing SMEs' chances to participate in the market indirectly as suppliers to other firms. There is no data regarding the impact of this measure. Algeria does not yet have an e-procurement system.
- In **Lebanon** some measures have been taken to increase the amount of information on public procurement opportunities online and in newspapers. Draft laws are under discussion for the modernisation of the procurement system.
- **Morocco** has simplified procedures related to the justification of technical criteria; introduced a cash advance for bid-winning SMEs; and created a unique identifier which facilitates accessing the financial information of the company.

For further action

All MED economies have made efforts to facilitate the participation of SMEs in public procurement. However, none has in place a comprehensive mechanism for monitoring the participation of firms engaged in public contracts. MED economies could therefore consider the introduction of procurement observatories. Several MED economies – namely Algeria, Lebanon and PA – could also benefit from the introduction of e-procurement mechanisms.

Some efforts have been made to promote exports and access to markets, but the links to SME policy remain weak in most cases.

Many factors determine the export potential/performance of a given company, and not all of them are (or should be) influenced by public policies. For instance, the sector in which an enterprise operates can be a key determinant of its international orientation. The size of the domestic market and the level of sophistication of a business are other important determinants. However, policies should be aimed at removing barriers and facilitating access to international markets for those companies with export potential and ambitions.

Progress since 2014

This interim assessment finds several initiatives aimed at increasing exports and market diversification, including the adoption of export strategies and the signature of new agreements. However, the concrete links to SME internationalisation and facts and figures on increased international business remain absent, except for Israel and Morocco.

Algeria, Egypt and PA have adopted new strategies to promote exports:

- **Algeria** is developing a National Export Promotion Strategy (as reported by the Agency for the Promotion of Foreign Trade) that will seek to eliminate administrative and technical barriers to international trade.
- **Egypt** has developed three interlinked strategies involving the promotion of exports: an industrial strategy, an export development strategy and an export strategy to Africa.
- **PA** has continued advancing in this policy area, in particular through the adoption of the National Export Strategy and the establishment of a public-private Export Council.

Other economies have introduced various measures such as financing programmes for SMEs (Israel), agreements with the EU on rules of origin (Jordan), and digitalisation of trade procedures (Morocco):

- **Israel** has implemented a number of new initiatives. This includes the Foreign Trade Administration's "Smart Money" programme for SMEs, which provides training and loans for marketing consulting services. Other example is Shalev programme which provides loans to micro firms so they can develop marketing activities, business planning and training.
- **Jordan** has undertaken various initiatives in this area, notably in co-operation with the European Union (EU). The most salient one is the simplification of the rules of origin set out in the EU-Jordan Association Agreement in order to incentivise integration of Syrian workforce in Jordan. But by July 2017 some estimates reported that only eight firms had been deemed to meet the conditions and just two of them actually benefit from it.
- **Morocco** has advanced towards a more internationalised environment for SMEs. A relevant improvement has been the implementation of PortNet, a virtual platform to deal with the formalities of foreign trade in ports. Morocco aims to reach the total digitalisation of foreign trade procedures by 2020.

Fewer measures have been introduced in Lebanon and Tunisia:

- **Lebanon** registers little progress in this area. A number of initiatives for SME internationalisation have been introduced over the past few years, although without a clear holistic or coherent framework. The *Integrated Vision for the Lebanese Industrial Sector 2025* includes a section on increasing industrial exports with a series of actions in this area and responsible parties. The export promotion agency has not been established and there is no export promotion strategy.
- **Tunisia** has undertaken several efforts in this area over the past few years with the technical support of multilateral bodies. Tunisia also joined the Europe Enterprise Network.

For further action

All MED economies have made efforts towards export promotion and market access. However, only rarely are these efforts clearly linked to SME internationalisation. Although export strategies and agreements have often included aspects related to SME internationalisation, the link to concrete actions and results is almost absent.

The way forward

Supporting enterprise creation and growth through BDS and better access to public procurement and international markets is an important policy area that most MED economies have addressed through a large number of programmes and initiatives. However, this interim assessment finds very little evidence in terms of actual results. This could suggest 1) that these initiatives have remained in declarations of intent without clear strategies for SMEs to benefit; 2) that linking actions to results has been a weak exercise, with no evidence available on the extent to which SMEs have benefited from the many initiatives in these policy areas; or 3) a combination of both.

More concretely, this interim assessment puts forward the following actions for MED economies:

- Consolidate and disseminate comprehensive information about SME and entrepreneurship support programmes provided by different institutions (e.g. government agencies, private sector providers, donors).
- Publish the results of these inventories and make them easily available for their beneficiaries through simple means such as brochures and through comprehensive mechanisms such as SME Observatories.
- Implement e-procurement systems and track the extent to which specific measures have actually benefited SMEs (splitting up tenders, easing procurement conditions, providing down payments, etc.). Procurement observatories could be a useful tool for assessing the effectiveness of these measures, and could be linked with SME Observatories.
- Better link export-promotion strategies with concrete measures for SMEs to benefit from these strategies, and better track whether exports or trade in general (exports and imports) actually increase – and to what extent these results end up benefitting SMEs (e.g. access to cheaper and better quality inputs, greater access to markets).

Notes

[1] https://etenders.gov.eg.

Bibliography

EBRD (European Bank for Reconstruction and Development) (2017), *Egypt country strategy report*, EBRD, London.

OECD (2016), *Stocktaking Report on MENA Public Procurement Systems*, OECD Publishing, Paris, https://www.oecd.org/governance/ethics/Stocktaking_MENA_Public_Procurement_Systems.pdf.

OECD/IDRC (2013), *New Entrepreneurs and High Performance Enterprises in the Middle East and North Africa*, Competitiveness and Private Sector Development, OECD Publishing, Paris, http://dx.doi.org/10.1787/9789264179196-en.

Chapter 5. Entrepreneurial human capital development

This chapter examines human capital development initiatives related to entrepreneurship and SME internationalisation in the MED economies. It focuses on three areas: entrepreneurial learning in upper secondary education (general and vocational); training for women's entrepreneurship; and skills development for SME internationalisation. The analysis finds that although MED economies have improved their policy frameworks in this area, challenges remain – including the implementation of policies, data collection and analysis on training provision and evaluation.

Key recommendations are as follows:

1. Governments should build multi-stakeholder and cross-ministerial partnerships to ensure the efficient implementation of action plans for entrepreneurial learning that may belong under different national strategies (such as education, vocational training, employment, economic development, exports). This could include promoting entrepreneurship as a key competence as well as business skills. MED economies could build on project-based initiatives to a systemic approach providing entrepreneurial learning into the national curricula at all levels of education.

2. MED economies could move towards holistic approaches to supporting women's entrepreneurship development rather than individual policy measures and actions. Holistic approaches could combine training with mentoring, coaching and networks set-up. Governments could also continue their efforts to produce and collect gender-disaggregated data to enable the design of policies tailored to the needs of entrepreneurial women.

3. All MED economies require more developed data on SME training, particularly in terms of export potential. One lead in-country institution should co-ordinate data and wider intelligence (e.g. good practice) to support the government in setting policy priorities and resource allocation.

The statistical data for Israel are supplied by and under the responsibility of the relevant Israeli authorities. The use of such data by the OECD is without prejudice to the status of the Golan Heights, East Jerusalem and Israeli settlements in the West Bank under the terms of international law.

One of the objectives of this interim assessment is to support the efforts of MED economies to develop more-entrepreneurial human capital as a lever to increase employability and reinforce competitiveness. Three targets have been identified in relation to the region's potential, its demographic structure and its main challenges: 1) *young people*, who constitute an important part of the overall population (ranging from 36.8% in PA to 20.9% in Tunisia); 2) *women*, in consideration of their particularly low levels of participation in the labour market in the Arab region (ranging from 16.6% in Algeria to 26.6% in Tunisia); and 3) SMEs with potential to *internationalise* as a means to foster innovation.

Building entrepreneurship as a key competence is the next challenge for policy makers and schools.

Youth employability remains a top priority for the region. Improving the employability of young people and promoting entrepreneurship through education is one of the possible solutions to the problem of high youth unemployment (between 25% and 40%) and the growing phenomenon of young people "not in education, employment or training" (NEETs). Recent data shows that NEETs represent around 30% of young people aged between 15 and 24 in Egypt, Morocco, PA and Tunisia, and 20% in Algeria and Lebanon. High NEET rates have a negative impact on employability, future earnings and access to quality jobs. Education and training have a key role to play in developing an entrepreneurial culture of young people to find a job more easily and to contribute to the economic growth and competitiveness of the countries.

This section looks at how entrepreneurial learning is being promoted in upper secondary education, both in general education and vocational education and training (VET). Particular attention is given to entrepreneurship as a key competence that employers increasingly seek in this fast-changing world. It describes where countries stand in terms of policy dialogue and partnership, as well as implementation of entrepreneurial learning in schools, including school-enterprise co-operation.

Progress since 2014

The assessment shows that entrepreneurial learning is still too focused on the development of business skills, such as financial literacy and business plans. More awareness-raising for school directors, teachers, student associations, parents associations and policy makers is necessary to ensure understanding on the need to develop entrepreneurship "as a key competence". This focuses on cultivating an entrepreneurial attitude characterised by a sense of initiative and agency, pro-activity, a forward-looking attitude, courage and perseverance in achieving projects (European Commission, 2018). Research shows that, by enhancing such attitudes, youth will have a higher chance of successful participation in society as active citizens and will better manage their lives in an increasingly complex world (European Commission, 2017).

Since 2014 all the MED economies have included entrepreneurial learning across different socio-economic policy documents:

- **Tunisia** has a separate entrepreneurial learning strategy, while **Morocco** clearly targets the promotion of entrepreneurial learning in its Strategic Vision of the Education System and in the Vocational Training Strategy 2021. In the other economies, entrepreneurial learning features across different strategies – for example, national development plans (**Algeria**), educational or youth strategies (**Lebanon and PA**), or economic strategies (**Egypt**, **Israel** and **Jordan**).

Because entrepreneurial learning has no single policy "home", it is important to build structured national partnerships to ensure that the various policy areas are aligned. Unfortunately, this is missing in most of the MED region. These national partnerships should include a wide range of stakeholders – including representatives from ministries of education, employment, and economy; civic society; social partners; employer's organisations; teachers and youth organisations; entrepreneurs; and donors – to properly drive (and then to monitor and evaluate) country initiatives for entrepreneurial learning. In this respect, action plans that establish how to integrate entrepreneurial learning into formal and non-formal education and training need to be established.

- **Lebanon** is currently working on a multi-annual action plan to integrate entrepreneurial learning into the national education system, including a budget estimate and a clarification of the roles and responsibilities of the different partners involved.

Practically all economies have made progress in the promotion of entrepreneurial learning in upper secondary education since 2014. However, entrepreneurship as a key competence is not yet embedded into the national curriculum framework for upper secondary education (general and VET) in any of the MED economies. The European Entrepreneurship Key Competence Framework, known as EntreComp (European Commission, 2018) is a useful tool for understanding and developing entrepreneurship as a competence.

- In **Egypt**, the IMKAN[1] pilot project in the Luxor governorate borrowed from the framework for reforming the curricula and formulating entrepreneurial learning outcomes for VET schools.
- In **PA**, the Palestine Polytechnic University, winner of the 2017 ETF good practice award for promoting entrepreneurship key competences in VET, is raising awareness amongst the wider higher-education community by using the entrepreneurship key competence framework (EntreComp).

There are several good practices where entrepreneurial learning is being implemented in general and VET schools at the secondary level. The challenge now is to move towards a systemic approach by inserting entrepreneurial learning into the national curricula at all levels of education. Good examples of entrepreneurial learning promotion include:

- In **Jordan**, My Entrepreneurial Project (MEP) is fostering creativity, teamwork, and initiative for young people to stimulate entrepreneurship and self-employment as a career choice. INJAZ[2] is an active partner in the region, offering opportunities for secondary-school students by creating practical business experiences.
- **Tunisia** has started a project across the whole VET system. This includes the production of a national Entrepreneurial Learning Charter to set this policy area as a priority. As part of an integrated approach, Tunisia is also putting in place a curriculum development and in-service and pre-service teacher training – including integrating entrepreneurship as a key competence.
- **Israel** has developed guidelines for teachers on how to enhance entrepreneurial learning in the classroom.

However, despite the fact that national policies are underlining the importance of school-enterprise co-operation in all MED countries, there is poor data on the number of upper secondary schools (including VET) that have established structured partnerships with enterprises. The collection of data on school-enterprise co-operation is key to adapting policies, setting targets and motivating enterprises and schools to set up common projects.

The assessment shows that, in general, school-enterprise co-operation is more prominent in VET. The challenge is to extend this co-operation to the general education system.

For further action

MED economies need to build national partnerships to implement the entrepreneurial learning policies recommended since the last assessment. These partnerships, which should build on concrete action plans, should include representatives from the ministries of education, employment, and economy; civic society; social partners; employer's organisations; teacher and youth organisations; entrepreneurs; and donors. Countries need to continue making efforts to move from project-based initiatives to a systemic approach by inserting entrepreneurial learning into the national curricula at all levels of education. A strategic focus on entrepreneurship as a key competence is the next challenge for all education and training systems and apprenticeships should include opportunities for young people to develop entrepreneurship skills e.g. through working within the enterprise administration.

Momentum is growing in women's entrepreneurship and requires a comprehensive policy response.

The Small Business Act for Europe (SBA) points to the impact of the gender gap on the low numbers of women entrepreneurs (European Commission, 2008). Modern policy thinking now recognises the complex undercurrents behind the low numbers of women entrepreneurs, and societal barriers limiting women's access to wealth and power. The EU's SBA policy framework sets targets for raising the share of women entrepreneurs and their participation in business activities across all sectors of economy.

In the MENA region, there are substantial gaps in women's participation in the labour market, self-employment and entrepreneurship, coupled with large gender differences in accessing better-paid jobs, managerial positions, and employment opportunities in general. Women's participation in the labour force is as low as 25.33% (ILO, 2017); only 8.38% of firms have a female top manager, compared to the global average of 18.6 % (IFC and WB, 2017). Women in the region have limited support, primarily coming from the family and some business development support programmes (European Union, 2017).

While these inequalities are attributed mainly to external legal, cultural, and socio-economic factors, the skills and competences of women should be key to enhancing the abilities which they possess to the same degree as men. Entrepreneurial skills and competences enable women to escape the constraints of the social and economic silos they have traditionally occupied, to achieve work-life balance, and to create jobs and income for themselves and for others.

This section summarises the findings on women's entrepreneurship development regarding 1) government policies and action plans; 2) evidence-based policy development, monitoring and evaluation, including data collection and partnership development; and c) measures to develop the SME-related skills and entrepreneurial competences of women. Overall, the current assessment identifies positive dynamics across all countries and much progress in terms of policy support for women's entrepreneurship since the last report.

Progress since 2014

In 2014, most of the MED countries – except for Algeria and Egypt – had *ad hoc* interventions in place. Since then, governments and their partners have joined forces, both at the policy level and through targeted initiatives in Israel, Jordan, Lebanon, and Tunisia:

- In **Algeria**, the government's plan (2017) puts a strong focus on the development of women's entrepreneurship in rural areas.
- In **Jordan,** the Economic Growth Plan (2018-2022) and the Strategic Plan for Empowering Women (2013-2017) set targets that benefit this policy area.
- Women's entrepreneurship is now among the objectives of government investment in **Lebanon**, promoted both through the National Strategy for Women in Lebanon (2011-2021) and the SME Strategy (2015-2020).
- In **Morocco**, support for women's entrepreneurship is part of the government's Plan for Equality (ICRAM 2012-206).
- Countries have also set up multi-stakeholder groups and platforms to co-operate in women's entrepreneurship; one example is a task force led by the Business Women Forum in **PA**.

The quality and scope of policy analysis has improved in the last years, strengthening the effectiveness of evidence-based policy and the monitoring and evaluation capacity of national governments:

- International organisations such as GIZ, through an EU funded regional programme, and UNIDO have developed research on women's entrepreneurship in the MENA region (GIZ, 2017, and UNIDO, 2017).
- National governments have also undertaken studies on the topic. For example, a feasibility study by the **Israeli** Agency for Small and Mid-Sized Enterprises (2017) examined gaps between female and male entrepreneurs and factors preventing women from engaging in high-value-added sectors; and the **Jordan** Enterprise Development Corporation (2017) conducted a study titled "Women entrepreneurship in Jordan: women empowerment".

In terms of providing training and support for women's entrepreneurship, governments and business-support partners are promoting entrepreneurial skills and competences of women across the MED region:

- In **Egypt**, through the Women's Strategy (2030), employability and digital skills are the focus of women's entrepreneurship support.
- In **Tunisia**, a rich supply of training programmes is a result of partnership between the government and women's entrepreneurship networks and associations promoting female entrepreneurs.
- In **Israel**, the government is gradually expanding the scope of women's entrepreneurship programmes from individual target groups to support measures based on a holistic view of women's roles and needs in entrepreneurship.
- The **Moroccan** government focuses on women entrepreneurs' access to technologies.

- In **PA**, the "Start-up Palestine" initiative provides a good example of how access to finance and training could be adapted to benefit women entrepreneurs.

For further action

Policy attention to women's entrepreneurship should be further structured and consolidated, with built-in policy partnership instruments, guided by a joint, holistic vision on the specific challenges and objectives across all policy areas impacting the state and spread of women's entrepreneurship. Governments should allocate their resources to the specific needs of women in starting-up and growing their businesses, while continuing gender-neutral entrepreneurship support programmes. This should be accompanied by systematic evaluations of programme relevance, quality, efficiency and accessibility for various groups of populations.

Systematic data collection on women's entrepreneurship – to inform policy formulation, monitoring and evaluation, and policy improvement – remains an objective for the coming years, and needs to become a feature of the national strategy and budget planning processes. It should be underpinned by the availability of sex-disaggregated data in each country, and by the engagement of policy partners in the systematic monitoring and evaluation of public and private programmes that benefit male and female entrepreneurs.

It is important to ensure that support for the enhancement of skills and competences to boost women's entrepreneurship goes beyond general gender-neutral SME training courses and targets women's specific needs: strengthening their self‐efficacy, ambition and creating gender-sensitive entrepreneurship development ecosystems. Mentoring, coaching and support to the establishment of women-led businesses are valued highly by women entrepreneurs, due to their positive effects on business start-up survival and on confidence building among women entrepreneurs (Bekh, 2014).

Moving SMEs forward in international trade – the case for improved training.

SMEs working in international markets are more innovative, more competitive and generate more jobs (Love and Ganotakis, 2013; European Commission, 2010) but poor management and vocational skills are barriers to international trading and SME engagement in global value chains (WTO, 2016). Despite more developed trade-enhancing arrangements provided by bilateral, regional (e.g. the Agadir Agreement[3]) and multilateral agreements (e.g. Euro-Mediterranean Association Agreements[4]), SMEs in MED economies are still weak players in the trade tables (OECD et. al., 2014). The trade gap between the EU and the Southern Neighbourhood countries is particularly accentuated. EU exports to the region increased by just over 50% between 2006 and 2016, compared to a 25% increase from the region to the EU for the same period (European Commission, 2018).[5]

This section addresses training for SME internationalisation, particularly in terms of exporting (i.e. outward trade in goods and services). Training is considered in its widest sense and includes knowledge transfer and online learning across three areas to support SME export potential: 1) administrative requirements (e.g. technical and legal obligations for exporting); 2) vocational training (e.g. skills needed to adapt products and services to the demands of foreign markets); and 3) management development (e.g. business skills, foreign language proficiency).

Progress since 2014

Intelligence on training for SME internationalisation is weak across the region:

- More-developed data is available in **Israel** through the range of support institutions (e.g. foreign trade administration, export institute).

Policy instruments as enablers for training for SME internationalisation are generally well developed in all countries:

- These range from national development plans (e.g. Egypt, Jordan and PA) to SME and trade development strategies (e.g. Algeria, Egypt, Lebanon, Morocco) through to dedicated trade promotion activities (Israel).
- While particular emphasis is given across all countries to training on the legal obligations (administrative and technical requirements) for SME exporting, as well as management training (e.g. international marketing), the assessment highlights relatively little evidence across the region of the vocational training implications for exporting SMEs.
- There is little interface between SME internationalisation policies and the wider education and training policies. The **PA** export strategy highlights both the management and vocational skills requirements within a number of sector-specific export strategies. In **Tunisia** a couple of sector-driven projects help SMEs in their efforts to increase exports. However, as in all countries, the vocational training ecosystem is still loosely aligned with sector export interests.

Training in administrative or regulatory issues is widely available from sector associations, chambers of commerce and export development authorities. While there is little effort to innovate the learning process there are examples of interesting approaches to SME training:

- **PA**'s cluster-based training of SME managers in areas like market mapping and e-commerce encourages know-how exchange between SMEs from diverse sectors, is good practice.
- E-commerce in particular opens up export opportunities to the region's SMEs and will require dedicated policy discussion and training support in all MED countries. In this regard, **Jordan**'s Inter-institutional Committee on e-Commerce is an important reference.

The assessment highlights good efforts in ICT learning applications, although more can be done:

- In **Egypt** the Centre for Distance Learning at the Foreign Trade Training Centre provides online courses on exporting.
- The **Israel** Export and International Co-operation Institute offers small exporters webinars, courses and other services and trains mentors to assist exporter companies.
- In **Morocco** webinars for harmonised standards are offered.

For further action

More effort is needed across all countries to co-ordinate and cluster available data to help policy makers set priorities and allocate resources. This should include intelligence on the administrative requirements of vocational and management training for SME exports. With all countries having already established training commitments in key economic sectors, sector organisations will have an important role to play in terms of intelligence build-up and monitoring.

Given the demands of foreign markets for high-quality goods and services, vocational training needs to be more explicitly integrated into wider SME policies in all countries, particularly in those areas promoting SME internationalisation.

Given the widespread availability of ICT infrastructure, online training should be explored at the national and regional levels to enhance SME access to training – particularly for administrative and regulatory export-related training, which lends itself well to e-learning options.

The way forward

Overall, the MED economies have improved their policy frameworks for developing entrepreneurial human capital. The main challenges across the three sub-dimensions include the implementation of policies, cross-stakeholder co-operation, including all relevant public and private stakeholders, data collection and analysis on training provision and evaluation.

More particularly, this interim assessment puts forward the following actions for MED economies:

- Concerning entrepreneurial learning promotion, governments should build multi-stakeholder and cross-ministerial partnerships to ensure an efficient implementation of the action plan(s) that may belong under different national strategies. More reflection is needed on the development of entrepreneurship as a key competence. As a first step, awareness raising for policy makers, teachers, school directors, students and parents organisations with regard to entrepreneurship key competences would be necessary. EntreComp the European framework to promote entrepreneurial spirit can be a valuable tool to inspire policies and training measures at national level. At the same time, countries need to continue making efforts to move from project-based initiatives to a systemic approach by inserting entrepreneurial learning into the national curricula at all levels of education and by (re)training teachers.
- MED economies could move from individual policy measures and actions supporting women's entrepreneurship development to holistic approaches built on hard evidence that goes beyond the social, gender equality agenda and that puts the policy discussions in economic context. Governments could also continue their efforts to produce and collect gender-disaggregated data to enable the design of policies tailored to the needs of entrepreneurial women – first of all being measures for skills development and support of women's intention to engage in entrepreneurship. Skills and competences development measures should go beyond general SME training courses to include mentorship, coaching, network support and creation of women's entrepreneurship enabling systems that foster growth and innovation of women-led and women-owned enterprises. Systematic monitoring and evaluation of public-funded programmes with involvement of policy partners would ensure the effectiveness and efficiency of the above policy measures, generate a solid stock of data, and underpin further policy improvements.

- More developed data on SME training, particularly in terms of export potential, is required in all countries. One lead institution in-country should co-ordinate data and wider intelligence (e.g. good practice) to help the government decide policy priorities and resource allocation. Further, trade and SME policies require alignment 1) to ensure training meets external trade interest and 2) to include a closer interface with the vocational training environment – particularly to address quality improvements in sectors with improved export potential. Innovation in both training design and delivery through better use of available ICT technologies will require more developed engagement of the training community and the export-driven private sector.

Notes

[1] United Nations Industrial Development Organisation (UNIDO) initiative to support youth employability and entrepreneurship on upper Egypt.

[2] A youth-centred non-profit organisation established in Jordan in 1999 active in the European Union and worldwide, including in the Middle East, North-Africa and Pakistan.

[3] http://www.agadiragreement.org.

[4] https://eur-lex.europa.eu/legal-content/EN/TXT/?uri=LEGISSUM%3Ar14104.

[5] Data covers trade in goods only.

Bibliography

Bekh, O. (2014), "Training and Support for Women's Entrepreneurship", ETF Working Paper, European Training Foundation, Turin.

European Commission (2010). *Internationalisation of European SMEs,* Final Report, Directorate General for Enterprise and Industry, Brussels, http://ec.europa.eu/DocsRoom/documents/10008/attachments/1/translations/.

European Commission (2018). *Proposal for a Council Recommendation on Key Competences for Lifelong Learning*, Brussels, 17.1.2018 COM (2018) 24 final, https://ec.europa.eu/education/initiatives/european-education-area/proposal-council-recommendation-key-competences-lifelong-learning_en.

European Commission (2018). *European Neighbourhood Policy (South): international trade in goods statistics,* retrieved from http://ec.europa.eu/eurostat/statistics-explained/index.php/European_Neighbourhood_Policy_-_South_-_international_trade_in_goods_statistics.

European Commission (2017), *Taking the future into their own hands, Youth Work and entrepreneurial learning,* DG Education, Youth, Sport and Culture, https://publications.europa.eu/en/publication-detail/-/publication/8f5910d8-6b64-11e7-b2f2-01aa75ed71a1.

European Union project for ENP South Countries EUROPEAID/133918/C/SER/MULTI (2017), *Enhancement of the Business Environment in the Southern Mediterranean: Arab Women Entrepreneurs,* Consolidated Report, Brussels, http://www.ebesm.eu/template/default/files/WE_reports/1%20Arab%20Women%20Entrepreneurs%20Report%20.pdf.

International Labour Organization, ILOSTAT database (2017). "Labour force participation rate, female (% of female population ages 15+) (modelled ILO estimate)". Retrieved from https://data.worldbank.org/indicator/SL.TLF.CACT.FE.ZS.

Kelley, D., B. Baumer, C. Brush, P. Greene, M. Mahdavi, M. Cole, M. Dean, R. Heavlow, Babson College, Smith College and the Global Entrepreneurship Research Association (GERA) (2017), *Women's Entrepreneurship 2016/2017 Report.* https://www.babson.edu/Academics/centers/blank-center/global-research/gem/Documents/GEM%202016-2017%20Womens%20Report.pdf.

Love, J.H., and P. Ganotakis (2013). "Learning by exporting: lessons from high-technology SMEs." *International Business Review* 22 (1), pp. 1-17, https://www.semanticscholar.org/paper/Learning-by-exporting-%3A-Lessons-from-SMEs-Love-Ganotakis/079776eb0fcc1456ebd261a20dee8298e1773ed7.

OECD, European Commission, ETF (2014). *SME Policy Index for the Mediterranean Middle East and North Africa 2014: Implementation of the Small Business Act for Europe.* OECD Publishing, Paris, http://www.etf.europa.eu/web.nsf/pages/SME_Policy_Index_MENA_2014.

UNIDO (2017), *Promoting Women Empowerment for Inclusive and. Sustainable Industrial Development in the Middle East and North Africa region: A study on women entrepreneurship development in Egypt, Jordan, Lebanon, Morocco, Palestine and Tunisia*, https://www.unido.org/sites/default/files/2017-04/MENA_REPORT_Eng_interactive-1_0.pdf.

World Bank, Gender Equality Data & Statistics (2017). "Firms with female top manager (% of firms)". Retrieved from https://data.worldbank.org/indicator/IC.FRM.FEMM.ZS/.

WTO (2016). World Trade Report 2016. *Levelling the trading field for SMEs.* https://www.wto.org/english/res_e/booksp_e/world_trade_report16_e.pdf.

Part II. Mediterranean Middle East and North Africa Economy Profiles

Chapter 6. Algeria

The foundations of SME policy: definitions, statistics and institutions

One of the main steps Algeria has taken over the past few years has been the issuance of the SME Law 1702 of 2017, which formally establishes four important aspects of SME policy making: 1) an official definition of micro, small and medium-sized enterprises; 2) the mechanisms designed to support SMEs; 3) measures to promote sub-contracting (*sous-traitance*) by SMEs as a means of promoting industrial development and import substitution; and 4) the development of a system of economic information of SMEs (SME Observatory).[1]

Concerning the establishment of an official **SME definition,** the SME Law builds on a number of principles and international practices, notably the following (see Table 6.1):

1. The identification of SMEs as business entities producing goods and services regardless of their status (limited liability, incorporated, individual entrepreneur, etc.);
2. The combination of employment and financial criteria to better identify and target SMEs operating in different economic activities or sectors; and
3. The inclusion of SME independence criteria (e.g. an SME should not be more than 25% owned by another entity or more than 49% owned by a private equity firm).

The adoption of the SME Law 1702 makes Algeria the only MED economy with a fully-fledged SME definition officially enshrined in legislation.

Table 6.1. SME definition

Criterion	Micro	Small	Medium
Employment criterion	1-9 employees	10-49 employees	50-250 employees
Financial criterion	Annual turnover < DZD 40 m	Annual turnover < DZD 400 m	Annual turnover < DZD 4 bn
	Year-end statement < DZD 20 m	Year-end statement < DZD 200 m	Year-end statement <DZD 1 bn

Source: SME Law 1702 of 2017.

Chapter 3 of the SME Law 1702 also lays the foundation for establishing a **System of SME Economic Information** under the responsibility of the National Agency for SME Development (ANDPME) to serve as a planning and decision-making tool. This system (in principle an SME Observatory) would consolidate information from several statistical and administrative sources, namely the National Statistics Office (ONS), the business registry, the National Social Security Institute (CNAS), the Institute for Social Security for the Self-Employed and Independent Professionals (CASNOS), the tax administration, the customs administration, the chamber of commerce and industry, and the association of banks and financial establishments. If implemented successfully, such a system would provide timely and complete information on private enterprises at a low cost and with a lower burden on firms than the enterprise or establishment censuses undertaken in most countries.

This would increase the already good availability in Algeria of SME data, which are published regularly (about twice per year) in the statistical bulletins of the Ministry of Industry and Mines[2] and include total SME population, SME entries and exits, employment, and exports and imports. They also comprise information on SMEs broken down by economic activity and territorial distribution. The data is obtained from official sources such as the National Social Security Institute (CNAS) and its equivalent for self-employed and independent professionals (CASNOS).

The wider **economic agenda** in which SME policy is framed remains almost unchanged. The SME Policy Index 2014 noted that the overall economic policy framework was set by the Five Year Economic Plan (2010-2014), which placed private sector development as one of the country's key priorities (together with public investment in infrastructure, housing and social services), with the aim of reducing reliance on the hydrocarbon sector and diversifying the country's economic structure.

The 2015-2019 Economic Development Plan continues to place a high priority on economic diversification through private sector development. As part of the Plan, the *Governmental Policy on the Domain of Industry and Mines* mentions SME development as a priority, notably through the development of basic industries and "downstream SMEs" and import substitution.[3] This, combined with the consultations carried out for the purposes of this interim assessment, point to a strong orientation of SME policy towards the development of the industrial sector. Furthermore, it is surprising that other economic policy areas under the 2015-2019 Economic Development Plan barely mention the role of SMEs in sectors such as commerce; agriculture and fisheries; energy; tourism and handcrafts.[4]

In terms of the **institutional framework and co-ordination** for SME policy, the Ministry of Industry and Mines continues to be the main institution in charge of enterprise development policy, with the ANDPME and the National Agency for Investment Development (ANDI) under its umbrella. Other pertinent authorities in this area are the National Agency for the Support of Youth Employment (ANSEJ), the Credit Guarantee Fund for SMEs (FGAR) and the "SME Facilitation Centres" and business incubators across the country.[5]

The SME Policy Index 2014 noted that policy co-ordination between the various institutions was a major issue due to the lack of a comprehensive medium-term SME development strategy supported by short-term action plans. In this regard, the SME Law designates the ANDPME as the leading institution in charge of the SME policy agenda for enterprise creation, growth and survival. The Law establishes local authorities as the initiators of SME support, notably in terms of accessing land and immovable property. According to the consultations for this interim assessment, in order for the ANDPME to be more agile in its policy mandate the **SME agency** will need to gain autonomy – becoming a "public establishment of specific character" – and will have a board of directors that includes representation from the private sector (a model that is already applied in several countries in the region, including Morocco and Jordan).

The SME Law also notes that the "Algerian SME development policy should be based on consultation and co-ordination among relevant public and private actors and on appropriate studies leading to programmes, measures and support structures." It also foresees the creation of a public-private consultation body, the National Consultation Council for SME

Development (CNC), which should be formed by organisations and professional associations representing SMEs. The CNC was officially launched in November 2017. (See Chapter 1, section 4, for more on public-private dialogue.)

Importantly, the SME Law puts into place a **special fund to finance the actions and support** stated in the text as well as the operations of the ANDPME: the National Fund for Upgrading SMEs, Supporting Investment and Promoting Industrial Competitiveness.[6] According to the Finance Law (*loi des finances*) 2018 and to the consultations, the Fund is to be financed by a new tax on industrial land designed to raise of DZD 395 million (about EUR 2.8 million).

The SME Law sets the legal framework for a more complete and coherent SME policy in Algeria. Nonetheless, the implementation of a concrete **SME strategy and action plans** with detailed activities, responsibilities, budgets and monitoring and evaluation (M&E) mechanisms is *still* missing. According to the consultations conducted for this interim assessment, an SME strategy is being developed in the context of the Project for the Support of SME Development (PAD-PME) supported by the African Development Bank (AfDB).[7] The project also supports the reorganisation of the ANDPME, capacity building for the Agency, and the establishment of the SME information system (the SME Observatory).

On **public-private dialogue**, the broad economic issues continue to be tackled by the Tripartite Council (*la Tripartite*) formed by the government, the General Union of Algerian Workers (UGTA) and many private sector associations. More precisely, on SME policy the most important recent development is the creation of aforementioned CNC, which represents several business organisations in various economic sectors. According to the consultations for this assessment, the CNC is working with the EU Technical Assistance and Information Exchange instrument (TAIEX) to develop an action plan between the CNC and the ANDPME. During the launch of the CNC in November 2017 the Algerian authorities revealed a road map for developing the SME Strategy. [8]

For further action: Through the SME Law and the initial implementation of some of its actions, Algeria has made an important step towards the adoption of a more comprehensive and coherent SME policy. The SME Law, albeit brief, is a complete document that stipulates how the most important aspects of SME should be conducted. Its full implementation, including the execution of an SME strategy, is now essential to put words into action. Furthermore, the creation of the CNC is expected to provide a formal consultation mechanism allowing SMEs and entrepreneurs to contribute to policy making; that said, its success will be highly influenced by the degree to which the CNC is representative of the SME and entrepreneur population.

In contrast, as earlier noted in the SME Policy Index 2014, structural factors – including the difficult regulatory and business environment and the lack of economic diversification and openness – create important distortions for SME and entrepreneurship development. In addition, although SME policy is seen as an important instrument for industrial policy and economic diversification, not much is said about the role of SMEs in services and non-industrial sectors. Hence, the Algerian authorities also could extend their vision on the role of SMEs for the whole economy and consider the measures necessary to support the promotion of entrepreneurship and SMEs outside industrial activities.

Improving business environments for SMEs and entrepreneurs

The SME Policy Index 2014 noted that Algeria was stepping up efforts for **regulatory reform and administrative simplification**. It mentioned in particular the creation of a number of inter-ministerial working groups designed to improve the business environment, including the Tripartite Council formed by the government, the General Union of Algerian Workers (UGTA) and many private sector associations (see Chapter 1, section 4). However, the lack of a clear regulatory strategy and mandates for administrative simplification were hampering these efforts. Furthermore, there were neither pilot nor formal efforts to introduce regulatory impact analysis (RIA) or the SME test.

This interim assessment finds no significant progress in this area. Indeed, according to the consultations, the government is lifting constraints that hinder strong and sustained growth through the improvement of the business environment and investment in terms of procedures, deadlines and costs, as well as through the implementation of improved business promotion policies. The consultations also point to the fact that the SME Law 1702 aims at encouraging the creation and competitiveness of SMEs and the role that is given to local authorities in this regard. However, as noted above, although the SME Law provides the legal basis for improving the business and regulatory environment for SMEs, its approval does not automatically translate into results. At the end of the day, Algeria continues to have the most complicated business environment of all the MED economies, according to *Doing Business*.

According to this interim assessment, Algeria has no plans to introduce formal mechanisms for **RIA** (*ex-ante* and *ex-post*) and therefore no indications of an SME test. This endeavour, though, could be undertaken in the context of the recently created CNC mentioned earlier.

In terms of efforts to facilitate the **creation of new enterprises**, the SME Policy Index 2014 called for Algeria to introduce a single identification number to better exploit the synergies between the different institutions involved in the registration process. The introduction of such a number is being contemplated in the establishment of a System of SME Economic Information mandated by the SME Law 1702 under the responsibility of the ANDPME. Under this system, the relevant agencies and institutions will be required to provide the various types of information they have on SMEs. Those agencies are the ONS, the National Centre of the Commercial Register (CNCR), the CNAS, CASNOS, the tax office, the customs administration, the Chamber of Commerce and Industry, and banks associations and financial establishments.

The SME Policy Index 2014 also noted the existence of an online business registration system – although the platform was only accessible to notaries who, on behalf of their clients, could use the CNRC web portal to reserve a company name, upload summaries of articles of incorporation, and publish the registration in the *Official Bulletin of Legal Announcements*. Entrepreneurs could only download business creation forms from the CNRC and ANDI websites.

One of the main actions reported by this interim assessment is the creation in May 2017 of an **electronic portal devoted to enterprise creation** which is hosted, administered and maintained by the ANDPME.[9] The portal provides important information regarding the creation of a firm either as a natural person or a legal person. The platform is accessible to the public, although *it is still necessary to choose a notary* registered in the CNRC to carry out necessary formalities – such as transferring the information and the documents necessary to the relevant agencies, namely the CNRC, the tax register and the social security (CNAS-CASNOS). By the end of the third quarter of fiscal year 2018 (March 2018), about 80 enterprises had been created through the portal and 276 notaries had been trained to use the portal. The hurdles for a further deployment of the initiative though are the lack of recognition of electronic signatures and e-payments.

The SME Policy Index 2014 also noted the measures that were taken to reinforce the role of the one-stop shops managed by the ANDI throughout the country's 48 *Wilayas,* or governorates. However, the one-stop shops had only limited decision-making capacity and acted mainly as single initial contact points. In this regard, the ANDI reports in this interim assessment that the one-stop shops were reorganised following the adoption of the 2016 Investment Law 16-09, with the introduction of the notion of "centres" charged with investment promotion and facilitation. What these reforms mean in terms of facilitating enterprise creation, though, is not clear. There is no evidence that investment promotion and facilitation activities are explicitly linked to the facilitation of the creation of new firms across the country.

As in 2014, the framework governing **bankruptcy** continues to be the Code of Commerce (Order 75-79) of 1975. According to *Doing Business* 2018, Algeria continues to have a relatively effective bankruptcy system featuring relatively speedy resolution (1.3 years, faster than the OECD average) and a cost of 7% of estate (also below average OECD costs). However, the recovery rate is 50 cents per dollar, below the 71 cents in the OECD. The SME Policy Index 2014 indicated that Algerian courts were not generally trained in matters related to the reorganisation of enterprises and therefore often opt for liquidation, which can lead to the closure of businesses that could have survived bankruptcy. Therefore, the recommendation was that Algeria could benefit from capacity-building programmes for judges dealing with insolvency. To this end, the Ministry of Justice notes that there have been training programmes to strengthen judges' insolvency skills since 2000. These programmes focus on general business, business law, bankruptcy, international commercial arbitrage, etc. According to the consultations, about 25 magistrates undergo training, in addition to other training courses abroad in partnership with countries such as France and Belgium. The total number of judges benefiting from this training since 2012 is 800 according to the consultations. However, there is no evidence of concrete results for this programme – for example, whether the training has resulted in fewer liquidations and business exits and more business restructurings.

For further action: There is ample space for Algeria to continue improving its business environment, particularly since the country is ranked last in the region in terms of *Doing Business* (166) and second last in terms of starting a business (145). Algeria could take the opportunity of the creation of the CNC as a multipartite platform for the creation of a formal RIA system and/or an SME test. Furthermore, in order to expand business creation through the new electronic portal, the authorities could work to establish a system of electronic payments and the recognition of digital signatures so that entrepreneurs do not have to rely only on physical procedures. Finally, the effectiveness of the training system for judges dealing with enterprises in difficulty could better tracked. Indeed, although Algeria ranks second in the MED region on this aspect of *Doing Business*, it still ranks 71st globally.

Fostering access to finance

The **legal and regulatory framework** for access to finance has remained mostly unchanged over the past few years. A recent reform is the modernisation, in September 2015, of the Credit Registry (*Centrale de risques*) to include information about households and consumer credit. The Credit Registry, which is over 20 years old, is now better placed to manage risks to the financial system and to help households avoid over-indebtedness, hence contributing to the expansion of consumer credit. However, the provisions of the decree leading to this reform[10] apply to loans not exceeding 60 months, meaning that longer-term loans (which could be funding productive investments by entrepreneurs or small firms) are not included in the Credit Registry. Furthermore, according to the consultations for this interim assessment, the Credit Registry includes only loans above MAD 2 million (nearly EUR 189 000). This relatively high figure would result in the exclusion of several entrepreneurs and micro firms with access to smaller loans.

In addition, no efforts have been made either to create a credit bureau or to improve the register of moveable assets. This indicates that progress on access to credit information remains limited compared to the rest of the region.

Concerning the availability of **sources of finance**, the SME Policy Index 2014 noted that credit guarantee schemes were sponsored by public institutions, state banks and international donors, and no private market existed for these vehicles. This interim assessment found no reforms in this area. The main players are still the public actors, the Credit Guarantee Fund for SMEs (FGAR) and the Fund of Guarantees for Credit Investment (CGGI).

Similarly, equity investments for SMEs continue to be dominated by public vehicles. The most salient is the *Wilaya*s (governorates) Investment Fund, which is funded by public sources and is focused on supporting youth entrepreneurship across the country. This vehicle finances up to 49% of the investment required by the venture and has a total envelope of DZD 48 billion, or DZD 1 billion per *Wilaya* (about EUR 7 242 000). The Fund is managed by three public financial institutions (Finalep, Sofinance and El Djazair Istithmar) and two public banks (BEA and BNA). The Fund provides venture capital (*capital de risque*) for new firms, growth capital and business restructuring to ensure the survival of firms and the jobs they sustain.

For further action: This interim assessment indicates limited progress on financing SMEs and entrepreneurs. Algeria does not have yet plans to create a credit bureau or a registry of moveable assets and the state continues to have a dominant role in the provision of financing through credit guarantees or through direct funding. Furthermore, although the consultations for this assessment point to a number of decrees and legal provisions designed to facilitate access to finance, there is no evidence of the implementation or impact of these provisions. Algeria could therefore take a series of measures to foster the participation of private actors in the SME financing market, including through the establishment of credit bureaus and credit rating agencies, credit guarantee schemes, and venture capital and business angels. It could also better track the impact of legal provisions on the actual access to finance by SMEs and entrepreneurs.

Nurturing entrepreneurship and SME growth

There have been no significant changes in the provision of **business development services** (BDS) in Algeria since the SME Policy Index 2014. The main actor in the BDS market continues to be the Ministry of Industry and Mines through its a flagship support scheme, the National Upgrading Programme (*Programme de mise à niveau*), which has been implemented by the ANDPME since 2010. The programme provides technical training and assistance for SME competitiveness, including supporting tangible and intangible investments on standardisation, quality certification, intellectual and industrial property, ICT, special equipment, etc. The SME Policy Index 2014 and the website of the National Upgrading Programme note that the objective to attain was 20 000 beneficiary firms during the period 2010-2014. According to the consultations for this assessment, however, there are just over 5 300 beneficiary firms, and there is no evidence of any impact on the competitiveness of these firms. Furthermore, the second programme mentioned by the

SME Policy Index 2014 (the SME Support Programme or PME II), which focused on promoting the use of ICT in SMEs with growth potential, is no longer operational.

Access to **public procurement** for SMEs, on the other hand, continues to be a relatively positive policy area. Decree 15-247 of 16 September 2015, which regulates public procurement, reserves a quota of 20% of this market for SMEs. The decree also states that a company which has been awarded a public procurement contract can subcontract up to 40% of it to other firms, giving SMEs a chance to participate indirectly in this important market. However, there are no figures on the impact of this decree on SME development. There is no e-procurement system either.

In terms of **SME internationalisation**, several platforms that disseminate information on foreign markets continue to operate, including the Algerian Company of Export Guarantees (CAGEX), the Algerian Agency for the Promotion of Foreign Trade (ALGEX), the Office of Promotion of Foreign Trade (PROMEX), and the Algerian Chamber of Commerce and Industry (CACI). Furthermore, according to ALGEX, a National Export Promotion Strategy is being developed with the participation of various ministries and the co-ordination of a committee in order to eliminate logistical, administrative and technical barriers to international trade.[11] Nonetheless, there is no clear link between the strategy and the direct promotion of SME exports and several of the sectors identified as a priority are rather capital intensive or dominated by large firms (chemical industry, pharmaceutical industry, construction materials, electronics, etc.).

For further action: This interim assessment finds that although most of the mechanisms and initiatives for SME growth identified by the SME Policy Index 2014 continue to operate, there are no new initiatives. Algeria could therefore increase its efforts to expand the market for business development services beyond the initiatives provided by public institutions and in particular the National Upgrading Programme. Indeed, there is no evidence on the role of private sector providers of business development services. Furthermore, no progress is evident with regard to the promotion of SME internationalisation, and Algeria is not yet part of the Europe Enterprise Network (EEN). Finally, the authorities could track and publish facts and figures on the impact of measures to promote SME access to public procurement and could also work towards the establishment of e-procurement.

Investing in entrepreneurial human capital

In terms of **entrepreneurial learning in upper-secondary education**, the government's Action Plan[12] refers to the introduction to "entrepreneurial know-how" in general education through students' project development and company visits. For vocational training, the action plan aims to train young people to better prepare them for the professional world and for the creation of a business. A framework agreement was signed in 2014 between the Ministry of Professional Education and Training and 14 ministerial departments as well as social partners. The *Institut National de la Formation et de l'Enseignement Professionnels* developed a training module on "the roadmap for entrepreneurs" targeted at schools.

Ten years after the reform of the education system in 2008, entrepreneurial learning as a key competence is still not sufficiently integrated into secondary education programs (general and vocational). Nevertheless, vocational training has made more progress in this area thanks to a gradual strengthening of the partnership between vocational schools and businesses and the establishment of a legal framework for apprenticeship.

The policy dialogue at the national level on the integration of entrepreneurial spirit is at an initial stage, and it has not yet resulted in a concrete action plan. It would be relevant to create a multidisciplinary working group including the various stakeholders (relevant ministries, organisations of employers, entrepreneurs, teachers, civil society) and identify a leader.

Several actions have taken place to promote **women entrepreneurship** since 2013. The Government Plan 2017 aims to support women entrepreneurs, especially in rural areas. The 2014 Charter of Working Women recognises the importance of awareness campaigns and support programmes, including training. The Ministry of National Solidarity, Family and Women's Affairs is preparing an action plan on women entrepreneurship.

Training programmes for women are available also at the regional level, as are awareness campaigns like the Caravan to the *Wilaya*s. But the offer is often scattered and focuses on the start-up phase. The National Microcredit Agency (ANGEM) and ANSEJ support self-employed women and women entrepreneurs. Several training modules have been developed in the context of the Women for Growth project supported by the International Labour Organisation (ILO): "Manage Your Business Better (GERME) and Get Ahead".

In the context of the new SME law, **training for the internationalisation of SMEs** should have an important role. The offer of training programmes is scattered and information about it fragmented. The Algerian Chamber of Commerce and Industry and AlGEX provide courses and support companies' participation in international fairs. But the content of the training programmes is not sufficiently tailored to SMEs, which would benefit more from capacity building regarding procedures, packaging, risks, rules of origin, etc.

For further action: Entrepreneurship as a key competence should be better integrated into secondary schools. Awareness raising campaigns directed at teachers and school directors could help, as could more partnerships between schools and local companies. Systemic actions to support women entrepreneurship training could build on the policy documents that have been developed, which should become an opportunity to provide a more cohesive offer and develop modules that support businesses beyond the start-up phase. Training programmes to support SME internationalisation could be improved by undertaking a mapping of needs and focusing on sectors with high export potential, such as the agro-food sector. Institutions that deliver these types of training would also benefit from capacity building to upscale their offer.

The way forward

The establishment of the SME Law and the implementation of some of its actions constitute an important but initial step for Algeria to increase policy co-ordination and efficiency, as recommended by the SME Policy Index 2014. Unfortunately, beyond the SME Law and the establishment of the CNC, this interim assessment finds no substantial progress in the policy areas analysed. In this view, the actions recommended by this report are as follows:

- Developing a comprehensive and multi-annual SME strategy, including measures to address structural factors and distortions preventing the development of the private sector. The strategy could take a wider perspective beyond a narrow focus on industrial activities; this is particularly relevant given the comparative advantages of SMEs in sectors such as tourism, trade and services, as well as innovative activities.

- Using the CNC as a platform for improving the business environment and, in particular, establishing an RIA mechanism and the SME test.
- Fostering greater private sector participation in financing SMEs and entrepreneurs. This includes a number of actions, ranging from the establishment of one or more credit bureaus (and related services such as credit ratings) to the creation of a registry of moveable assets and the introduction of tools and sources of finance (credit guarantees, venture capital funds, business angel networks, etc.).
- Fostering greater private sector participation in the provision of business development services, which are so far dominated by a few schemes and public actors.
- Further facilitating SME access to public procurement and to international markets, and better tracking the impact of existing laws and measures in these areas.
- Create a multidisciplinary working group (including the different ministries concerned, organisations of employers, entrepreneurs, teachers, civil society) to promote entrepreneurship as a key competence.
- Develop an action plan to implement the Government Plan 2017 in favour of women entrepreneurs.
- Identify sectors with high export potential such as the agro-food and design specific training offers.

Notes

[1] Official Journal of the Algerian Republic No 02, 11 February 2017; www.droit-afrique.com/uploads/Algerie-Loi-2017-02-orientation-developpement-pme.pdf.

[2] Algerian National Statistics Office, http://www.ons.dz, and "Bulletins d'information statistique de la PME" (SME Bulletins), http://www.mdipi.gov.dz/?Bulletin-de-veille-statistique.

[3] Algerian Prime Minister's website, economic development section www.premier-ministre.gov.dz/fr/ in particular "Politique gouvernementale dans le domaine industrie et des mines" (2015), www.premier-ministre.gov.dz/ressour ces/front/files/pdf/politiques/industrie-mines.fr.pdf.

[4] Algerian Prime Minister's Website, Politiques Publiques, www.premier-ministre.gov.dz/fr/gouvernement/politiques-publiques/developpement-economique.

[5] www.mdipi.gov.dz/IMG/pdf/mise_a_niveau_des_pme.pdf.

[6] Compte d'affectation spécialc n° 302-124 intitulé "Fonds national de mise à niveau des PME, d'appui à l'investissement et de promotion de la compétitivité industrielle."

[7] www.afdb.org/fr/projects-and-operations/project-portfolio/p-dz-kf0-002/.

[8] Algérie Presse Service (4 December 2017), "Industrie : un plan d'action pour le développement de la PME pour 2018", www.aps.dz/economie/66584-industrie-un-plan-d-action-pour-le-developpement-de-la-pme-pour-2018; and S. Vidzraku (6 December 2017), "Algérie: le government dévoile les axes de son plan d'action pour le développement des PME", *La Tribune Afrique*, https://afrique.latribune.fr/economie/strategies/2017-12-06/algerie-le-gouvernement-devoile-les-axes-de-son-plan-d-action-pour-le-developpement-des-pme-760501.html.

[9] *Le portail Algérien de creation d'entreprise en ligne*, www.jecreemonentreprise.dz/index.php?lang=fr.

[10] Published in the Official Gazette No 24 of 13 May 2015.

[11] L'Agence Nationale de Promotion du Commerce Extérieur (1 February 2018), "La stratégie nationale exportations – SNE: la 2ème consultation les 29 et 30 janvier 2018 au siège d'algex", www.algex.dz/index.php/blog-export/item/1074-la-strategie-nationale-des-exportations-sne-la-2eme-consultation-les-29-et-30-janvier-2018-au-siege-d-algex.

[12] Gouvernement Algérien (2017), *Plan d'action du gouvernement de la mise en œuvre du programme du président de la République,* Service du premier Ministre, www.premier-ministre.gov.dz/ressources/front/files/pdf/plans-d-actions/plan-d-action-du-gouvernement-2017-fr.pdf.

Chapter 7. Egypt

The foundations of SME policy: definitions, statistics and institutions

Egypt is in the process of redesigning its institutional and policy framework for SME and entrepreneurship and is starting to address one of the key recommendations of the SME Policy Index 2014 – which noted that the country should address the fragmentation of the institutional framework by defining the role of the various institutions and government agencies, co-ordinating support instruments and developing synergies among programmes.

As part of these efforts the Ministry of Trade and Industry and the Central Bank of Egypt (CBE) are working towards the development of a unified **SME definition**, which is expected to be included in the upcoming SME law. Currently, there are three definitions, i.e. those of 1) the Central Agency for Public Mobilisation and Statistics (CAPMAS) the Establishment Census; 2) the Egyptian Small Enterprise Law No. 141 of 2004; and 3) the CBE. Each institution applies a different definition (see Table 7.1).

Table 7.1. SME definitions in Egypt

<table>
<tr><th rowspan="2">Class</th><th colspan="2">Existing companies</th><th colspan="2">Newly established companies</th></tr>
<tr><th>Annual revenues (EGP Mn.)</th><th>Number of employees</th><th>Paid-up capital (EGP Mn.)</th><th>Number of employees</th></tr>
<tr><td>Micro</td><td>< 1</td><td><10</td><td>< 0.5</td><td><10</td></tr>
<tr><td>Small</td><td>1 : 50</td><td rowspan="2">< 200</td><td>Industrial companies 0.05 : 5
Non-industrial companies 0.05 : 3</td><td rowspan="2"><200</td></tr>
<tr><td>Medium</td><td>50 : 200</td><td>Industrial companies 5 : 15
Non-industrial companies 3 : 5</td></tr>
</table>

Source: Central Bank of Egypt, http://www.cbe.org.eg/ar/BankingSupervision/Pages/Circulars.aspx?p=4.

In terms of **SME statistics**, the main source of information is the Establishment Census undertaken by CAPMAS. This census is usually conducted every ten years, and the latest was issued on 2017. According to the Census, there are 3.8 million micro enterprises and 67 600 small and micro enterprises in Egypt. In 2010-2011, the Egyptian Banking Institute (EBI), the financial development arm of the Central Bank of Egypt, and CAPMAS conducted an SME survey, which was expanded by the Economic Census of CAPMAS in 2013. There are plans to create an SME Observatory in the context of the new SME agency.

Egypt's overall **economic policy framework** is being shaped by a number of important structural reforms, including those launched in November 2016 in the context of the International Monetary Fund's (IMF) Extended Fund Facility. These reforms have been mostly oriented at redressing macroeconomic imbalances and structural challenges (such as low growth and investment rates, rising inflation, high government debt and an overvalued exchange rate) that had negative effects on the current account deficit and international reserves. The implementation of these reforms has yielded positive results such as increased economic growth and declining inflation (despite the negative immediate effects of the floatation of the currency and the removal of subsidies). Yet, as noted by the IMF in its latest Article IV Consultation for Egypt, the state continues to play a prominent role in the economy, either as the employer of choice given the better job conditions and security it offers, or through its direct participation through state-owned enterprises in sectors such as banking, energy, manufacturing, agriculture, transport, tourism and services.[1]

Another important initiative guiding the overall economic, social and environmental orientations is the Sustainable Development Strategy: Egypt Vision 2030. The economic development pillar of Vision 2030 focuses on mega infrastructure projects, notably the expansion of the Suez Canal, the construction of a new administrative capital and the development of a 4 million-acre project. Vision 2030 also includes a series of reforms designed to improve the investment climate and the regulatory environment for businesses, but it makes no direct reference to SME and entrepreneurship policy.

According to the SME Policy Index 2014, the **institutional SME policy framework** in Egypt was highly fragmented, with a blurred separation between the functions of policy development and policy implementation. The Social Fund for Development (SFD) was in charge of micro and small enterprises, while the General Authority for Investment and Free Zones (GAFI) focused on SMEs with high growth potential. The Ministry of Trade and Industry, through the Industrial Modernisation Centre (IMC) and other affiliated organisations, supported small-to-large enterprises operating in industrial sectors. Policy development responsibilities were split between different ministries: Trade and Industry, Investment and Finance, and Planning. Some form of co-ordination took place through cross-board representation in the implementation agencies (SFD, GAFI, IMC), but co-ordination remained difficult in the absence of a comprehensive SME development strategy. In 2013, the SFD was mandated to co-ordinate the development of the new SME strategy with other stakeholders and work had already started in parallel with the launching of a wide consultation process.

Egypt has taken important steps to address the fragmentation of the SME policy framework. First, in November 2016 the Ministry of Trade and Industry launched a National Strategy for Enhancing Industrial Development and Foreign Trade until 2020, which had been developed with support of the EU.[2] This strategy includes a thematic pillar on developing SMEs and entrepreneurship, under which the "National MSME & Entrepreneurship Development Strategy & Operational Plan 2018-2023" is developed with the support of Global Affairs Canada (GAC) and the International Labour Organization (ILO).

- In April 2017, a Prime Ministerial Decree established the new **MSME Development Agency** (MSMEDA) under the direction of the Minister of Trade and Industry. MSMEDA absorbs the responsibilities of the SFD, the Industrial Training Centre (ITC) and the IMC's responsibilities related to entrepreneurship and SME support. One of the main role of MSMEDA will be to ensure co-ordination among the different government structures dealing with SMEs. MSMEDA is in charge of:
- Developing SME and entrepreneurship policy and strategic planning;
- Putting in place the necessary frameworks for implementing, co-ordinating and monitoring SME support initiatives;
- Designing and executing support programmes on skills, supply chain, marketing, participation in trade fairs, collective negotiation for suppliers, etc;

- Facilitating access to finance for MSMEs; and
- Working with concerned and relevant authorities to facilitate and streamline license issuance procedures for MSMEs to start up activity.

MSMEDA is working on finalizing the Performance Measurement Framework (PMF) of the National MSME and Entrepreneurship Strategy. It has also developed a new **National Strategy for MSME Development 2020** and its Operation Plan, which was endorsed by its board and should be officially approved in the next months. The new National Strategy for MSMEs is divided into six pillars, and the Operational Plan includes 115 measures. The European Union (EU) is supporting the implementation of the strategy through the "Support for the Implementation of Strategies to Foster MSME Development in Egypt" (MiSMESIS) project. The project is developing a corporate strategy for MSMEDA to implement the National Strategy around three main pillars: 1) knowledge and centre of excellence; 2) business environment; and 3) enterprise-level support. The project has also undertaken a donor mapping exercise to identify ongoing activities within the six pillars of the strategy.

The seven "government directions" regarding SMEs are influenced by the SBA principles and their adaptation to the MED region through the SME Policy Index assessments. These are:

1. Creating an environment in which entrepreneurs and SMEs can thrive and where entrepreneurship is rewarded – in particular for future entrepreneurs – by fostering entrepreneurial interest and talent, particularly among young people and women, and by simplifying the conditions for business transfers.
2. Ensuring that honest entrepreneurs who have faced bankruptcy quickly get a second chance. The government will promote a positive attitude in society towards giving entrepreneurs a fresh start, making it easier and quicker to apply for non-fraudulent bankruptcy, and ensuring re-starters are treated on an equal footing with new start-ups.
3. Designing rules according to the "think small first" principle, in particular by:
   a. Ensuring that the impact of all government legislation and regulation on small businesses are carefully considered before they are introduced;
   b. Making public administrations responsive to SMEs' needs; and
   c. Adapting public policy tools to suit SME needs and facilitate SMEs' participation in public procurement, and to make better use of small-business support programs.
4. Facilitating small business access to finance and developing a legal and business environment that supports timely payments in commercial transactions. In particular, the government will facilitate the promotion of risk capital, microcredit and mezzanine finance and develop a legal and business environment supportive to timely payment in commercial transactions.
5. Promoting the upgrading of skills in SMEs and all forms of innovation by encouraging investment in research by SMEs and their participation in research and development (R&D) support programs, transnational research, and clustering and active intellectual property management by SMEs.

6. Enabling MSMEs to turn environmental challenges into opportunities by providing more information, expertise and financial incentives to help small businesses exploit opportunities of new "green" markets and increased energy efficiency, partly through the implementation of environmental management systems in SMEs.
7. Encouraging and supporting SMEs to benefit from the growth of international markets. The government will facilitate the provision of market-specific support and business training activities.

Concerning **public-private dialogue** (PPD), as in 2014, there is a large number of private sector organisations in Egypt, including the Federation of Egyptian Chambers of Commerce; the Federation of Egyptian Industries; the Egyptian Business Association; the Egyptian Junior Business Association; the Egyptian Federation of Investors; the Alexandria Business Association; and the Women Business Association. According to this interim assessment, private sector organisations are considering establishing departments for SMEs and the establishment of the MSMEDA is expected to lead to increased PPD. Of the three boards in the MSMEDA (Advisory Board, Board of Directors, and Board of Trustees), the first two include representatives from the private sector and from non-governmental organisations (NGOs).

For further action: Egypt is moving forward in terms of one of the key recommendations of the SME Policy Index 2014: the need to address the fragmentation of the SME institutional framework. The creation of the MSMEDA as an authority with policy co-ordination and direct support powers is a concrete step, although there are still no details on the precise role and responsibilities of the agency: the institutional strategy of MSMEDA and the national SME strategy are still under development and there is no clarity on when and how they will be approved and implemented. Furthermore, although the consultations for this interim assessment pointed to plans for establishing a formal public-private dialogue mechanism for SME policy, there is no concrete evidence on how these plans will be developed and implemented. Similarly, there is talk of the development of an SME Law and an official SME definition, but no evidence on how and when that would happen. Hence, Egypt could continue and increase its efforts to develop and implement its new legal and institutional framework for SME policy beyond its initial plans and steps.

Improving business environments for SMEs and entrepreneurs

Since 2008 (albeit with a temporary suspension from 2012 to 2013) Egypt has undertaken an ambitious, comprehensive multi-year **regulatory reform** programme, the Egyptian Regulatory Reform and Development Activity (ERRADA).[3] The initiative is supervised by the Ministry of Trade and Industry and is set as a priority in the governmental agenda for business climate reform.

The current activities of ERRADA include an inventory of all regulations related to the business environment and their publication in the e-registry for free consultation;[4] and the participation in the review of laws such as the Franchise Law, the Agency Law and the Bankruptcy Law and the law on Joint Stock and Limited Liability Companies. According to the consultations for this assessment and to the ERRADA website, Regulatory Impact Analysis (RIA) has been applied in some cases, such as the revision of the Franchise Law, the allocation of arable land and shipping agencies.[5] However, there is no evidence of the consistent application of RIA on business regulations. Furthermore, although the SME test and the "think small first" principle are said to be fully reflected in the SME Strategy that is under preparation, there is not yet evidence of its actual implementation.

A new Law on the Simplification of Industrial Licensing Procedures was issued in May 2017 as a response to outdated industrial laws from the 1950s. According to the Law, the license of the Industrial Development Authority (IDA) became the sole license required for establishing and operating an industrial facility. The EU's MiSMESIS project includes a component on regulatory simplification as well as the enhancement of single windows and one-stop shops. In addition, the Ministry of Investment introduced reforms at the Investor Service Centre, which extends the necessary approvals, certifications and licences needed for the establishment, operation and dissolution of a company. Those reforms include new windows, the introduction of a tool to measure users' satisfaction and new centres in different governorates.

Concerning reforms to facilitate the **creation of new enterprises**, in 2014 Egypt was working on introducing a single identification number through its extensive network of one-stop shops, managed by GAFI, SFD, IDA and the chambers of commerce, throughout the country. The consultations under this interim assessment note that the new Investment law no. 72 of 2017 states (in Article 51) that "each facility or company, regardless of its legal form, shall have a unified national number to be used for all the investor's dealings with all the different authorities and bodies in the state once it is activated." There are ongoing discussions for the EU to support a project to activate the single identification number.

In terms of online registration, the 2014 report noted that online registration facilities were available, albeit on a limited scale. The responses to this interim assessment note that companies can be created online by uploading the necessary documents. The entrepreneur is nonetheless requested to physically sign the documents at GAFI's premises in order to obtain the tax card and the social insurance number. These steps are done in a single step, while the relevant fees can be paid online. Furthermore, according to *Doing Business,* in 2016 Egypt improved its one-stop shop for business registration by introducing a unit to liaise between the tax and labour authorities on one the hand, and the firm on the other.[6] This means that the investor (or entrepreneur) now obtains the certificate of incorporation and the tax card, and registers for social insurance, in one window and one step.

In terms of **bankruptcy procedures**, a new law was approved by parliament on 28 January 2018. The Law, according to the consultations for this assessment, effectively decriminalises bankruptcy by abolishing prison sentences and allows companies more time and options for restructuring by introducing mechanisms to help settle commercial disputes outside the courtroom and simplify bankruptcy proceedings. The Law also mandates the formation of special bankruptcy courts within the Economic Courts system, which would mediate and arbitrate cases. Under the Law, a restructuring plan must be completed within 60 days of filing for a standstill, and bankruptcy court judges will have the right to extend that period at their discretion. The Bankruptcy Law also reduces the liquidation period for companies to nine months, instead of the current average of more than two years.

For further action: Egypt continues to perform relatively well in this policy area, although the overall business environment remains challenging. The reactivation of ERRADA is an important opportunity to enhance the regulatory environment, especially if RIA and the SME test are formally introduced. Furthermore, the implementation of a single identification number, mandated by the new Investment Law, should facilitate dealings with different public agencies; nonetheless, there is no information of how and when this would be implemented. There is also work ahead regarding the implementation of the reforms to the bankruptcy framework, especially given Egypt's rather low performance on resolving insolvency in *Doing Business* (ranked 115 and a distance to frontier of 38.89).

Fostering access to finance

The SME Policy Index 2014 noted that Egypt had a relatively good performance on the **legal and regulatory framework** for access to finance, especially given the existence of both a credit registry and a credit bureau. The credit bureau, I-Score, issues credit reports based on data provided by banks and by the credit registry of the Central Bank of Egypt (CBE). I-Score has increased the coverage of the adult population since the last assessment from 19.6% to 25.3% and has introduced a credit rating system. Furthermore, on September 2017 the Financial Supervisory Authority (EFSA) awarded I-Score the contract for the creation of a registry of moveable assets, addressing in principle one of the shortcomings identified by the SME Policy Index 2014. The initiative for a registry of moveable assets builds on efforts undertaken after the SME Policy Index 2014, in particular the issuance of a law governing secured transactions over movable assets (Moveable Security Law), which was enacted in December 2016.[7] The Movable Security Law regulates the pledging of movable assets and specifies the types of assets that can be taken as collateral. It aims to facilitate the granting of funds and to reduce the risks of small and medium-sized projects. Also, a new leasing law is being developed.

In terms of the availability of **sources of finance,** by 2014, credit guarantee schemes were both publicly and privately funded and the Credit Guarantee Company (CGC) was the main actor, with nine commercial banks and one insurance company as stakeholders. However, there were no monitoring mechanisms measuring the impact of the schemes.

Since then, the CBE has bought the shares of banks in the CGC and has injected money into the company for the purpose of incentivising banks to disburse loans under the CBE MSME lending initiative. The Board of Directors of the Central Bank approved on December 2017 a guarantee of 2 billion Egyptian pounds for the CGC and modified capital adequacy ratio rules.

Egyptian authorities are also trying to stimulate the supply side of finance and to establish tailored funding schemes. In 2016, the CBE launched an initiative to increase finance for SMEs and mandated national banks to dedicate at least 20% of their total loans to SMEs.[8] In 2017 the Central Bank also launched an initiative to stimulate financing for microbusinesses by injecting a total financing of EGP 30 billion (EUR 1.4 billion) into the banking sector, which would benefit 10 million customers over the next few years.[9] In addition, in 2018 the CBE launched an initiative of EGP 200 billion (EUR 9.3 billion) to finance SME projects over the next four years. The CBE also started three plans to support SMEs by 1) exempting banks from the reserve requirement for specific credit facilities; 2) creating financing facility for medium enterprises in the industrial, agricultural & renewable energy sectors to invest in equipment; and 3) with short term facilities for working capital.

In order to stimulate access to finance, the EBI, part of the Central Bank, has developed the Small and Medium Enterprises Portal summarising a number of financial instruments and other support available to SMEs and banks. The portal gathers information regarding financing instruments, training programs, studies and research, as well as SME statistics. The goal of the portal is to inform SME managers in their decision making.[10] The portal seems to be a useful source for SMEs to learn about different sources of support available.

In terms of access to equity, a number of platforms continue to operate including Cairo Angels, Flat6labs, Sawari Ventures and others. Furthermore, the MSMEDA, in collaboration with the World Bank and the International Finance Corporation (IFC), is working on the establishment of a venture capital programme for early-stage entrepreneurs.

In addition, on May 2017 the Ministry of Trade and Industry announced the creation of *Misr* Venture Capital Company, a private fund with a capital of EGP 150 million (EUR 7.1 million), which aims to help distressed but viable SMEs through the provision of short-term financing mechanisms.[11]

For further action: This interim assessment finds that Egypt has achieved incremental progress on the legal and regulatory framework for access to finance, notably through the new Moveable Security Law and the initial steps to set up a registry of moveable assets by I-Score, the already well-established credit bureau. These initiatives are positive, although too recent to show any results yet. Furthermore, over the past few years, government actors, notably the Central Bank and the MSMEDA, have initiated a number of initiatives to increase SME access to credit and equity. However, there are no details and evidence on the characteristics, targets and results of these initiatives and hence their impact is unknown. This indicates that Egypt could do much more in terms of tracking and reporting the results of efforts by public actors. There is also no evidence on an increasing role of private sector actors in providing funding for SMEs and entrepreneurs.

Nurturing entrepreneurship and SME growth

As reflected in the SME Policy Index 2014, Egypt had a well-developed market for **business development services**. The main service providers were government bodies including the SFD through technical support programmes, the IMC through its business development programmes, and GAFI's Bedaya Centre for Entrepreneurship and SME Development. This interim assessment finds that government bodies and donor initiatives continue to be the main actors in this area, including recent initiatives such as:

- The United States Agency for International Development (USAID) Strengthen Entrepreneurship & Enterprise Development programme, which runs from 2015 to 2019 and mobilises USD 22.9 million (EUR 19.3 million) to improve the quality, availability and accessibility of business development services for SMEs.
- GIZs' Promotion of Small and Medium Enterprises Programme (PSME) running from 2015-2020 to increase SME competitiveness by developing a services marketplace and helping the Ministry of Trade and Industry to strengthen the services of its technology and innovation centres.
- The "Nilepreneurs" initiative by the Central Bank, Nile University and the MSMEDA to develop business development services centres in all governorates. The Nilepreneurs programme has a training service unit, a BDS hubs, a media service unit, a design house focusing on product design, a caravan unit for on-the-ground events, an innovation challenge unit, a growth program unit, and mainstreams women empowerment
- The EU launched a new initiative, Promoting Inclusive Growth in Egypt, to improve access of SMEs to different business development services, including in terms of regional coverage.
- MSMEDA launched an Electronic MSME Platform,[12] which will become fully operational by end of 2018. The platform will function as an Enterprise Hub providing comprehensive information and data on all types of services offered by the Agency and by the other entities involved in enterprise financing and business development.

- The ministry of investment has launched in 2017 a new initiative to support entrepreneurs and start-ups entitled "Your idea, your company "Fekratek Sherkatek and one of its main pillars is to establish the "Entrepreneurship Service Centre" based in GAFI, that provides BDS for SMEs and entrepreneurs

These initiatives aim at fostering the availability and access of SMEs to different business development services and eventually to strengthen the market of these services across the country. It will therefore be important to track their results over their five years of implementation. No concrete results of these programmes are publicly available or provided in the responses to the consultations for this interim assessment.

In terms of facilitating SME access to **public procurement**, the SME Policy Index 2014 noted that although there were some legal provisions on this area (e.g. splitting tenders into lots, a suggested quota of 10% for SMEs in procurement contracts, deadlines on payments, etc.) the enforcement of these provisions was not common. This interim assessment finds that Egypt recently reduced by 50% the guarantee bond required from SMEs during the application to a public tender. Also, a protocol expected to be signed between the MSMEDA and the Authority for Government Services for facilitation of SME access to public procurement. However, no details on the nature and characteristics of the protocol have been published.

The SME Policy Index 2014 also pointed to the absence of e-procurement in Egypt. This has been addressed through the creation of a portal where interested parties can consult information on opened, closed and awarded tenders. Interested parties can also use the portal to bid for tenders and consult the status of applications for projects. There is no information on the use of the portal by SMEs though.

Concerning **SME internationalisation**, the SME Policy Index 2014 highlighted that Egypt was developing a new export strategy for 2014-2018 although political events were expected to slow the process. This interim assessment finds some progress in this regard, notably the development and implementation of three internationalisation strategies:

- The Ministry of Trade and Industry Strategy 2016-2020, which involves a pillar for export development. The strategy focuses on export promotion, trade facilitation and agreements, logistics and infrastructure, quality control and inspection procedures, competitiveness, and export regulations and procedures.
- Egypt Export Development Strategy 2017-2020, aligned with the above mentioned strategy, including the required institutional reform, potential sectors, target markets, export incentives, export development services, trade facilitation and economic integration policy. The strategy aims to support 200 new exporters.
- Egypt Export Development Strategy to the African Markets, which determined potential products, target markets, market entry support services, logistics centres, export finance services, and trade agreements.

Egypt also established a new plan for the Export Development Authority (EDA) to implement the export strategies and to coordinate amongst the different entities. EDA is specifically keen to engage SMEs in the development of the export sector.13 EDA for instance launched an export portal (www.expoegypt.gov.eg) which aims to act as a national trade platform that supports (SME) exporters throughout the whole export process.

The SME Policy Index 2014 also noted that several institutions provided export related services and that the online one-stop shop was not yet operational. This is still the case. Although there are plans to implement a national electronic single window through the project EgyTrade (project also mentioned in the SME Policy Index 2014), there have not been significant concrete measures over the past few years. The only activities cited for this interim assessment are the passing of a decree by the Minister of Finance to develop a consolidated customs declaration and a decree by the Minister of Industry and Trade amending import and export regulations to facilitate electronic exchanges.

For further action: This interim assessment does not point to significant progress in this area over the past few years. The provision of business development services continues to be led by government agencies and donors, although ongoing initiatives are geared towards developing the market for these services over the medium term. Efforts towards SME internationalisation are also preliminary, with the adoption of export promotion strategies and the passing of decrees to facilitate international trade through electronic platforms as very initial steps. Hence, Egypt could continue working towards more concrete results directly linked to SME characteristics and needs.

Investing in entrepreneurial human capital

Egypt has undertaken several actions to support **entrepreneurial learning in upper secondary education**, in line with the country's "2030" vision to have a knowledge-based economy. Promoting entrepreneurship in upper secondary education is formally addressed in the National MSME Strategy and in the Trade and Development Strategy, but it is not included in vocation education strategic plans. Moving forward, it will be important that general secondary education schools are eventually integrated into the wider entrepreneurship key competence developments.

The IMKAN initiative[14], which borrows on the European Entrepreneurship Key Competence Framework has been piloted in vocational schools in the Luxor governorate. It has achieved positive results and could be replicated in other governorates before taking legislative decisions in this regard. The initiative involves curriculum reform and teacher training, including development of learning outcomes. A committee was created comprising international aid organisations to bring forward entrepreneurship as a key competence. Additionally, the Ministry of Education and Technical Education (METE) has proposed to mainstream entrepreneurship as a key competence within all vocational schools.

Regarding **women's entrepreneurship training**, Egypt's "2030" vision includes a strategy for women empowerment which comprises the twin challenges of improved education and work experience, and women's entrepreneurship. The strategy emphasizes the need to develop digital skills for women, and to promote a culture of entrepreneurship. "Early start" initiatives at schools where girls and boys have exposure to successful women entrepreneurs will be important in tackling social stereotypes. The National Women's Council is planning to develop an action plan to support the 2030 Women's Strategy, which could provide an opportunity to develop systematic data on women's entrepreneurship and related support measures. Research and analysis of women's entrepreneurship should not be left only to international organisations. National expertise and knowledge networks around government departments, universities and NGOs should fill the gap in critically evaluating both policy and practice. Data and intelligence development, to include good practice build-up on training for women's entrepreneurship, should interface with a system-wider monitoring and evaluation of women's entrepreneurship to include assessment of effectiveness of training.

In terms of **training for internationalisation of SMEs**, the 2016-2020 industry and trade development strategy sets an overall objective of a 10% annual export growth rate. It targets four sectors (chemicals, engineering, textiles and building materials), and includes a skills development pillar within the ecosystem support framework. The strategy aims to increase Egyptian high-value exports, which requires high-level skills and innovation. The strategy also aims to identify the export potential of SMEs already at the start-up phase. This has implications for managerial and trade skills and wider entrepreneurship development. To meet these priorities, the national vocational training network will require significant adaptations to training design, and the necessary involvement of sector consultations.

The BEMT initiative is an excellent example of a joint-venture between training providers and the private sector. It involves four universities, the ITC and the Egyptian Chamber of Engineering Industries and allows university students to be trained on business and manufacturing technologies, quality and ISO standards with a view to facilitate the international competition of Egyptian products. Another good practice includes online export training for SMEs, provided by the Foreign Trade Training Centre through its Centre for Distance Learning. Information on training for SME internationalisation remains scattered, although the Export Development Authority and the Agency for Micro, Small and Medium Enterprise Development plan to cluster data providing an opportunity to monitor developments in the area.

For further action: More actions should be taken to improve entrepreneurship promotion within vocational training programmes by fostering more school-enterprise co-operation and ensuring coherence between the National MSME and technical and vocational education and training (TVET) strategies. The government should develop measures to implement the 2030 Vision in relation with women economic empowerment, and ensure girls' access to entrepreneurship key competence development through formal and non-formal education. Data collection and the development of statistics and indicators would be particularly important to allow for in-depth analysis and evidence-based policy making and monitoring of training programmes.

The way forward

Egypt has been addressing the main recommendation provided by the SME Policy Index 2014 in terms of adopting a more coherent approach to SME policy and redressing the fragmentation of the institutional framework. The most important initiative or series of initiatives over the past few years have been the establishment of a dedicated SME agency, the MSMEDA, and the ongoing development of a comprehensive SME strategy, which would result in a more intelligible framework for support. However, in contrast to other MED economies also reshuffling their SME institutional framework, Egypt does not seem to be working to establish a structured public-private dialogue platform to improve SME policy making. The SME Law and an official SME definition are expected to be adopted by the end of 2018.

Progress in other areas analysed by this interim assessment seems to be much more modest. In this view, the actions recommended by this report are as follows:

- Continuing and increasing efforts to develop and implement the new legal and institutional framework for SME policy beyond the initial plans and steps.
- Implementing a formal RIA mechanism and SME test, building on the efforts by ERRADA to improve the business environment.

- Moving forward with the implementation of the new bankruptcy framework and the establishment of a registry of moveable assets, which are also in their initial stages.
- Better tracking the results of support schemes for SME access to finance, including credit and equity.
- Promoting a greater role of the private sector in the provision of funding and business support services to SMEs. These markets are currently dominated by public actors and to a lower extent, donors.
- Better tracking the results of support schemes for SME access to public procurement and SME internationalisation.
- Ensuring implementation of high-level strategies regarding human capital development, including developing training programmes for SMEs with high-export potential, in consultation with sectoral associations.
- Elaborate a framework strategy and action plan for women's entrepreneurship to include data and wider intelligence on training services backed up by data and indicators to measure progress.
- Mainstreaming entrepreneurship in upper secondary education to include further efforts to promote understanding and application of the entrepreneurship key competence across the school network.

Notes

[1] IMF (2018), *Arab Republic of Egypt: 2017 Article IV Consultation, Second Review Under the Extended Arrangement Under the Extended Fund Facility, and Request for Modification of Performance Criteria*, IMF Country Reports, International Monetary Fund, Washington.

[2] Egyptian Ministry of Trade and Industry (10 November 2016), "Minister of Trade and Industry announces strategy for enhancing industrial development and foreign trade until 2020", www.mti.gov.eg/English/MediaCenter/News/Pages/Tarek-Kabil-announces-strategy-for-enhancing-industrial-development-and-foreign-trade-until-2020.aspx.

[3] Egyptian Regulatory Reform & Development Activity, www.errada.gov.eg/index_en.php.

[4] Egyptian Regulatory Reform & Development Activity, "e-registry", http://eregistry.errada.gov.eg/.

[5] Egyptian Regulatory Reform & Development Activity, "Achievements", www.errada.gov.eg/index_en.php?op=module_page_en&id=10.

[6] The World Bank Group Doing Business (2018), "Business Reforms in Egypt, Arab Rep.", www.doingbusiness.org/Reforms/Overview/Economy/egypt.

[7] Law No.115/2015.

[8] Oxford Business Group (30 June 2016), "SME financing ramps up in Egypt", www.oxfordbusinessgroup.com/news/sme-financing-ramps-egypt.

[9] Enterprise (24 May 2017), "CBE Microfinance to push out EGP 30 bn in subsidized financing to as many as 10 mn borrowers within four years", https://enterprise.press/stories/2017/05/24/cbe-

microfinance-to-push-out-egp-30-bn-in-subsidized-financing-to-as-many-as-10-mn-borrowers-within-four-years.

[10] Central Bank of Egypt, "Small and Medium Enterprises Portal", http://sme.ebi.gov.eg.

[11] Egyptian Ministry of Trade and Industry (29 May 2017), "Misr Venture Capital launched soon", www.mti.gov.eg/English/MediaCenter/News/Pages/Misr-Venture-Capital-launched-soon.aspx.

[12] www.msme.eg

[13] Mounir, H. (May 20, 2018), *"Egypt adopts three pointed plan to develop exports: EDA chairperson",* Daily News Egypt

[14] United Nations Industrial Development Organisation (UNIDO) initiative to support youth employability and entrepreneurship on upper Egypt

Chapter 8. Israel

The foundations of SME policy: definitions, statistics and institutions

As in 2014, Israel continues to have two main **SME definitions**. The first is set forth in Government Decision no. 2190 as follows:

- Micro business: a company or practitioner employing up to five employees and a sales turnover of less than ILS 10 million a year (approximately EUR 2.31 million).
- Small business: a company or practitioner employing up to 50 employees and a sales turnover of less than ILS 25 million a year (approximately EUR 5.78 million).
- Medium business: a company or practitioner employing up to 100 employees and a sales turnover of less than ILS 100 million a year (approximately EUR 23.12 million).

The second definition is that of the Small and Medium Business Agency (SMBA). The SMBA definition, which is shown in Table 8.1, is based on much lower financial (turnover) criteria for micro enterprises than are used in Government Decision no. 2190.[1] The SMBA definition has been revised as a result of research that was part of the strategic plan of the agency.

Table 8.1. SME definition by the Small and Medium Business Administration

Type of enterprise	Number of employees	Turnover
Micro	1 to 4	ILS 2 million (EUR 482 000)
Small	5 to 20	ILS 20 million (EUR 4.8 m)
Medium	21 to 100	ILS 100 million a year (EUR 20 m)

Note: The SMBA defines SMEs as companies or practitioners.
Source: Periodic Status Report - Small and Medium Businesses in Israel, 2017, page 21.

Although there are no plans to unify the SMBA and government definitions, the SMBA classification is the *de facto* official definition. For example, the SMBA definition was used in a bill passed by the Knesset (parliament) on first call in August, 2016.[2]

The statistical data for Israel are supplied by and under the responsibility of the relevant Israeli authorities. The use of such data by the OECD is without prejudice to the status of the Golan Heights, East Jerusalem and Israeli settlements in the West Bank under the terms of international law.

Israel has a very complete set of **SME statistics,** including data comparable at the international level. The main source of official data is published by the Central Bureau of Statistics (CBS) *Yearly Statistical Abstract.*[3] Israel also takes part in the OECD-Eurostat Entrepreneurship Indicators Programme (EIP) which presents a wide set of internationally comparable statics on SME and entrepreneurship performance based on official sources. This includes extensive information on the structure and performance of the enterprise population (firm demographics, value added, employment, etc.), productivity, business dynamics (entry, exit, high growth firms, etc.), job creation, international trade and other indicators. Israel also participates in the OECD Scoreboard on Financing SMEs and Entrepreneurs, which comprises an important set of indicators on debt, equity, asset-based finance and framework conditions for access to finance.

In terms of the wider **economic context**, Israel's diversified economic structure and vibrant start-up and innovation scene represent important drivers for the development of SMEs and entrepreneurship. Manufacturing activities represent around 20% GDP, of which advanced manufacturing such as machinery, electronics, chemicals and medical instruments account for important shares (about a quarter of manufacturing output). At around 50% of the economy, trade and services (excluding public administration and defence) are also important contributors to GDP, especially IT and other information services. Yet, according to the latest OECD Economic Survey of Israel[4], productivity performance is weak since highly dynamic tradable goods industries co-exist with inefficient sheltered sectors. This is derived from deficiencies in product market regulation and competition, particularly in the food chain, banking and electricity sectors. Furthermore, poverty and income inequality are high, especially among specific segments of the population.

Concerning the **institutional framework and co-ordination**, the Ministry of Economy and Industry is the main authority in charge of economic reform and development. As such, it hosts the Foreign Trade Administration, the Investment Authority, the Industrial Co-operation Authority and the **Small and Medium Business Agency**. The SMBA operates since 2010 a large network of business support centres (MAOF centres). Over the past few years the SMBA has increased and improved the provision of support services to SMEs by reshuffling and extending its network of business development centres. Yet, as noted in the OECD's *review of SME and Entrepreneurship Policy in Israel 2016*, although the co-ordination of SME and entrepreneurship policy is one of the functions assigned to the SMBA, there is no formal mechanism in place for this purpose. There is no inter-ministerial SME and entrepreneurship policy committee and there are no focal points in government ministries and agencies. Furthermore, the 2014 **SME Bill** that is cited by both the SME Policy Index 2014 and the OECD 2016 review, and which is intended to strengthen the co-ordination role of the SMBA is not yet approved by the Knesset (parliament). In addition, the OECD 2016 report notes, there is no integrated policy document (i.e. SME strategy) setting out a **strategic policy framework** for SME and entrepreneurship development.

The SME Policy Index 2014 reported that Israel had a well-developed system of **public-private dialogue** (PPD). The SMBA held quarterly meetings with the SME community. Organisations such as LAHAV (Independent Businesses Association), the Federation of Israeli Chambers of Commerce (FICC), or the Manufacturers Association of Israel and the Enterprise Europe Network Partners were very active in PPD processes. This interim assessment finds that PPD continues to be active, especially in terms of regulatory reform (see section on "Improving business environments for SMEs and entrepreneurs").

For further action: Israel has in general a well-established framework for SME and entrepreneurship policy, yet policy co-ordination could be improved through the development of an SME strategy, the establishment of a co-ordination mechanism and the adoption of the SME Bill. Indeed, although the SMBA is the main agency in charge of enterprise policy, its role appears as being limited to the co-ordination of business support services through the MAOF centres and providing support to some horizontal initiatives such as the introduction of regulatory impact analysis. As recommended by the OECD's review of *SME and Entrepreneurship Policy in Israel 2016*, the government could craft a single strategic policy document which lays out the vision, objectives, target groups, policy measures and budgets dedicated to the support of SMEs and entrepreneurs. This could be particularly important given the already noted dual nature of the economy in which a highly productive and innovative sector co-exists with less productive and dynamic firms. An SME strategy could for instance devise measures to increase productivity spill over effects from the dynamic sectors into the rest of the economy. This could be also important given the regular consultations which are already happening between the SMBA and the private sector, and which could be a good starting point for integrating other relevant government institutions into a wider public-private dialogue platform.

Improving the business environment for SMEs and entrepreneurs

According to the SME Policy Index 2014, the **regulatory environment** was one of the weak areas in the Israeli policy framework. To address this issue, Israel established three inter-ministerial committees working on 1) improving the general business climate (the *Doing Business* Committee), 2) the system of business licensing, and 3) the introduction of regulatory impact analysis (RIA) for new legislation and regulations. Although the *Doing Business* Committee is no longer operational, the two other committees remain active.

One of the main improvements was the issuance in October 2014 of Government Resolution 2118, which provides the basis for a comprehensive, whole-of-government regulatory policy.[5] The resolution includes provisions to reduce the current regulatory burden (stock) and to undertake *ex ante* **regulatory impact analysis**.

In compliance with Government Resolution 2118, an official responsible for RIA has to be designated in each ministry or government agency involved in matters related to regulations. A special unit at the Prime Minister's Office is tasked with determining the methodology for RIA and its implementation. Nonetheless, the implementation of the Resolution 2118 started only in January 2017. According to the resolution, the ministries have to formulate five-year action plans to reduce the regulatory burden, including a reduction of 25% of administrative costs. The ministries have also to formulate and disseminate detailed action plans to be implemented every year.

The SMBA is not directly involved in the RIA process since it is not a source of legislation and regulations. However, the SMBA provides substantive analysis of the impact of regulations on SMEs and provides comments to the relevant ministries and the RIA co-ordination unit hosted at the Prime Minister's Office. The analytical work undertaken by the SMBA is the product of consultations with business organisations and takes the form of white papers. For example, as part of the wider RIA efforts the SMBA has published guidance for the implementation of an SME test. However, the guidance is not yet part of the RIA efforts. Furthermore, the SMBA white papers are not exclusively focused on RIA; they comprise other relevant areas for SME development – for example, timely payments for public procurement contracts or value-added tax (VAT) payments.

Israel has been implementing reforms to simplify **start-up procedures** over the past few years. In 2013-14, three main agencies were involved in the registration process for corporations and self-employed individuals: the Registrar of Companies (part of the Israeli Corporations Authority at the Ministry of Justice), the Tax Authority and the National Insurance Institute. According to the *Doing Business* indicators, starting a business has become easier over the past few years due to several improvements, notably the adoption of a single identification number to deal with different government agencies and the establishment of an online registration platform. Also, the tax and social security registration were merged: the National Insurance Institute receives information about the opening of the tax file, and opens, without the employer's request, a file for the new employer as well. Furthermore, in November 2015 an optional electronic system for company registration was launched which now, according to interviews, handles 75% of all applications and provides registration within two to four days. Through the system, users can upload the articles of association and pay the registration fee of about ILS 2500 (about EUR 600). The use of the electronic system does not require the involvement of a lawyer if the company has an electronic certificate.

Nevertheless, there are reports that obtaining licenses for businesses in the food industry is becoming more cumbersome due to new requirements by the Ministry of Health. Requirements on nutrition labelling,[6] government-approved Good Manufacturing Practice (GMP) certifications and the use of the *Codex Alimentarius*[7] as a reference for food standards, which makes food imports much more difficult. On the other hand, municipalities seem to apply different standards, so local requirements vary from one place to another.

Results in terms of obtaining business licenses and permits are inconclusive based on the information available for this interim assessment. A review of SME and entrepreneurship policies in Israel noted that the complex system of licenses and permits is one of the main factors holding back SME growth (OECD, 2016).[8] This complexity is due to the fact that licenses and permits are issued mainly by municipal authorities, following approval by relevant government departments (e.g. Ministry of Health, Ministry of Environmental Protection), and must be renewed annually. According to the review, approximately 40% of enterprises need a license in Israel, but one quarter of them does not have one.

The government has been working to address these shortcomings for several years. In 2005 it launched an inter-ministerial committee (the Haber Committee) to review business licensing and issue recommendations for reform. In 2006 a subcommittee was created to develop a plan to implement the recommendations of the Haber Committee. However, according to the website of the Ministry of Environmental Protection, "it took years for all the parties involved, some of whom had opposing interests, to agree on how best to implement the recommendations."[9] The result was the amendment to the Business Licensing Law (2010) and the Government Decision 1007, which unites licensing requirements throughout Israel, "making it difficult" for municipalities to add additional local requirements and reducing delays in obtaining licenses, especially in industries that do not pose environmental risks.

The government continues working on improving licenses and permits. According to the consultations for this interim assessment, the municipal authorities now apply a harmonised licencing system and even act as a one-stop shop for different local institutions (e.g. police, fire department). However, there is no evidence on the effectiveness of the system. Furthermore, according to the OECD's Indicators of Product Market Regulation – which, among other matters, measure barriers to entrepreneurship including the complexity of the licenses and permit system – Israel is a "less competition friendly" economy.[10] The specific indicators measuring the restrictiveness of the licenses and permits system show that Israel is the third most restrictive country in this regard.[11]

Over the past few years Israel has introduced reforms to its **bankruptcy framework**, which is governed by three statutes: the Bankruptcy Ordinance dealing with individuals; the Companies Ordinance dealing with corporate liquidations and receiverships; and the Companies Act for corporate reorganisations. The latest is the Official Receivers' Reform of 2013, which provides a specific structure and a target time frame (18 months) for the procedure. Its aim is to facilitate the "fresh start" policy by providing certainty and predictability for all parties.[12]

On March 2018, the Knesset approved a new Insolvency and Economic Rehabilitation Law overhauling insolvency procedures for individuals (bankruptcy) and companies (liquidation, receivership, stay of proceedings and restructuring). It aims to advance debtors' financial rehabilitation; to maximise the return to creditors; and to increase the certainty and stability of the law, shorten procedures, and reduce the bureaucratic burden.[13]

For further action: Israel has adopted the initial steps to address the difficult regulatory environment identified by the SME Policy Index 2014 and subsequent reports. The mandate by Government Resolution 2118 of 2014 to undertake *ex ante* and *ex post* RIA and the establishment of a RIA co-ordination unit provide ripe ground for improvement of the business environment for SMEs, including through the eventual adoption of an SME test following the guidance developed by the SMBA. However, this interim assessment is inconclusive regarding the role of local authorities in providing business licences. On the one hand, the consultations indicate that business licenses have been harmonised and that local authorities now even act as one-stop shops for licencing procedures. On the other hand, the OECD indicators of Product Market Regulation still note that Israel is one of the most difficult economies in this area. Apart from this, this interim assessment finds progress in terms of the introduction of a single identification number and the creation of an online registration platform.

Fostering access to finance

The SME Policy Index 2014 noted that Israel had an advanced **legal and regulatory framework** for access to finance, with a functioning credit registry and two credit bureaus. Concerning the credit registry, the Central Bank's Banking Supervision Department continues to publish information on "restricted accounts and restricted bank customers" on its website.[14] The information is freely available and includes details on debtors restricted by courts in the course of bankruptcy procedures and debtors in debt collection proceedings, among other things.

Furthermore, following the Credit Data Law 5776 of 2016, the Central Bank is establishing a Central Credit Register to provide data to credit bureaus for uses such as credit ratings, credit reports, and financial consulting.[15] This is leading to the establishment of a new credit bureau that is expected to enter the market in 2019; however, this credit bureau is intended to target households and not firms, given that households are seen as facing greater difficulties in accessing credit.[16] The two credit bureaus mentioned by the SME Policy Index 2014 continue to operate (managed by international companies Coface[17] and Dun & Bradstreet[18]) and provide various types of credit information such as restricted accounts, lawsuits, liquidation proceedings, and returned cheques. According to *Doing Business*, the credit bureaus cover 71.4% of the adult population, the highest level in the MED region and above the OECD average of 63.7%.

A registry of moveable assets also continues to operate under the Pledges Registry of the Ministry of Justice.[19] According to the SME Policy Index 2014, the registry was fully operational and had several offices.

According to the consultations for this interim assessment, the low levels of bank competition are a major impediment for greater SME access to credit: the sector is dominated by six major banks, with two of them holding 60% of the market. This has resulted in comparatively high interest rates for SME loans despite the very low levels of non-performing loans; and has caused SME lending growth to lag the growth in SME GDP. To address this shortcoming a Committee for Increasing Competitiveness in Common Banking and Financial Services ("Strom Committee") was founded in 2015, and the government has recently begun to implement some of its recommendations. For example, a law that separates credit card companies and banks was passed in January 2017 as part of a series of moves to enhance the competition level in the banking industry and to lower financing costs for SMEs. In addition, in March 2016 a credit data law was passed, according to which in 2018 a central households and SME credit database will be established, which is expected to improve competition and data accessibility in the Israeli credit market.

Other reforms are also intended to foster SME access to alternative sources of finance. For example, in October 2016 the Tel Aviv Stock Exchange relaxed its listing requirements to facilitate initial public offerings of R&D-intensive companies, and hence their access to capital in their early stages.[20] However, there are no facts and figures on the impact of this measure for innovative SMEs. In addition, to promote competition among institutional investors and to help expand the funding options for SMEs, the authorities are working to establish a legal framework for the issuance of collateralised debt obligations. Nonetheless, there are no details of how and when this would be implemented.

Israel is also promoting access to crowdfunding and peer-to-peer (P2P) lending by allowing these transactions when they are ILS 1 million (about EUR 233 000) or less. Loans above that are supervised by the Israel Securities Authority.

In terms of the availability of **sources of finance** for SMEs, the main credit guarantee scheme is the Small and Medium Businesses Fund (SMBF), which is sponsored by the SMBA and the Ministry of Finance and managed by two private companies. The SMBF guarantees about 70% of a loan for an existing SME and up to 85% for a new firm. According to the OECD's 2016 review of SME and Entrepreneurship Policy, the SMBF's rejection rate was a very high 45%, and the fees charged by the Fund were low compared to international standards. The recommendation by the review in this regard was to increase fees and address the high rejection rates. However, the consultations for this interim assessment noted that these rejection rates and low fees were needed in order to keep credit guarantees accessible and sustainable. This argument could seem surprising, though, given the lack of competition between banks and the consequent limited or expensive access for SMEs and households to credit. In addition, according to official figures and as cited above, non-performing loan rates are low; hence the justification for a 45% rejection rate would seem uncertain.

The market for private equity in Israel is one of the most dynamic in the world given the high prevalence of innovative and technological firms. However, according to the consultations for this interim assessment, there is a financing gap for the funding of the growth of medium-sized firms. To address this gap, in 2016 the SMBA and the Ministry of Finance launched two equity funds managed by private companies Kogito Capital and Peninsula.[21] The funds target companies with a turnover of between ILS 10 million and

100 million (EUR 2.4 million -20 million).[22] The funds have a total capital of ILS 900 million with a contribution by the government of ILS 200 million. To incentivise investments in high potential firms, the government takes a share of the losses if there are any. No information on the results of this fund was provided for this interim assessment so there is no evidence on its effectiveness.

For further action: The SME Policy Index 2014 had already noted that Israel had a well-developed legal and regulatory framework for access to finance and a well-diversified market for sources of funds for SMEs and start-ups. The main recommendation in that report was to facilitate equity investments in non-technological firms. This interim assessment finds that there are several new initiatives in that and many other areas of access to finance – such as fostering banking competition (which is identified as a main issue by the authorities) and developing alternative sources of finance other than bank credit. These measures represent important areas of progress. However, almost no evidence exists in terms of the results of these initiatives, even if many of them have been operational for over one year. Israel could therefore track their progress so as to assess the concrete results of the new and older initiatives.

Nurturing entrepreneurship and SME growth

SMEs in Israel continue to have access to a wide array of **business development services** (BDS), including through the expansion of the network of small business development centres (MAOF centres) from 26 in 2014 to 40 now. Following a model that is prevalent in Israel, the MAOF centres are funded by the public resources of the SMBA but managed by private firms, which have to participate in a tender process to be able to operate these centres. The MAOF centres offer a wide array of BDS at subsidised prices and through a vast network of specialised consultants which provide personalised support. The MAOF centres receive funding according to the levels of satisfaction of their clients. This is assessed through surveys, some of them using control groups to better measure performance – although, according to the consultations for this assessment, it is often difficult to find the right firms for the control groups. The network of MAOF centres also acts as a one-stop shop for other government agencies, hence maximising their impact and value for money.

Israel has also registered progress in terms of SME access to **public procurement**. The Government Procurement Administration (GPA) in the Ministry of Finance is in charge of publishing centralised tenders and of disseminating regulations and administrative codes on public procurement. Local authorities, however, have their own rules and their regulations and do not need to abide by the GPA, although there are ongoing efforts to align local and central processes (procurement by schools, for example, is under municipal responsibility).

In 2016 amendments were made to the Mandatory Tender Law and the Mandatory Tender Regulations in order to prevent the exclusion of SMEs from these markets. These amendments included the screening of tender processes for potential barriers for SME participation, the elimination of fees for the participation in tenders of less than ILS 50 million (EUR 10 million), and the publication (from 2018) of information on tenders granted to SMEs.

In addition, there are new and ongoing efforts to establish e-procurement, an area that was considered weak in the SME Policy Index 2014 and the 2016 OECD review of SME and Entrepreneurship Policy. These efforts have been inspired by international experiences from other OECD countries and include pilot platforms where SMEs can consult and submit their bids (e.g. *Menorah* and *Na'ama* systems for conventional e-procurement and *Zohar* system to promote public access to innovative products and services).

The SME Policy Index 2014 pointed to the existence of three key institutions promoting **SME internationalisation**:

1. The Foreign Trade Administration (FTA) of the Ministry of Economy, which had a network of 35 economic and trade representatives and offices in 50 countries.
2. The Israel Export and International Co-operation Institute (IEICI), a non-profit organisation operated by the government and the private sector promoting the export of Israeli goods and services, as well as trade relations and co-operation and strategic alliances with overseas companies.
3. The Manufacturers Association of Israel (Department of Foreign Trade and International Relations), which advocates for local industry in terms of foreign trade policy, while at the same time promoting international collaboration and the principles of free trade.

Through their websites, these institutions provide extensive information for SMEs regarding international markets and trade. Furthermore, the IEICI also acts as a one-stop shop, while the FTA assists firms with setting up partnerships/alliances and determining market entry strategies.

Since the publication of the SME Policy Index 2014, a number of new programmes and initiatives have been introduced by these institutions. For example, the FTA introduced a "Smart Money" programme for SMEs with turnover of up to ILS 200 million (double the size of the SMBA definition). This programme provides loans for marketing consulting services and training. Another new programme, *Shalev*, was launched in June 2017 to support mostly micro firms through loans for marketing activities, business planning and training. The programme aims to benefit about 100 firms per year.

Overall, according to the consultations for this interim assessment, Israel's foreign trade is concentrated in a few companies and in a few sectors; hence, the strategic objective of the government is to promote small exporters as a means for diversification and also to foster higher productivity in the economy (given the link between productivity and international competition). There is also interest in diversifying the markets for exports away from the tradition markets (the United States and Europe) and into Asian markets, notably China, India and Japan, countries with whom there are ongoing trade negotiations.

For further action: Israel has introduced several initiatives to foster entrepreneurship and SME growth since the SME Policy Index 2014. These include the expansion of the MAOF centres, the introduction of reforms on public procurement and the introduction of new programmes for SME internationalisation. These appear as very positive efforts that could be better linked to maximise results. For example, according to the consultations for this interim assessment the MAOF centres, which build on a public-private co-operation model recurrent in Israel, have very limited direct involvement in SME internationalisation. These centres constitute an extended network of one-stop shops that could maximise the impact of the internationalisation programmes implemented by the FTA, IEICI and others. Along the same lines, the MAOF centres could disseminate information on public procurement opportunities and actively promote the participation of SMEs in that market.

Investing in entrepreneurial human capital

Regarding **entrepreneurial learning in upper secondary education**, Israel has been strategically moving from mainly project-based initiatives to system-level actions and is integrating entrepreneurship key competence into a life-long learning perspective. Nowadays, entrepreneurial learning is part of the national youth, education and economic policies and includes school-enterprise co-operation across different education levels. The new socio-economic strategy 2030 of the Israeli government features mainstreaming of key competences and entrepreneurial learning in all parts of general education, and technical and vocational education and training (TVET).

The education system benefits from networks that are inspired by a strong vision of entrepreneurship and industry-education co-operation. These networks (e.g. Amal[23] and ORT[24]) have established structured partnerships with the business community serving as mentors for entrepreneurial youth. They engage more than 15% of junior-high and high-schools in Israel. Similarly, Unistream, a government-funded programme operated by the Israeli Innovation Authority, supports training of underprivileged Israeli teenagers and young adults in entrepreneurship and leadership to promote youth start-up and ventures with steady mentorship by local business leaders.

The government furthermore provides funding, regulatory support and guidelines for the development of entrepreneurship competence and enhancement of entrepreneurial culture in education institutions. An example of this is a recent recommendation for teachers on the promotion of entrepreneurship and business skills amongst underprivileged and at-risk youth, aiming at value creation, development of entrepreneurial mind-set, and including aspects of practical entrepreneurial experience. Moving forward, the Israeli authorities need to concentrate further efforts on the systemic integration of entrepreneurship key competence into the national curriculum and teacher training. The European Entrepreneurship Competence Framework (EntrComp) can be a possible source of inspiration.

The Israeli government has made a substantial step forward in addressing **women's entrepreneurship**. In 2017, the SMBA commissioned a feasibility study to analyse the state of women's entrepreneurship. The study looks at the gap between female and male entrepreneurship and is used to develop a fact-based solution to increase women's entrepreneurship, especially in high-value added sectors. Furthermore, Parliament recently engaged actively with the issue of women's entrepreneurship, with a new parliamentary lobby on female entrepreneurs established in January 2017.

Training for women entrepreneurs is part of a national institutional framework for SME support, and several official government programmes provide training to women entrepreneurs (e.g. MAOF and KIEDF's Arab Israeli Loan Fund [SAWA]). Non-governmental programmes and organisations similarly provide support measures and training. The Economic Empowerment of Women Centre (EEWC) for instance supports entrepreneurial aspirations of around 1.000 women annually, providing them with start-up training, as well as financial literacy, computer literacy, social media marketing, business site tours and "marathon-style" training courses. A 2015 evaluation of the EEWC program reported that 40% of the women owned their own business at the end of the program, and that the five-year survival rate of these businesses was 71%. The programme-level data are collected by MAOF, KIEDF and non-government partnerships and show a positive trend: women make 52% of all entrepreneurs participating in these programmes.

Israel's FTA acts as the "backbone" for the state's **SME internationalisation support** system. It has a chain of economic missions around the world tasked with helping SMEs expand into foreign markets by providing advice, helping them complete tender bids, and connecting them to local businesses.

The government also invests major resources in skills development for internationalisation. The Ministry of Economy, through the FTA, offers support training (e.g. online courses and webinars) to eligible exporters. It also operates the "Smart Money" initiative which finances marketing consulting services. A variety of quality training and mentorship programmes are delivered through the Administration's Centre for Learning, including a certified exporter course, country-specific courses, digital trade, marketing, logistics and transportation, legal and finance courses. Webinars, courses and other services for small exporters are also available from the Israel Export Institute, which trains and prepares mentors to assist exporter companies. Information on training programmes and providers is publicly available, and more than 20% of SMEs in key economic sectors (e.g. medical technology, high-tech and new-tech) have participated in training on SME internationalisation since the last assessment.

For further action: Israeli authorities need to concentrate further efforts on the systemic integration of entrepreneurship key competence into the national curriculum and teacher training. The government might consider scaling up the high-quality, gender sensitive, modern services for exporting SMEs to other key economic sectors, and adopt policy measures to increase women's entrepreneurship, especially in high-value added sectors. Given the major investment in programmes and the high importance of export promotion for the Israeli economy, more attention should be given to assessing the impact of the training programmes. A well-developed monitoring and evaluation system should be set in place to provide feedback on how to further increase the quality and efficiency of such services.

The way forward

Israel has continued progressing in the areas analysed by this interim assessment, especially in terms of policies for entrepreneurship and SME growth and access to finance, and to a lesser degree on improving the business environment and the building blocks of SME policy. Overall, Israel has one of the most advanced policy frameworks of the MED region. Beyond this, the actions suggested by this report are as follows:

- Considering adopting a unified SME definition, given that several support programmes use definitions other than the ones cited in the first section of this chapter (the SMBA definition and the Government Decision 2190).
- Giving the SMBA a greater policy co-ordination role, beyond the management of the network of MAOF centres and based on models applied in other countries, including OECD and MED economies. This interim assessment notes that the SMBA has some role in the implementation of RIA and an advocacy role in the eventual introduction of an SME test; but this role seems rather limited in terms of access to finance, public procurement and access to international markets.
- Building on the above, and as suggested by the SME Policy Index 2014 and the OECD review of SME and Entrepreneurship Policy 2016, Israel could develop an SME strategy to increase policy co-ordination and adopt more-articulate objectives between policy areas. This interim assessment finds that Israel does indeed have specific strategic objectives in terms of regulatory reform, access to finance (e.g.

increasing bank competition and access to alternative sources of finance for SMEs) and access to international markets (diversification of markets, products and exporting companies), to mention a few. These strategic orientations could be combined into a single SME or private enterprise development strategy consolidating efforts and identifying institutional responsibilities. The development and implementation of the strategy could build on the already active system of public private dialogue outline in the first section of this chapter. The strategy could also consider specific SME aspects such as the introduction of the SME test in the ongoing RIA efforts.

- The implementation of an SME strategy could also help to better track policy results. This interim assessment finds for instance that there is little evidence on the impact of measures on access to finance and public procurement.
- The well-established network of MAOF centres, managed by the SMBA could also provide a well-positioned mechanism for the delivery of the different policy aspects of the SME strategy, beyond the provision of business development centres.
- Entrepreneurship as a key competence could be further scaled up at system level into the national curriculum and in teacher training programmes.
- The modern services for exporting SMEs could be scaled up to additional key economic sectors. More attention could be given to assessing the impact of the training programmes.

Notes

[1] Another difference between the definitions is that the SMBA definition is an enabling definition – that is, it is enough for a business to be in *either* the employees group size *or* in the turnover group size in order to be classified as a certain enterprise type. By contrast, the definition in Government Decision no. 2190 is a restrictive one: the business has to be in *both* the employees size group *and* in the turnover size group in order to be classified as a certain enterprise type.

[2] Amendment No. 25 to the Mandatory Tenders Law.

[3] Central Bureau of Statistics (2017), "Statistical Abstract of Israel 2017", www.cbs.gov.il/reader/shnatonenew_site.htm.

[4] OECD (2016), *OECD Economic Surveys: Israel 2016*, OECD Publishing, Paris. http://dx.doi.org/10.1787/eco_surveys-isr-2016-en.

[5] OECD (2015), "Country Profile: Israel", in *OECD Regulatory Policy Outlook 2015*, OECD Publishing, Paris, http://dx.doi.org/10.1787/9789264238770-en; and Government Resolution No. 2118 (22 October 2014), www.pmo.gov.il/policyplanning/Regulation/Documents/Reducing%20the%20Regulatory%20Burden.pdf.

[6] This requirement will enter into force in January 2021.

[7] FAO (2018), Codex Alimentarius, www.fao.org/fao-who-codexalimentarius/en/.

[8] Together with the product market regulation constrains also highlighted by the 2016 OECD Economic Survey of Israel, and a lack of systematic entrepreneurship education.

[9] Israel Ministry of Environmental Protection, "Business Licensing Process", www.sviva.gov.il/English/env_topics/IndustryAndBusinessLicensing/BusinessLicensingProcess/Pages/default.aspx.

[10] OECD, "Indicators of Product Market Regulation", www.oecd.org/eco/growth/indicatorsofproductmarketregulationhomepage.htm#indicators.

[11] OECD, "Economy-wide Product Market Regulation (PMR)", www.oecd.org/eco/reform/Indicators_PMR.xlsx.

[12] No statutory amendments were needed for this reform, which consists on: 1) filing a proof of claims and allowance/disallowance; 2) an economic study (investigation) of the debtor; 3) and the establishment of a repayment plan for up to three years or filing immediate discharge if NINA (no income no asset) debtors.

[13] www.globalforumljd.org/sites/default/files/docs/cop/Questionnaire%20Israel.pdf.

[14] Bank of Israel, "Customer Information on Restricted Accounts and Customers", www.boi.org.il/en/ConsumerInformation/RestrictedAccountsAndCustomers/Pages/Restrictedac.aspx.

[15] Bank of Israel (20 September 2016), "The Bank of Israel publishes a draft licensing policy for credit bureaus and business information bureaus", www.boi.org.il/en/NewsAndPublications/PressReleases/Pages/20-09-16c.aspx.

[16] Scheer, S. (11 November 2015), "Israel regulator sees credit bureaus helping to lower loan costs", Reuters, www.reuters.com/article/israel-banking-regulator-idUSL8N1362XF20151111.

[17] CofaceBdi, www.bdi.co.il/EngDefault.aspx.

[18] Dun & Bradstreet, "Private Customers Management", www.dbisrael.co.il/business-protection/private-customers-management/.

[19] Ministry of Justice, "Israeli Corporations Authority", www.justice.gov.il/Units/RasutHataagidim/units/RashamHakdasot/Pages/default.aspx.

[20] Tel Aviv Stock Exchange, "R&D Companies", https://www.tase.co.il/Eng/Listings/IPO/ResearchandDevelopmentCompanies/Pages/RDCompanies.aspx.

[21] Ministry of Economy and Industry (1 April 2016), "Cogito Capital and peninsula Chosen to Establish Growth Capital Funds for Investment in Small and Medium-Sized Businesses: Total Investment NIS 1 billion", http://economy.gov.il/English/NewsRoom/PressReleases/Pages/GrowthCapitalFundsInvestment1Billion.aspx

[22] This definition does not align with the medium-sized firm definition by the SMBA.

[23] A network of (junior) high schools and colleges working in partnership with enterprises to promote technology, science and arts.

[24] A network of comprehensive and vocational schools and colleges in the area of science and technology education.

Chapter 9. Jordan

The foundations of SME policy: definitions, statistics and institutions

Jordan has made little progress since the publication of the SME Policy Index 2014. The main positive development back then was the finalisation of the National Entrepreneurship and SME Growth Strategy, developed with the support of the EU. Four years later, the SME Strategy is yet to be approved, funded and implemented. The SME Strategy puts forward an official **definition of SMEs** which would enter into force once the strategy is adopted (Table 9.1).

Table 9.1. SME definition in the SME Strategy

Type of enterprise	Employees	Turnover
Micro	1 to 4	≤ JOD 100 000 (EUR 115 438)
Small	5 to 19	≤ JOD 1 m (EUR 1 154 382)
Medium	20 to 99	≤ JOD 5 m (EUR 5 771 912)

Source: Jordan National Entrepreneurship and Small and Medium Enterprise Growth Strategy 2016-2020, p. 36.

On **SME and entrepreneurship statistics**, the main source of data continues to be the Establishment Census undertaken every few years by the Department of Statistics (DOS). The latest census was published in 2011 and the new one will be realised later in 2018.[1] Furthermore, one of the main developments in this area over the past few years has been the creation of an SME Observatory hosted by the SME agency, the Jordan Enterprise Development Corporation (JEDCO). The SME Observatory collects data from different sources including the Establishment Census and the Global Entrepreneurship Monitor (GEM) and has published comprehensive studies of the state of SMEs in the country based on that data.[2] It is also planning to launch a web portal to widely disseminate its information. The OECD is working with the DOS, the Companies Control Department, the Customs Department and others to improve the SME data collection and dissemination mechanisms under the MENA Transition Fund project SME Policy Effectiveness in Jordan.

The **wider economic context** in Jordan and its policy agenda continue to be highly affected by the large number of refugees escaping conflict from neighbouring Syria and Iraq. It is estimated that Jordan hosts more than 1.3 million Syrians, with 83% of them living outside refugee camps. To help the country to cope with this burden, the Jordanian government and the international community signed the Jordan Compact in 2016, which has provided concessional loans and preferential trade terms in return for opening the labour market to refugees. However, the actual effects of the Jordan Compact on job creation and entrepreneurship among refugees remain unclear. Furthermore, according to the consultations for this interim assessment, two of JEDCO's flagship support programmes funded by donor money, the Jordan Upgrading and Modernisation Programme (JUMP) and the Jordan Services Modernisation Programme (JSMP), were closed due to the redirection of funds towards supporting refugees.

Jordan's wider economic policy is also guided by Jordan 2025: A National Vision and Strategy,[3] a long-term strategic plan to be implemented through three-year development programmes and development plans at governorate level. Jordan 2025 sets a number of priorities for private sector development including improving the business environment, increasing the availability of capital for growth, promoting clusters and SMEs. However, no clear monitoring and evaluation mechanism yet exists to track the effectiveness of Jordan 2025.

Concerning the **institutional framework and co-ordination** for SME development in Jordan, the Ministry of Industry and Trade continues to be in charge of enterprise and SME policy development, with the support of JEDCO. The Ministry of Planning and International Co-operation continues to be responsible for implementing the broader country development strategy and mobilising donor support, while SME policy implementation is delegated to a number of specialised agencies.

JEDCO, in its role of **SME agency** is supervised by a board of directors, chaired by the Minister of Industry and Trade and composed of representatives of key economic ministries and the private sector. JEDCO is identified by the **SME strategy** as the main SME policy co-ordination agency. Yet, the pending approval of the SME strategy has resulted in a reduced technical and financial capacity and a weak convening power for JEDCO to act as policy co-ordinator.

The SME strategy includes a complete policy framework covering six strategic pillars: 1) a more conducive legal and regulatory environment, 2) entrepreneurship awareness and culture building, 3) entrepreneurial skills and business development services, 4) access to finance, 5) innovation and technology adoption/development and 6) market access.

The SME strategy also puts forward a comprehensive governance structure that includes 1) a high-level committee (formed by relevant ministers, the governor of the central bank and private sector organisations); 2) a technical level committee composed of focal points in relevant public sector institutions; 3) an SME Advisory Committee composed of private sector and non-governmental organisations (NGOs), which are very active in providing SME and entrepreneurship support in Jordan; and 4) SME regional committees in each governorate. The SME strategy also foresees to designate JEDCO as the SME co-ordination agency and as the secretariat to the high-level committee. In this context, the OECD is working with JEDCO and other Jordanian counterparts in establishing the governance mechanisms of the strategy and in setting up a monitoring and evaluation mechanism.

In terms of **public-private dialogue** (PPD), the SME Policy Index 2014 noted that consultations were already a common practice through the Economic and Social Council which met at least twice a year. Furthermore, the preparation of the national SME strategy in 2013-2014 involved extensive consultations with different participants. However, the pending implementation of the SME strategy means that the PPD mechanisms foreseen in that document, especially the creation of an SME Advisory Committee composed of private sector and non-governmental organisations, are not yet operational. JEDCO and the OECD are currently working on making such mechanisms operational through the MENA Transition Fund project SME Policy Effectiveness in Jordan.

For further action: One of the most important areas of progress found by this interim assessment in terms of SME policy co-ordination and implementation is the initial establishment of the SME Observatory to better disseminate data and information on SMEs and entrepreneurship in Jordan. Yet the main stumbling block is the lack of implementation and funding of the SME strategy developed in 2013 and expected to enter into force in 2015. The strategy is intended to increase the synergies and impact of the various support measures; however, one of the key impediments for its execution has been the difficult political environment in the country and the constantly changing leadership at JEDCO, the SME agency. Furthermore, political and economic instability linked to the Syria crisis has shifted attention and resources away from existing SME programmes, and the sustainability of some of the actions taken is at risk. This is particularly affecting programmes that had been developed to facilitate finance and business support services for SMEs (see respective section below); therefore, future attention could be paid to avoid the reversal of actions taken and to step up support programmes. The role of JEDCO as SME policy co-ordinator and secretariat for the implementation of the SME strategy could be reinforced. The OECD is supporting Jordan in this regard through the MENA Transition Fund project SME Policy Effectiveness.

Improving the business environment for SMEs and entrepreneurs

The SME Policy Index 2014 recognised Jordan's initial efforts to improve the **regulatory framework** and reduce the administrative burden for SMEs. These efforts were initially framed by the United States Agency for International Development (USAID) Jordan Economic Development (SABEQ) Programme (2006-2012) which laid the ground for a public-private Reform Steering Committee and three technical committees representing the regulating institutions and business associations. These committees implemented a pilot regulatory guillotine process although in very few areas (vocational licensing and construction permits) in order to systematically review, eliminate, and streamline business constraints and procedures.

After the closing of the SABEQ project and the ceasing of operations of the regulatory guillotine, a MENA Transition Fund project Jordan Economic Legislation Reform 2016-2018 continued to review and modernise laws and regulations in consultation with the private sector.[4] This project takes the regulatory guillotine further by, among other activities, enhancing the regulatory reform unit at the Prime Minister's Office to build its capacity to supervise reform activities; developing a comprehensive reform roadmap and identifying capacity building needs; and implementing the roadmap and conducting the capacity building. The project also aims to establish a **regulatory impact analysis** (RIA) mechanism to ensure the quality of new laws and regulations and the quality of regulatory delivery.

On the implementation of the **SME test**, a capacity building workshop was organised by JEDCO, the European Union (EU) and the project Enhancement of the Business Environment in the Southern Mediterranean (EBESM) in March 2016. The aim of the workshop was to raise awareness of international best practice concerning the measurement of the impact of new regulations on SMEs, the development of a simple SME test model for measuring the impact of new regulations on SMEs, and the creation of champions for the model who can initiate the development of the model in Jordan. However, an SME test is not yet in place.

Concerning the facilitation of procedures for the **creation of new enterprises**, the SME Policy Index 2014 noted that Jordan was one of the few MED economies to have a single identification number for firms, although this applied only for a few agencies (the Companies Control Department, the Chambers of Commerce and Industry, the Greater

Amman Municipality, and the Income and Sales Tax Department). Back then, however, there was no online registration system, although the forms could be downloaded from the Companies Control Department website.

Since then, a Local Enterprise Support project (LENS) has been established by USAID to, among other things, improve business registration. It is currently working with the Ministry of Industry and Trade and the Companies Control Department to improve the efficiency of business registration process for SMEs. This includes upgrading the Companies Control Department's server storage capacity to handle more data for registered businesses and developing a business registration manual (in co-operation with the Financial Services Volunteer Corps) that clearly outlines the registration process for different types of businesses in order to motivate people to formalise their businesses. The manual has been published and widely disseminated; however, there is no evidence on the impact of this initiative on new enterprise registration. Furthermore, there is no evidence on progress on online registration services and one-stop shops for companies' registration.

In terms of **bankruptcy**, a new Reorganisation, Bankruptcy and Liquidation Law was approved in April 2018, aiming to establish a legal framework for distressed companies. Furthermore, the *Doing Business* indicators note that this is a particularly complex procedure in Jordan, with the lowest recovery rates in the MED region (USD 27.7 cents on the dollar, compared to over 71 in the OECD) and a cost of 20% of real estate.

For further action: In recent years Jordan has continued its efforts to improve the business environment by implementing donor-sponsored projects towards the establishment of regulatory impact assessments and an SME test. These efforts, however, remain initial and need continuation and formalisation beyond pilot projects. Indeed, the SABEQ project and the MENA Transition Fund project Jordan Economic Legislation Reform, as well as the initial efforts with the EBESM project to introduce an SME test should be continued and be translated into the implementation of permanent RIA mechanisms. This interim assessment did not find any details of how that will be achieved, though. Jordan could also move forward with the implementation of its new Bankruptcy Law, which, like the SME strategy, is pending final government approval.

Fostering access to finance

In terms of the **legal and regulatory environment** for access to finance, the SME Policy Index 2014 noted the existence of a credit register at the Central Bank, although its coverage was limited and individuals and firms could not consult its information. Since then, a new credit bureau (CRIF), was launched in December 2015. The new credit bureau aims to centralise and aggregate credit information on individuals and businesses provided by financial institutions, microfinance organisations, insurance companies, and eventually public agencies such as JEDCO. The credit bureau is intended to increase transparency of companies and to help to mitigate the information asymmetries that obstruct lending to SMEs. This would accelerate lending processes and minimise default rates. The credit bureau collects information from 39 sources and, according to *Doing Business*, covers 15.3% of the adult population, still much lower than the OECD average of 63.7%.

There has also been some progress in the establishment of a collateral registry of moveable assets. An Online Movable Collateral Registry was made operational on April 2017. This project is led by the Ministry of Industry with the support of the International Finance Corporation (IFC) and USAID. During its first phase, the collateral registry focused on leasing contracts. On May 2018, the Secured Lending Law was approved, which will allow the registry to provide services for a full range of assets and contracts.

The new Companies Law, which was approved in September 2017, contains provisions on venture capital. The Companies Control Department has begun working on the relevant regulations as identified in the Law, including those governing the registration of venture capital companies.

Regarding access to **sources of finance** for SMEs, the Jordan Loan Guarantee Corporation (JLGC) is the main body in charge of the provision of credit guarantee schemes for SMEs. The JLGC has a capital base of nearly JOD 30 million (about EUR 35.7 million) and provides five major programmes including an SME loan guarantee, export and domestic credit insurance, a microbusiness loan guarantee, an Islamic financing guarantee and a financial leasing guarantee.[5] The JLGC is a well-established organisation producing regular reports on its activities.[6] This interim assessment finds progress in the provision of credit guarantees by the JLGC, in particular the establishment of two special funds in 2016 to provide guarantees for start-ups. The first fund focuses on loans by commercial banks whereas the second one is devoted to loans extended by Islamic banks. These programmes provide a guarantee of 85% of the value of the loan for up to JOD 100 000 and a fee of 1%. In addition, JLGC also launched the Jordan Renewable Energy and Energy Efficiency Fund to provide a guarantee of 70% for households and SMEs to increase their use of renewable energy and reduce dependence on energy subsidies.

Other developments regarding access to finance include the continued operation of the Governorate Development Fund (GDF), which has supported 96 projects between 2012 and 2018. However, the staff of the GDF has been reduced due to budget constraints at JEDCO. In addition, the JLGC made efforts to set up an Early Stage Venture Capital fund to provide equity for innovative products; nonetheless, due to funding issues it has not yet become operational. The JEDCO's Banking Window Programme was also closed due to funding problems.

For further action: Although some progress has been made over the past few years in terms of access to financing, the efforts are still very preliminary. On access to credit, a new credit bureau and an online registry of moveable assets have been established but have yet to become fully operational. Approval of the Secured Transactions Law will allow the implementation of phase II of the collateral registry. Furthermore, other sources of finance and initiatives such as the GDF, the JLGC's early-stage venture capital mechanism and the JEDCO's banking window have seen setbacks due to lower availability of resources for their operations. On the other hand, a positive development has been the expansion of the guarantees by the JLGC. A general message, though, is that several efforts for increasing access to finance for SMEs have been negatively affected by the slow pace of reforms and the more general difficulties resulting from the political and institutional environment in Jordan.

Nurturing entrepreneurship and SME growth

Jordan continues to have a diversified and extensive market for **business development services** (BDS) for SMEs. Some of the most important and active organisations in this regard include JEDCO, the Business Development Centre, several NGOs and private service providers, and the Business Associations and Chambers of Industry and Commerce. The information about all these support services is scattered across a large number of sources, although one of the missions of the SME Observatory established at JEDCO is to facilitate an easier access to this information.

This interim assessment finds that new business development services have been introduced since the SME Policy Index 2014. For example, a MENA Transition Fund project – the Accelerate with JEDCO programme – is supporting the establishment of a programme aimed at supporting high potential firms. This programme provides comprehensive business diagnostics to help SMEs and start-ups managers to identify barriers to growth as well as a business coaching support to overcome these barriers. At the time of writing, Accelerate with JEDCO had received 373 applications from all governorates in Jordan, an initial diagnostic had been made for 313 companies, 124 growth plans had been developed, 70 business managers had been coached, and 15 employees from JEDCO had become growth managers. Regarding financial assistance initiatives, USAID's Local Enterprise Support Project (LENS) supports small business growth and provides direct support to micro and small enterprises. Also, JEDCO has launched the Rural Economic Growth and Employment Project (REGEP), which provides technical and financial support to small-scale farmers, farmers' associations and producers and exporters of agricultural crops and SMEs.

The MENA Transition Fund project SME Policy Effectiveness in Jordan is working to increase co-ordination and dialogue among all these initiatives to enhance their impact. The framework used is based on the SME strategy, which is still pending approval but which provides a good agenda to achieve greater policy impact given the large number of support services and agencies already operating in the country.

Unfortunately, this interim assessment found that other flagship initiatives – such as the Jordan Upgrading and Modernisation Programme (JUMP) for industrial firms, and its equivalent for services firms (JSMP), operated by JEDCO – were closed due to lack of funding.

On SME access to **public procurement** opportunities, this interim assessment finds that the most important area of progress since the SME Policy Index 2014 is the ongoing work to establish an e-procurement system. This is based on the publication of an update of the Supplies Act concerning the implementation of electronic systems for government inventory management and for e-procurement. In this area, a new e-procurement system is being developed with the support of the Korean International Cooperation Agency (KOICA) with the aim of centralising information for procuring entities and for bidders/suppliers, including SMEs.

Some progress has also been realised in terms of SME access to **international markets**. In June 2015, JEDCO and the Higher Council for Science & Technology (HCST) signed an agreement with the EU Executive Agency for Small & Medium Enterprises (EASME) for Jordan to join the Enterprise Europe Network (EEN). They have set up a consortium to provide support for companies seeking to export, and to facilitate technology transfers and business and research co-operation. In 2017, the Amman Chamber of Industry joined the consortium. Nonetheless, Jordan is not yet part of the EEN.

Additionally, in July 2016, an agreement was reached with the EU to simplify the rules of origin set out in the EU-Jordan Association Agreement in order to incentivise integration of Syrian workforce in Jordan.[7] But the challenge lies in implementation. By July 2017 some estimates reported that only eight firms had been deemed to meet the conditions and just two of them actually benefit from it.[8]

Several projects have been put in place to provide technical and financial assistance to support SME internationalisation. In September 2014, JEDCO, the International Trade Centre (ITC) and the World Bank launched the MENA Transition Fund project Development of SMEs Exports through Virtual Market Places (VMP) to develop e-commerce. The project is training export advisors and coaching exporting SMEs, and it has created an Inter-Institutional Committee on E-Commerce.

Finally, Jordan's Economic Growth Plan 2018-2022 foresees the creation of an export co-ordination unit at JEDCO to provide technical support to enterprises seeking to export. JEDCO is expected to establish a fund dedicated to supporting and financing exports, introduce an export coaching program, and provide technical support to enterprises seeking to export.

For further action: Nurturing entrepreneurship and SME growth is the policy area where Jordan has achieved the most progress in this interim assessment. Positive results include the expansion of business support services, despite the closure of some programmes. The SME Observatory will have an important role in facilitating easier access to the disperse information on the diversity of these services. Jordan also could continue its efforts towards the full implementation of the new e-procurement system, which remains in pilot stage. Jordan could also move forward in joining Europe Enterprise Network to facilitate SME internationalisation. And to improve access the EU single market, it could also assess, with the support of the EU, what have been the barriers to the success of the initiative to relax the rules of origin.

Investing in entrepreneurial human capital

Since the last assessment, Jordan has demonstrated progress in deploying **entrepreneurial learning in education**. Entrepreneurial learning promotion is part of the Jordan Economic Growth Plan for 2018-2022 (JEGP), and a national event (the Generation Dialogue Program) in 2016 presented a platform that includes key bodies of the government, private sector, young entrepreneurs and international partners for discussing the importance of entrepreneurial learning for youth.

INJAZ[9] supports the Ministry of Education and runs programmes in both public and private schools, such as the Company Start-up Program – Schools & Competition, which provides high school students with hands-on experience and practical training in business; the CP National Competition, which supports student teams in presenting their companies to a panel of business leaders and experts; and the My Entrepreneurial Project (MEP), which offers youth career opportunities in entrepreneurship and self-employment. The Business Development Centre (BDC) supports the application of the entrepreneurship key competence approach in vocational education and training (VET) schools. In co-operation with the Jordanian Ministry of Education, The BDC trained over the last period more than 120 vocational school teachers and technical community college instructors on the application of entrepreneurship key competence approach, thus benefitting 4,000 students in 20 pilot institutions. These initiatives are excellent examples of school-enterprise co-operation.

Women's entrepreneurship training has become a policy priority, as reflected in the JEGP, and in the Strategic Plan for Empowering Women of the Jordanian National Commission for Women 2013-2017. In Jordan, only 3.3% of women are involved in entrepreneurship (JEDCO, 2017), and the share of firms with a female top manager is as low as 2.4% (World Bank, 2013). Jordan demonstrated substantial progress in addressing this critically important policy area. The Women Economic Participation conference addressed women's entrepreneurship development, and a number of studies have been published focusing on women's entrepreneurship, such as JEDCO's 2017 *Women entrepreneurship in Jordan: women empowerment*, and the 2017 EBESM report *Women's entrepreneurship & SME development in Jordan*.

There are also publicly and privately funded programmes to support women entrepreneurs in the rural and urban areas. These include the BDC's programme with the Ministry of Tourism for to enhance the local tourism capacity of women entrepreneurs; BDC's business mentorship program, which focuses on training female graduates to be mentors (SEEDS); the *Shorouq* project, implemented by Etihad Bank to support financial services for women entrepreneurs, networking events, coaching, advisory services, and mentorship; and the Village Business Incubator, which promotes the role of rural women in economic development by encouraging them to establish micro and small enterprises far beyond traditional home or gender-based models.

In addition, Jordan has developed initiatives to provide **training for the internationalisation of SMEs**. One example is the activity of the Inter-Institutional Committee on E-Commerce, which provides independent recommendations to create an enabling environment for e-commerce, and supports SME internationalisation. Policy dialogue on skills development for SME internationalisation was advanced within an open policy consultation process that led to the National SME Strategy 2016-2020.

JEDCO has also been implementing SME internationalisation training programmes in the garment and services sectors. Information on training programmes and providers for SME internationalisation is extensive and publicly available from the key players: the Jordan Chamber of Industry, the National Fund for Enterprise Support (NAFES) and the BDC.

For future action: The Jordanian government should implement further system-level actions to embed entrepreneurship key competence in education curricula and teacher development in life-long learning perspective. National authorities could support practitioners' efforts to apply advanced tools for the development of entrepreneurial culture, such as the European Entrepreneurship Competence Framework (EntreComp). In order to better support women's entrepreneurship, cross-agency and cross-sectoral efforts are needed, given it is a transversal issue. JEDCO could play a critical role, building on the strength of its programmes engaging the key policy partners both from the public and private sectors. In order to continue supporting training programmes for the internationalisation of SMEs, the government could consolidate its international trade policies, and support JEDCO in scaling up its activities on this field.

The way forward

Overall, Jordan has made limited progress in the implementation of the reforms identified by the SME Policy Index 2014. The reasons for this seem to be derived from the difficult institutional situation and the large inflows of refugees which have diverted attention and resources from SME development policies. The SME Strategy is still pending approval. Furthermore, as in 2014, Jordan continues to be greatly reliant on donor and international assistance, which is not necessarily negative as long as these initiatives are sustainable in the long term and lead to greater domestic capacities for policy design and implementation. Nonetheless, that sustainability is not very clear. In this view, the main actions put forward by this interim assessment are as follows:

- Moving forward with the implementation and funding of the SME Strategy, including reinforcing the role of JEDCO as secretariat for its execution. JEDCO and the OECD will continue advancing on this area, but the ultimate impact will depend on the actual enactment of the strategic document and its action plan.
- Advancing with the full-fledged establishment of RIA and the SME test.
- Moving forward with the full implementation of e-procurement, the joining of EEN and the maximisation of the opportunities provided by a greater access to the EU market for those companies which can benefit from the relaxed rules of origin.
- Entrepreneurship as a key competence should be better promoted in education curricula and teacher development in life-long learning perspective.
- Cross-agency and cross-sectoral efforts are needed to enhance women entrepreneurship, given it is a transversal issue.
- Training programmes for the internationalisation of SMEs, would benefit from consolidated international trade policies, and support to JEDCO to scale up its activities on this field.

Notes

[1] Department of Statistics, "Economic Establishments Census", http://dosweb.dos.gov.jo/censuses/economic-establishments-census/.

[2] Jordan Enterprise Development Corporation, "SME's Observatory", www.jedco.gov.jo/Pages/viewpage.aspx?pageID=171.

[3] http://www.jordanembassyus.org/blog/jordan-2025-national-vision-and-strategy.

[4] Middle East and North Africa Transition Fund, "Jordan Economic Legislation Reform", www.menatransitionfund.org/documents/jordan-economic-legislation-reform.

[5] The Jordan Loan Guarantee Corporation, www.jlgc.com/en/page/about-us.

[6] The Jordan Loan Guarantee Corporation, "Annual Reports", www.jlgc.com/en/page/annual-reports.

[7] Decision No 1/2016 of the EU-Jordan Association Committee (19 July 2016), http://eur-lex.europa.eu/legal-content/EN/TXT/PDF/?uri=CELEX:22016D1436&from=EN.

[8] Ghazal, M. (24 July 2017), "Only two Jordanian companies benefiting from EU relaxed rules of origin", The Jordan Times, www.jordantimes.com/news/local/only-two-jordanian-companies-benefiting-eu-relaxed-rules-origin.

[9] A youth-centred non-profit organisation established in Jordan in 1999 active in the European Union and worldwide, including in the Middle East, North-Africa and Pakistan.

Chapter 10. Lebanon

The foundations of SME policy: definitions, statistics and institutions

Lebanon has yet to develop a full-fledged SME and entrepreneurship policy. Although the Ministry of Economy and Trade have developed an SME Strategy, the document lacks details about implementation and resources and several, if not all, of its stipulations appear to be proposals instead of guidelines. Although an SME **definition** is proposed (not set) in the Strategy, it has so far been adopted only by the Ministry of Economy (Table 10.1).

Table 10.1. SME definition in the SME Strategy

Type of enterprise	Employees	Turnover
Micro	< 10 employees	< LBP 500 m (EUR 271 110)
Small	< 50 employees	< LBP 5 bn
Medium	< 100 employees	< LBP 25 bn

Source: Lebanon SME Strategy: A Roadmap to 2020, p. 36.

A draft SME Law has also been developed and is pending approval by parliament. The draft SME Law's Articles 2 and 3, put forward slightly different definitions of SMEs than the one shown on Table 10.1. The definitions in the SME Law also differentiate between commercial and service enterprises, industrial enterprises and agricultural firms. The definition included in the SME Law is the one expected to be adopted once it is enacted.

On **SME and entrepreneurship statistics**, Lebanon is one of few MED economies without an official source of data. The Central Administration for Statistics does not undertake establishment or business censuses and there are no initiatives to exploit administrative sources of information such as business registries or tax information. The Ministry of Industry has launched the Permanent Industrial Statistical System, an annual statistic form to be filled by industrial SMEs applying for an industrial certificate (around 2000 factories) in order to collect general information about factories as well as financial information. The aim is to create an industrial database system within the ministry of industry to undertake an annual survey.[1] The Ministry of Industry is also conducting a census covering 8 200 factories (95% of them SMEs), of which 4 700 are registered at the Ministry of Industry and the rest obtained their license before the establishment of the Ministry of Industry or are unlicensed. This census will help regulate the sector in Lebanon.[2]

Along these lines, the draft SME Law that is pending parliamentary approval also stipulates that the SME Unit within the Ministry of Economy and Trade shall establish a database of enterprises and undertake an inventory and a classification of micro, small and medium-sized enterprises. The SME Strategy also calls for the establishment of an SME Observatory which should be tasked to regularly conduct and publish research, statistical and impact analysis on SMEs and support entities, and maintain a comprehensive database to ensure continuous and effective monitoring of support to SMEs. The Ministry of

Economy and Trade is working with the World Bank to establish such an SME Observatory as part of the National Job Creation Program.

In terms of the **wider economic agenda**, Lebanon has been significantly affected by refugee inflows from Syria and Iraq. In this context, an international conference (CEDRE) was held in April 2018 to support Lebanon in facing the important challenges and burden of the negative spillovers of regional conflict. At the conference, the international community pledged USD 11 billion in loans and grants to support Lebanon's investment and reforms programme.[3] The government also unveiled a Vision for Stabilisation, Growth and Employment, which includes a number of structural reforms such as revising the Code of Commerce, developing the regulatory framework for e-government and e-banking, and other reforms to improve access to finance and the judicial system. This reform agenda could improve the business climate and have a positive impact for SME and entrepreneurship development.[4]

Concerning the **institutional framework and co-ordination** for SME development, the Ministry of Economy and Trade continues to play the leading role in policy development and co-ordination while the Ministry of Industry focuses on industrial development, including co-operation in the context of the Euro-Med network of industrial policy experts.

The draft **SME Law**, which is yet to be approved by parliament, stipulates that one of its objectives is ensuring co-ordination among all bodies and institutions working in the field of enterprise development to achieve the objectives of the relevant Lebanese national strategy. The SME Law also specifies that the **SME Unit** of the Ministry of Economy and Trade will be in charge of developing and implementing a national strategic plan relating to enterprises, updating it on a permanent and continuous basis, and setting the necessary rules and regulations to co-ordinate with the concerned parties in the public and private sectors. According to the consultations for this interim assessment, a concrete action plan to operationalise the **SME Strategy** will be developed once the SME Law is published (although there are no details of when this will happen).

On **public-private dialogue** (PPD), at the time of the SME Policy Index 2014 the main initiative promoting PPD was the multipartite platform Improving the Business Environment in Lebanon (IBEL). However, IBEL is no longer operational and did not reach its goals of improving several aspects of the business environment. Furthermore, there are no published documents on the IBEL's achievements and several of the government and private sector officials consulted for this interim assessment were not aware of its existence.

The Ministry of Industry is developing an action plan in collaboration with national and international experts and as a product of seminars conducted under the EU-supported Enhancement of the Business Environment in the Southern Mediterranean (EBESM) project. The aim is to institutionalise PPD in the SME policy-making process through a ministerial decree. Furthermore, the SME Strategy to 2020 and its action plan include provisions to foster PPD through regular roundtables,[5] establish a web portal,[6] and a mobile application to facilitate SME engagement, and hold a yearly SME stakeholder forum.

For further action: Lebanon could significantly increase its efforts to establish a full-fledged SME policy by approving the draft SME Law and implementing a detailed, action-oriented SME strategy that identifies concrete goals, targets, responsible parties and budgets – elements the SME Strategy lacks in its current form. Furthermore, the SME Law and the SME Strategy could be better aligned by addressing divergences such as the proposed SME definitions. Lebanon has also plenty of space to improve official SME statistics, which are mostly absent. The Central Administration for Statistics could for instance launch an economic census that could be eventually substituted by the use of administrative sources of enterprise information such as tax records, social security, and the business registry. Administrative data could be complemented with surveys to cover the informal economy. Along these lines, Lebanon could establish the planned SME Observatory to disseminate data on SMEs and useful information for entrepreneurs and business managers. The authorities should empower the SME unit in the Ministry of Economy and Trade or consider the creation of an official SME agency with policy co-ordination and policy implementation responsibilities, following the models of other MED and OECD economies. The SME unit or agency could also act as secretariat for the implementation of an SME strategy. In terms of public-private dialogue, Lebanon could reactivate the IBEL initiative to foster multipartite co-operation in areas such as improving the business environment and enhancing targeted SME policies. Laying the building blocks of a complete SME policy could prove costly at the beginning and would require significant capacity building; the donor and international communities could support Lebanon in this important endeavour, always keeping in mind the sustainability and scalability of efforts in the medium-to-long term.

Improving business environments for SMEs and entrepreneurs

Since the publication of the SME Policy Index 2014 there appear to be no comprehensive efforts for **regulatory reform and administrative simplification**. First, as mentioned above, the IBEL is no longer operational. Furthermore, there is no evidence of concrete efforts towards the development and implementation of regulatory impact analysis (RIA) and the introduction of an SME test.

According to the consultations for this interim assessment some of the 40 initiatives to improve the business environment put forward by the SME Strategy are being implemented by an EU-supported project under the co-ordination of the Office of the Minister of State for Administrative Reform (OMSAR) and in co-operation with relevant ministries involved in business regulations. Yet the information provided refers to an e-government initiative aimed at facilitating business procedures (the OMSAR e-government programme) and not to the establishment of a mechanism for regulatory impact analysis.[7]

Concerning the facilitation of procedures for the **creation of new enterprises**, the Ministry of Economy has created an electronic platform to register online for several services.[8] Yet there is no online registration for new enterprises. Business registry is done through the Commercial Registry and the Chambers of Commerce and is paper-based. There has been no progress with regards to one-stop shops for company registration, although according to the consultation the OMSAR project is to be staged in two phases: 1) the simplification of regulations and 2) the creation of one-stop shops.

In terms of **bankruptcy**, according to the SME Policy Index 2014 the government was revising the legal framework for insolvency and drafting a modern bankruptcy law through the IBEL initiative. There have been no changes in this regard since then.

For further action: There is plenty of space for action to establish initiatives to improve the business environment for SMEs and entrepreneurs. OMSAR could spearhead an initiative to introduce regulatory impact analysis and an SME test in Lebanon, in co-operation with relevant ministries and government agencies. Such an initiative could be accompanied with the re-activation of a platform for public-private dialogue, as seen in the previous section. The establishment of a single identification number for enterprises (of which there is no evidence) could also facilitate these efforts by making it easier for firms to deal with different public agencies. A single identification number could also have the advantage of helping to improve data collection, as noted in the previous section. Much greater effort could also be made to modernise the bankruptcy system, which is one of the most difficult in the MED region.

Fostering access to finance

In terms of the **legal and regulatory framework** for access to finance, the SME Policy Index 2014 noted that a credit registry was operational at the Central Bank. The registry back then was covering nearly 20% of the adult population (the figure now is 22.9%), higher than the OECD average. The consultations for this interim assessment noted that a public announcement issued by Central Bank (BDL) mandated that both legal and physical persons will be now allowed to request a credit information report from any BDL branch and not only from the headquarters. This initiative aims at making the provision of credit information decentralised and faster. In contrast, this interim assessment finds no progress or plans for the establishment of a credit bureau.

The SME Policy Index 2014 also pointed to ongoing work with the International Finance Corporation (IFC) towards establishing a legal framework for a registry of moveable assets. A draft law has been approved by the Council of Ministers on 27 March 2018 to allow the use of movable assets as collateral, and, once enacted, should be followed by the creation of a collateral registry.

In contrast, some progress has been made in terms of the availability of **sources of finance** for SMEs. In 2016 the Central Bank amended the regulatory framework to increase the margin of funds that banks can dedicate to financing firms in the knowledge economy sector, by authorising them to invest, with a BDL guarantee of 75%, up to 4% of their own capital, compared to 3% previously. The measure would raise the funds available for this purpose from USD 400 million to more than USD 600 million. In addition, about eight venture capital funds were created following this reform and thanks to the funds made available in the change of legislation.

In terms of access to credit, the BDL has also given incentives for banks to finance enterprises in different sectors and give them loans at very low interest rates (1% from the BDL to banks and up to 3% from banks to firms). This measure, first launched as a USD 1.47 billion stimulus package in 2013, has been renewed for the fourth consecutive year, with an average of USD 1 billion per year. The stimulus package targets, among other things, SMEs, although there is no evidence on its impact. This measure is intended to fund loans for investments and not for working capital (unless the loan is accompanied by a guarantee from Kafalat, the main credit guarantee scheme).

There have also been new initiatives by Kafalat introduced since 2014, notably the Kafalat iSME programme, a USD 30 million fund borrowed by the Republic of Lebanon from the World Bank and entrusted to Kafalat SAL to manage. The programme provides Concept Development Grants (of up to USD 15 000) for innovative projects and equity co-investments (between USD 100 000 and 1.2 million) provided alongside other capital investments by venture capital funds, holding companies, formal business angel groups and investment banks. To date the programme has given 70 grants and four equity investments.[9]

Another new initiative to provide equity investments and support to start-ups is IM Capital, supported by the United States Agency for International Development (USAID) through the Middle East Investment Initiative and managed by Berytech, a business incubator and provider of services to start-ups.[10] IM Capital is a USD 15 million investment fund and provides matching capital, equity guarantees and support programmes to a broad range of qualified early-stage businesses and investors in Lebanon. In addition, IM Capital established the Seeders Masterclass for Business Angels, a year-long programme to form individual angel investors through a "learn & earn" methodology consisting of an education and investment track in SMEs.[11] The aim of the programme is to create an informed community of investors. As a result, a community of business angel investors has been created and invested in four start-ups.

For further action: Lebanon has seen impressive progress in the introduction of new sources of access to finance in recent years, especially in initiatives aimed at equity investments and innovative start-ups. The initiatives appear to be well-aligned and consider synergies and they seem to be well-monitored. To advance even further in this area, Lebanon could work on the establishment of a credit bureau and registry of moveable assets in order to also facilitate access to credit.

Nurturing entrepreneurship and SME growth

The SME Policy Index 2014 noted already a vibrant market for **business development services** (BDS) in Lebanon, with several governmental, private and non-governmental players across the country providing a diversity of support schemes. Three business development centres (Berytech, BIAT and SouthBIC) were the main entities supporting SMEs. A number of co-working spaces and accelerators had been established (Cloud 5, ALTCITY and Co-working 961). The Euro-Lebanese Centre for Industrial Modernisation (ELCIM) offered more advanced services such as assessing business strategies and assisting businesses in improving production technology and production planning. And the SME Support Unit/Enterprise Team at the Ministry of Economy and Trade was developing a new support strategy for SMEs to provide a strategic framework (see the first section in this chapter).

Apart from these initiatives, most of which are still active,[12] the World Bank provided in 2016 a grant facility, the Lebanon MSME TA Facility, to promote business development service providers. The facility was disbursed within one year and provided a 50/50 matching grant to established and registered BDS providers in order for them to enhance their capacity in specific institutional areas including product innovation, monitoring and evaluation of services. This grant of USD 400 000 was managed by Kafalat and aimed to support very specific projects (i.e. not for general support and not for new BDS providers). The grant benefited eight business development services providers including the Business Angels Masterclass and the Tripoli Entrepreneurs Club Programme aimed at enabling the employability of computer programmers. According to the consultations for this interim assessment, the facility was meant as a pilot programme that could be replicated in other countries and continued in Lebanon, although there were no further actions.

In addition, to facilitate SME access to information on the many services available, the Ministry of Economy published the guidebook *What's in Lebanon for SMEs 2017*.[13] Apart from information on business development services, the guidebook includes descriptions of support programmes on innovation, finance and market access. This guidebook could represent a good practice for the dissemination of information at a reasonable cost.

The SME Policy Index 2014 indicated that the **public procurement** system in Lebanon was relatively open to the participation of SMEs. Information on public procurement was centralised at the national level and made available online and in newspapers. However, further efforts were needed to mainstream e-procurement. A law to regulate late payments existed but the penalty was not effectively enforced. This interim assessment finds no significant progress yet in this area. However, the Vision for Stabilisation, Growth and Employment presented by the Lebanese Prime Minister at the CEDRE conference in Paris in April 2018 notes that there are draft laws presented to parliament for the modernisation of the procurement system.[14] The laws aim at enhancing the transparency and efficiency of public procurement, which becomes even more important in view of the sharp increase in procurement activity that would result from the implementation of the Capital Investment Programme (CIP). The CIP is a long-term scheme to make use of the loans and pledges made at the CEDRE conference (see first section in this chapter).

Concerning measures to promote SME access to **international markets**, the SME Policy Index 2014 mentioned the existence of ad hoc initiatives (as opposed to strategic measures) such as trade missions and trade fairs. The Investment Development Agency (IDAL) assisted the promotion and marketing of Lebanese products, in particular agricultural products and materials used in the agro-industry. A draft law for the establishment of an export promotion agency was being discussed in parliament but there was no evidence of the development of a clear export promotion strategy.

This interim assessment finds little progress in these areas. A number of initiatives for SME internationalisation have been introduced over the past few years, although without a clear holistic or coherent framework. The export promotion agency has not been established and there is no export promotion strategy. IDAL continues to play a role in the promotion of Lebanese products in foreign markets; however, no published results are available on the impact of the agency's activities. Furthermore, although IDAL publishes online valuable information on investment opportunities and incentives in key tradable industries (agribusiness, information technology, etc.), the booklets available are not organised in a user-friendly manner (e.g. by topic).[15] In terms of the strategic promotion of exports, the Integrated Vision for the Lebanese Industrial Sector 2025 includes a section on increasing industrial exports with a series of actions in this area and responsible parties.[16] The more recent Vision for Stabilisation, Growth and Employment presented in the CEDRE conference includes a specific pillar for the diversification of Lebanon's productive and services sectors and the realisation of the country's export potential. To implement that pillar the Vision foresees the development of a strategy in this area based on an assessment by McKinsey consultancy.

For further action: There have been positive developments over the past few years in terms of the availability of business development services, but less so on SME internationalisation and even less on public procurement. New initiatives have been undertaken to strengthen the already mature BDS market in Lebanon and to facilitate SME access to information on the various support schemes available. The development and implementation of a full-fledged SME strategy could give even more coherence and impact to these efforts. The same is also true for support measures for SME internationalisation, which have increased in numbers but which still lack a strategic approach. Finally, Lebanon could increase its efforts for a greater participation of SMEs in public procurement, including by establishing an e-procurement platform.

Investing in entrepreneurial human capital

Since 2014, little progress has been made in the field of **entrepreneurial learning in upper secondary education**. There is a no national vision on lifelong entrepreneurial learning, which should be integrated within the ongoing discussions on the future national education plan. In fact, the Ministry of Education and Higher Education (MEHE) has recently reconfirmed it wants to integrate entrepreneurship as a key competence in the national education system, meaning there is the necessary political commitment.

A pilot project had been finalised in 2014 to develop entrepreneurial learning modules for general secondary schools and for technical and vocational education and training (TVET) schools, as well as training material for teachers.[17] The Steering Committee established under the pilot project is currently revising the action plan on how to integrate entrepreneurship key competences into the national curriculum, together with a budget estimate.

There are a number of ad hoc examples of school-enterprise co-operation, mainly driven by INJAZ.[18] However, more efforts should be made to increase school-enterprise co-operation in secondary general education with the aim to develop the entrepreneurial mindset of young people. In the case of TVET schools, school-enterprise co-operation is mainly addressed through the in-company training. However, it is important that besides learning professional skills there is room for entrepreneurship skills development, including the entrepreneurial mindset.

Significant progress has been made in the field of **women's entrepreneurship training**. The National Strategy for Women in Lebanon (2011-2021), spearheaded by the National Commission for Lebanese Women (NCLW),[19] aims to ensure gender equality and to empower women through the development of their business skills. In addition, the 2015-2020 SME Strategy promotes women's entrepreneurship. Yet, according to the survey carried out in 2016 in the MENA region, Lebanese business women feel that they do not receive the same business support as men.

The Lebanese League for Women in Business (LLWB) is an active partner in promoting women's entrepreneurship through providing a platform for networking, sharing experiences, developing their skills and accessing funds. The LLWB has a skills development committee that is responsible for training provision, including mentoring, and is planning to develop on-line trainings. The Cherie Blair Foundation for Women and the Lebanese Association for Development, *Al Majmoua* implemented in 2016 the Women's Economic Empowerment in the Bekaa Region project, where more than 250 Lebanese women entrepreneurs gained confidence and built capacities to run a viable business. The Ministry of Agriculture has co-ordinated several projects to raise awareness of women's entrepreneurship in the rural areas.

Despite Lebanon's political commitment to support exporting firms, there is little emphasis on **training for SME internationalisation**. There is an ongoing policy dialogue on how to better prepare Lebanese businesses to improve the competitiveness of their products, and the 2015-2020 SME Strategy provides a good basis to enhance capacity building for SME's in this respect. The SME Strategy foresees the creation of a Lebanese Export Promotion Agency, which could play an important role providing coherence and upgrading the training offer supporting SMEs' internationalization, as well as collecting data and monitoring support services.

The Ministry of Economy and Trade (MOET) has published a guidebook for SME's (MOET, 2017) that includes an overview of the different financial support schemes and provides a list of all institutions that deliver training for start-ups and for SMEs that are willing to grow (i.e. scale up) and export.

The more prominent agencies providing training are the Lebanese Training Centre (LTC) within the Chamber of Commerce, the Business Incubation Association in Tripoli (BIAT), the Lebanese Standards Institutions (LIBNOR), and several incubators and accelerators. IDAL, a national investment promotion agency, also assists Lebanese companies with growing their business in the international market. Several large projects that supported SME's internationalisation through training have been finalised and have yet not been replaced by other projects. The next phase of the QUALEB project (Quality Programme funded by the EU) will support SME's in the food sector through practical training, mentoring and coaching.

For further action: The government should introduce entrepreneurship learning within ongoing discussions about the national education plan in order to mainstream entrepreneurship as a key competence into the national curricula for general education and TVET. This would require the adoption of a new decree and the provision of sufficient financial and human resources for implementation, as well as a monitoring mechanism. In order to implement the National Strategy for Women in Lebanon, the next progress report of the National Action Plan should have a chapter dedicated to training for women entrepreneurs as well as data collection evaluate training programmes. A stronger emphasis should be put on training for SMEs (including mentoring and coaching) to help prepare them for international markets in different sectors such as agriculture, agro-food, ICT, and industry.

The way forward

Lebanon has seen the introduction of an important number of initiatives to promote the competitiveness and innovation of SMEs and start-ups, including the establishment and expansion of equity investment vehicles and the improvement of business development services. However, there is still plenty of room to improve the business environment for SMEs through RIA and an SME test, bankruptcy procedures, e-procurement and other areas. Furthermore, as it was the case already in 2014, Lebanon could make much greater efforts to strengthen multipartite co-ordination and dialogue. The recommendation put forward by the SME Policy Index 2014 on the introduction of a consultative committee on SME policy – a committee open to all stakeholders including independent experts, donors and private sector representatives – is still very much pertinent. In this view, the main actions put forward by this interim assessment are as follows:

- Approving the draft SME Law and implementing a detailed, action-oriented SME strategy identifying concrete goals, targets, responsible parties and budgets (elements lacking in the current form of the SME Strategy).
- Re-establishing a multipartite public-private dialogue platform to improve co-ordination and to obtain guidance on the design, implementation and evaluation of SME policies. The SME Unit at the Ministry of Economy could serve as secretariat for such platform. Eventually, Lebanon could consider the establishment of an SME agency building on existing models in OECD and MED economies.
- Improving the availability and dissemination of SME and entrepreneurship statistics, first through the establishment of a census or similar mechanism and eventually through the use of administrative sources of information (also building on international practice).
- Setting up a mechanism for regulatory impact analysis and the SME test.
- Creation of a "one-stop-shop" to simplify registration procedures and improve access to information.

- Establishing a credit bureau and a registry of moveable assets to facilitate access to credit.
- Approving the public procurement law, either by updating the existing draft or developing a new one.
- Establishing an e-procurement platform.
- Introducing entrepreneurship learning within ongoing discussions about the national education plan.
- Including training for women entrepreneurs in the next progress report of the action plan of the National Strategy for Women in Lebanon.
- Strengthening training for SMEs with a sectoral focus to help prepare them for international markets.

Notes

[1] 2016 Industrial Statistics, www.industry.gov.lb/Arabic/Arabic/Documents/%D9%86%D9%85%D8%A7%D8%B0%D8%AC%20%D8%A7%D9%84%D8%B7%D9%84%D8%A8%D8%A7%D8%AA/Questionnaire%20Industrielle%202015.pdf.

[2] http://www.industry.gov.lb/Arabic/Arabic/Pages/PublicationsAndStudies.aspx

[3] Of the total pledged, USD 10.2 billion has been pledged for loans, including 9.9 billion in concessional terms, and USD 0.86 billion as grants (including grants to subsidize loans).

[4] Joint Statement of the Economic Conference for Development through Reforms with the Private Sector (6 April 2018), www.diplomatie.gouv.fr/IMG/pdf/cedre_statement-en-_final_ang_cle8179fb.pdf.

[5] http://www.economy.gov.lb/en/services/-support-to-smes-/roundtables

[6] http://www.economy.gov.lb/en/what-we-provide/support-to-smes/

[7] Lebanese e-Government website, www.e-gov.gov.lb/Cultures/en-us/aboutEgov/Pages/ListSubChannels.aspx, and Dawlati website, www.dawlati.gov.lb/.

[8] Ministry of Economy and Trade Portal, "Applications List", https://portal.economy.gov.lb/MOET/ApplicationTypes.

[9] iSME Programme, www.kafalatisme.com.lb.

[10] Insurance and Match Capital, www.im-capital.com.

[11] Seeders, www.seeders.co.

[12] SouthBIC is no longer active.

[13] Ministry of Economy and Trade (2017), *Guidebook: What's in Lebanon for SMEs*, http://www.economy.gov.lb/en/services/support-to-smes/whats-in-lebanon-for-smes.

[14] Vision for Stabilization, Growth and Employment, www.pcm.gov.lb/arabic/ListingAndPDFWithDropdown.aspx?pageid=11224.

[15] The Investment Development Authority of Lebanon, Publications, http://investinlebanon.gov.lb/en/InformationCenter?pageNumber=0.

[16] Ministry of Industry, Publications and Studies, www.industry.gov.lb/Pages/Publicationsandstudies.aspx. Operational plan accessible at: http://www.industry.gov.lb/Pages/Publicationsandstudies.aspx.

[17] Multi annual project (2010-2014) "Support to the development of a framework for Lifelong Entrepreneurial Learning in Lebanon" developed by the Ministry of Education and Higher Education with the support of the European Training Foundation (ETF), International Labour Organization (ILO), and the United Nations Educational, Scientific and Cultural Organization (UNESCO).

[18] A youth-centered non-profit organisation established in Jordan in 1999 active in the European Union and worldwide, including in the Middle East, North-Africa and Pakistan.

[19] The NCLW is an official institution affiliated to the Presidency of the Council of Ministers.

Chapter 11. Morocco

The foundations of SME policy: definitions, statistics and institutions

Morocco has had for many years a relatively well-developed and structured SME policy. Since 2002 it has had an operational SME Law (*Charte de la petite et moyenne entreprise*) determining the most important policy principles including the establishment and responsibilities of an SME agency; the recognition of associations for the support of SMEs at the local, regional and national levels; and support mechanisms.[1] The **SME definition** used by Morocco SME, the SME agency (previously known as National Agency for SME Development, or ANPME), continues to refer only to financial criteria, with no headcount criterion (Table 11.1).

Table 11.1. SME definition by Morocco SME

Type of enterprise	Turnover
Micro	Annual turnover ≤ MAD 10 m
Small and medium	Annual turnover** ≤ MAD 200 m

Source: Contractual Framework between the State and Morocco SME for 2015-2020.

In terms of **SME and entrepreneurship statistics**, the National Statistics Office (HCP) publishes extensive economic and demographic indicators. Furthermore, one of the most important initiatives over the past few years has been the establishment of an MSME Observatory aimed to produce and disseminate ample information on this area. It is based on a collaborative approach between eleven founding agencies, namely Morocco SME; the Central Bank (BAM); the Ministry of Industry, Investment, Trade and the Digital Economy; the National Confederation of Moroccan Enterprises (CGEM); the credit guarantee agency (CCG); the National Banks Association; the statistics office (HCP); the Ministry of General Affairs and Governance; and the General Directorate for Taxes (DGI).

The MSME Observatory is already operational and has signed several collaboration agreements with other agencies to share information on businesses.[2] The agreements being signed are to provide a legal framework for the collection of information while ensuring the confidentiality of disaggregated data. However, no information has yet been published and its website is not yet operational. The ultimate goal is to have a confederated source of information using administrative data. These efforts are aligned with the creation of the single identification number (ICE) described in the section on improving the business environment.

The SME policy agenda in Morocco is in large part driven by the **wider economic development agenda**. At the same time the Ministry of Industry, Investment, Trade and Digital Economy is in charge of overseeing SME policy and developing and implementing two industrial development strategies: the National Pact for Industrial Emergence (PNEI) for 2009-2015; and the Industrial Acceleration Plan for 2014-2020, which is the current strategic framework driving industrial policy, including SME policy.[3]

In this context, Morocco SME, the **SME agency**, adopted a new "Contractual Framework" for 2015-2020.[4] In line with the Industrial Acceleration Plan 2014-2020, the contractual framework aims to increase SME competitiveness and to foster entrepreneurship, including high impact entrepreneurs.

One of the most important initiative undertaken by Morocco in recent years has been the introduction of a set of measures and incentives under the "auto-entrepreneur status" in 2015. The auto-entrepreneur status aims to foster the entrepreneurial spirit among Moroccans, to support aspiring entrepreneurs, to facilitate youth self-employment and to formalise the informal economy. Its main goals are:

1. To encourage independent work through a series of support measures that allow the possibility to easily undertake professional activities;
2. To reduce costs by simplifying administrative procedures related to enterprise creation; and
3. To ensure appropriate social security coverage for beneficiaries.

In terms of **public-private dialogue**, the National Committee of the Business Climate (CNEA) continues to be an example of good international practice by providing a multipartite platform involving public and private actors to lead the efforts to improve the business environment through a multi-year strategy and yearly action plans.

From the private sector the most important organisation representing SMEs is the General Confederation of Moroccan Enterprises (CGEM), with about 88 000 members from across the country and from different sectors. The CGEM is formed by "commissions", one of which is devoted to representing the interests of SMEs.

Since its creation in 2009 the CNEA has contributed to different reforms efforts leading to significant improvements of the business climate in Morocco, as reflected in the *Doing Business* and the Global Competitiveness Index rankings.

For further action: The Industrial Acceleration Plan 2014-2020 and Morocco SME's 2015-2020 Contractual Framework provides a coherent and strategic approach towards enterprise development. For example, the Industrial Acceleration Plan includes actions to support SME competitiveness whereas the Auto-entrepreneur status focuses on promoting employment and addressing informality. Through the CNEA, Morocco also has a well-established and formalised platform the foster dialogue. These elements are being used as vehicles to continuously move on the reform agenda (e.g. access to finance, regional development, etc.). Morocco could continue on this path and move forward with ongoing initiatives such as the MSME Observatory and the improvement of sources of statistics. Given the rich information available, Morocco could join the OECD Scoreboard on Financing SMEs and Entrepreneurs and the OECD-Eurostat Entrepreneurship Indicators Programme so that it can compare its conditions and performance with international peers. Morocco SME could also review whether its definition responds to the diversity of SMEs and could use more criteria (not just financial) to better differentiate between firms.

Improving business environments for SMEs and entrepreneurs

The CNEA continues to be the main driver of **regulatory reform and administrative simplification** in Morocco. The CNEA operates on the basis of a longer-term vision and yearly action plans with concrete targets.[5] Several of these targets have been structured around specific aspects of the *Doing Business* indicators. This has resulted in a significant improvement in the country performance in *Doing Business* rankings since 2012 and until the 2018 edition.[6] These improvements have been the result of very targeted reforms, such as the suppression of a minimum paid-in capital for the creation of an enterprise; the digitalisation of the process to have a business permit and to pay taxes; etc.

However, the CNEA is not a regulatory impact analysis (RIA) initiative in the sense of this report (i.e. a systemic approach to critically assessing the positive and negative effects of proposed and existing regulations and non-regulatory alternatives). According Article 19 of the Law on the Functioning of Government Bodies and the Statue of their Members, every new law proposal should be accompanied by an impact assessment.[7] This Article provides an adequate framework to introduce the SME test, and it has been subject to a feasibility study.[8]

In terms of the **operational environment for business creation**, as part of the *Doing Business* reforms Morocco streamlined the process to start a company by eliminating the minimum capital requirement, reducing registration costs and simplifying documentation requirements.[9] The government is aware of the importance of digital government. In fact, CNEA's 2017-2018 Action Plan[10] foresees the introduction of an online system for enterprise creation. This project is implemented by the National Office for Intellectual and Commercial Property (OMPIC), and takes over the formerly known Online System for Enterprise Creation (CREOL) project. In addition, the Cabinet adopted Bill 88-17 on the creation of enterprises online in February 2018. There are three bills in total:

- Bill 87-17 amending and supplementing Law 13-99 establishing the Moroccan Office of Industrial and Commercial Property (OMPIC);
- Bill 88-17 concerning the creation of businesses online and their accompaniment;
- Bill 89-17 on the revision of Book IV of the Commercial Code.

All three bills concerning the creation of enterprises online were adopted unanimously by the House of Representatives.

A single identification number (ICE) has also been introduced for both natural and legal persons.[11] Although the ICE does not yet replace other numbers (tax identification number, trade registry number and social security number) it is expected that in the future it will do so. Several fiscal provisions make it compulsory to have an ICE, given it is now a requirement for receipts to be accepted by the tax authorities and to benefit from tax exemption, and a fine is imposed in the absence of an ICE.[12]

The ICE will allow government agencies to exchange information (although the exchange of information is not yet widespread). The ICE will also be a tool to address the informal economy since documentation without ICE will not be valid (e.g. invoices without ICE are not be valid for fiscal purposes). Finally, as noted before, the ICE also serves SME statistical purposes by facilitating the operation of the MSME Observatory.

The legal framework for **bankruptcy** was recently overhauled through the approval in April 2018 of Law N. 17-73, which replaced Law N. 15-95 related to Book V of the Code of Commerce. The reform introduces changes on procedures for prevention and treatment of difficulties for enterprises, following the principles set by the United Nations Commission on International Trade Law (UNCITRAL) and the World Bank. The objectives of the new law are reflected in the proposed change of name, from "Enterprise difficulties" to "Procedures for the prevention, rescue and treatment of the difficulties of enterprises."[13] The Law dedicates several chapters to mechanisms aiming to resolve trans-border disputes, setting a framework for collaboration with foreign judiciary bodies.

For further action: Morocco could continue working to step up its initial efforts to develop the single identification number (ICE), the online registration (CREOL) and the revision of the bankruptcy framework. Additionally, apart from the targeted reforms to improve the performance in key *Doing Business* indicators Morocco could work on the implementation of a full-fledged RIA mechanism (building on Organic Law No. 065-13) and an SME test.

Fostering access to finance

On the **legal and regulatory framework** for access to finance, Morocco had both a credit information system (*Centrale des risques*) regulated by the Central Bank and managed by a private firm (*Experian Maroc*)[14] and a credit bureau (*Credit Info*).[15] Since then, more measures have been taken to increase access to information and credit transparency. One of these measures is the expansion of the services provided by the credit bureau, including the provision of credit scores in 2016, the monitoring of portfolios and alerting systems. The credit scoring actually allowed Morocco to increase its note to seven (on a scale of eight) in the depth of credit information index of *Doing Business*.[16] Furthermore, the opening up of the market for private credit bureaus in 2016 has led the way for the opening of a second bureau by Quantik Credit Bureau Maroc. There are also plans to expand the sources of information that can be integrated into the credit bureaus to include utilities and other service suppliers.

Concerning the registration system for moveable assets, an area where Morocco has lagged behind the rest of the region, there is a draft proposal to reform the law on moveable assets. The proposal is the product of a number of consultations taking place since 2015 and is presented as a priority by the CNEA, together with the reform of Book V of the Code of Commerce (bankruptcy), adopted in April 2018. The aim of the proposal, which was developed with the help of the European Bank for Reconstruction and Development (EBRD), the International Finance Corporation (IFC) and the Arab Monetary Fund, is to address a number of complex and dispersed procedures in this area.[17] Notably, the proposal seeks to extend the array of goods that can be pledged when accessing credit.

Concerning the availability of **sources of finance**, the SME Policy Index 2014 noted an expanding credit guarantee market formed by public and private actors. This trend appears to have continued over the past few years. In 2016, the total activity of Morocco's Central Guarantee Fund (CCG), both for businesses and private individuals, totalled MAD 21 billion of mobilised loans (about EUR 1.9 billion), an increase of 23% compared to 2015. Furthermore, the CCG created a dedicated Guarantee Fund for SMEs "*Mouwakaba*."

Overall, the credit guarantee system in Morocco seems to be working well since almost 52% of firms in the *Enterprise Surveys* say they have a bank loan or line of credit (compared to 28.6% in the rest of the MENA region) and nearly 35% are using banks to finance investments (compared to 25.9% in MENA).[18] In contrast, Morocco's performance in the getting credit indicator of *Doing Business* is rather low, especially given the weak strength of legal rights index, which measures the degree to which collateral and bankruptcy laws protect the rights of borrowers and lenders and thus facilitate lending (i.e. there is work needed on the Secured Transactions law and on the Bankruptcy Law).

New initiatives on access to credit have also taken place. The Central Bank has implemented some measures to support SMEs in access to finance, including a refinancing window for banks' loans to SMEs, targeting in particular companies in the industry sector and exporting firms.

Commercial banks are also becoming more interested in working with SMEs. For instance, the Moroccan Bank for Foreign Trade (BMCE Bank), created the "Club PME" to provide training to SMEs on financial products. BMCE Bank has also created a number of funds and products targeting SMEs. These include "BMCE Business Express" (loans to cover short term needs, complemented by a guarantee from the CCG), the "*Fonds de soutien financier des TPME*" (a co-finance mechanisms that looks to support companies going through punctual cash-flow difficulties, and focusing particularly on exporting companies), "*BMCE Cap Energie*" (to finance projects in the energy sector), and "Energy Lease" (to fund energy efficiency investments). In 2013, Bank Al-Maghrib and the CCG established a fund to co-finance SMEs going through cash-flow difficulties. Since then, 406 companies have been supported for a value of MAD 2.6 million. The Central Bank has also created a refinancing window for SMEs, and Morocco SME has launched the programmes "*Imtiaz Croissance*" and "*Istitmar Croissance*", which aim to support investment projects of industrial SMEs.

For further action: For Morocco to continue its progress on access to finance, it could step up its efforts to streamline the moveable assets law and establish a registry of moveable assets (in line with efforts already being done in the rest of the MED region). Furthermore, building on the many efforts being made on access to credit (and on the apparent good results based on international gauges), Morocco could work more on developing alternative sources of finance, including equity investments. This interim assessment did not find clear evidence on efforts to develop alternative sources of finance such as venture capital, business angels and other sources.

Nurturing entrepreneurship and SME growth

Morocco has a well-developed market for personalised **business development services** (BDS), with a high level of internal competition among service providers, including private ones. SMEs have access to support services from government agencies such as Morocco SME, and from several associations and private providers.

Morocco SME has developed support programmes for SMEs and self-entrepreneurs in the context of the Industrial Acceleration Plan 2014-2020. Two main programmes target micro-enterprises (*très petites enterprises*): *Istitmar Croissance* supports investment and technology development projects through investment premiums; TAHFIZ supports system modernisation and IT upgrades through co-financing. Support to SMEs is channelled through *Imtiaz Croissance*, which provides investment premiums of up to 20% of the total investment, and Moussanada, which funds technical assistance and consulting services at between 60-80% of the project. The impact of the programmes is evaluated by an external auditor every two to three years.

As mentioned in the first section of this chapter, one of the main areas of progress is the creation of a system of incentives and support measures to promote employment and entrepreneurship through the *Statut de l'auto-entrepreneur*.[19] Among the main pillars are: a simplified administrative procedure to benefit from this status, tax incentives, customised support and others. The auto-entrepreneur status was created in 2015 and has a target of 20 000 beneficiaries per year. As of May 2018, 32% of beneficiaries were women, and 54% were less than 34 years old; the activities engaged in were 43% in commerce, 35% in services, 15% in industry and 7% in handcrafts. The auto-entrepreneur status is also an innovative and comprehensive initiative to incentivise the formalisation of the economy.

In terms of **public procurement**, Morocco has a wide array of measures to support SME participation in this important market. First, a public procurement regulation reserves 20% for national SMEs since 2013. Since then, all relevant public entities have to reserve 20% in its yearly programmes and have to explicitly define whether a contract is reserved for SMEs only. Furthermore, the General Treasury has put into place a scheme to simplify the analysis of submissions and company profiles and has set up an electronic bidding system and database of suppliers with ready information for some companies. This adds to the existence of a 2014 decree on down payments for procurement to facilitate the financing for SMEs.[20] Finally, and most importantly, an online platform for public procurement exists that SMEs to acess and apply for public contracts..[21]

In terms of outreach and training courses for SMEs and the government on public procurement, the General Confederation of Moroccan Enterprises (CGEM), the main business association in the country, is playing a key role. The CGEM has developed several initiatives contributing to the dissemination of information and provision of training to expand the use of the e-procurement system.

Efforts have been made to promote the **internationalisation** of SMEs, mostly through the digitalisation of procedures. PortNet, a virtual platform to deal with the formalities of foreign trade in ports, has continued progressing and has now several documents in digital format (import and export licences, engagements, etc.). PortNet has now reached 26 000 users including exporters/importers, banks, etc.

Furthermore, a Decree of 19 May 2015 made these documents mandatory in digital form.[22] There are also efforts towards the computerised exchange of information between PortNet and other technical departments, such as the ONSSA (National Office for the Sanitary Safety of Food Products) and EACCE (Autonomous Agency for the Control and Co-ordination of Exports). The goal is to reach the total digitalisation of foreign trade procedures by 2020.

Beyond the digitalisation of trade procedures, there have been increasing efforts to help SMEs integrate the global value chains and profit, technologically and financially, from the presence of multinational enterprises in Morocco. The main focus has been on the development of linkage programmes. The Industrial Acceleration Plan aims to nurture industrial ecosystems to improve the competitiveness of SMEs, and therefore includes a plan tailored to support their needs. It also aims to create a new dynamic between the heads of SMEs and large firms through strategic alliances that allow all to benefit and produce an overall stronger value chain. The government launched a programme in collaboration with business associations to support SMEs in their export activities, aiming to create 200 major exporters among SMEs in 4 years.

Some programmes have been put in place to enhance the capacity of support organisations to develop marketing opportunities for SMEs. On December 2017, the Moroccan Agency for the Development of Investment and Exports (AMDIE) was created, merging the Agency for Investment (AMDI) with the Export Promotion Centre (Maroc Export) and the Casablanca Exhibition Office (OFEC) into a single agency. The objective was to improve co-ordination with the private sector and investors and to streamline human and financial resources. It also aims to provide an integrated support for companies and therefore develop investment opportunities and promote Moroccan exports.

Also, the Islamic Centre for the Development of Trade (ICDT), in partnership with the firm Reload Consulting and the Moroccan Association of Exporters (Asmex), launched the "*Pas à Pas Export*" training program for Moroccan SMEs. The goal of the program is to promote internationalisation among small entrepreneurs by providing the necessary strategic and operational skills.

For further action: Morocco has made important progress in the promotion of SME growth and entrepreneurship, notably through the establishment of the *Statut de l'auto – entrepreneur* and numerous initiatives to increase access to public procurement and international markets. Morocco could keep track of the impact of these measures on SMEs and start-ups by implementing monitoring and evaluation techniques, in the context of Morocco SME impact evaluation programmes. Given the large number of actors involved, Morocco could also work towards ensuring that these actions are not disparate and remain co-ordinated towards its strategic goals.

Investing in entrepreneurial human capital

Regarding **entrepreneurial learning in upper secondary education**, Morocco has adopted a clear strategic vision and has reinforced the provision of formal education and vocational training as well as non-formal education. The strategic vision of the Educational System Reform advocates the need to train entrepreneurship and encourage the involvement of companies in technical and vocational training courses. This vision was adopted by the Higher Council of Education, Training and Scientific Research, the representative constitutional body of all stakeholders (including the state, companies and unions, civil society and the world of schools, teachers, trainers, students and parents). Similarly, the National Strategy for Vocational Training 2021 adopted by the Government Council in 2015 highlights the promotion and development of entrepreneurial, and financial education.

The training offer aiming to reinforce the entrepreneurial spirit has developed significantly in Morocco during the last years. Several initiatives encourage trainees to become more entrepreneurial. A number of companies and economic actors support education and vocational training initiatives. The Casablanca Stock Exchange promotes financial education. Professional bodies are active integrating entrepreneurship education within professional *baccalaureates*. International donors work with schools and training centres to develop soft skills, and to open schools to the business world. For example, the "ALEF Project" and the "PDEE, Entrepreneurship Development Program" value the contributions of the local ecosystem. Several projects promote self-employment and entrepreneurship as viable career prospects, including UNICEF's "Pathway to Life" and "Pathways Project", and the International Labour Organization's (ILO) "Understanding the Enterprise Program" (CLE). The program "Student Innovative Social" (EIS), in partnership with the British Council, supports the creation of the social enterprises. INJAZ[23] Maghreb works with the Regional Academies of Education and Training to simulate business start-ups ("CP, Company Program" and "EMC, Entrepreneurship Master Class"), and together with businessmen promotes an entrepreneurial spirit ("It's My Business Project" and "Business Leaders").

The main strategic document framing Morocco's policies for women's economic empowerment is the Second Government's Plan for Equality (ICRAM 2), adopted in 2017 by the Ministry of Solidarity, Women, Family and Social Development. Several initiatives support **women's entrepreneurship**. Several networks target women in the different regions, some of them focusing on providing access to technology to women entrepreneurs coming from low income backgrounds ("*Entre Elles*", Tatmine, Mobadara). The European Union (EU) has supported the implementation of ICRAM 2 with 45 million Euro.

In line with the National Strategy for Development and Promotion of Exports 2011-2016, the Moroccan government has supported **training for internationalisation of SMEs**, such as "Training days for Export Excellency", putting forward specific funding mechanisms. The government has adopted a sectoral approach, as reflected in the "*Les métiers mondiaux du Maroc*".

For further action: In order to implement the strategic vision to include entrepreneurial learning in upper secondary education, an action plan should be developed to define the roles and responsibilities as well as the results to be achieved, integrated by monitoring and evaluation mechanisms as well as specific funding enabling to ensure good conditions of implementation. An equally necessary measure is the establishment of a systematic training of teachers and trainers on entrepreneurship as a key competence. The government should also develop a mechanism to monitor and evaluate the impact of measures implemented to support women's entrepreneurship and SME internationalisation. More innovative training methods, such as online modules, could be developed to better support SME in their internationalisation efforts.

The way forward

It is clear that Morocco is a case from which other MED economies could draw inspiration to improve their SME policies. But it is also clear that there is still much to do to make of SMEs a vehicle for competitiveness and development. For example, although Morocco has a relatively diversified economy, it still relies on low value-added activities such as the extraction of natural resources and rain-fed agriculture; the informal economy, underemployment and unemployment are not uncommon; and the Human Development Index is lower than that of other MED economies, especially in terms of income. Morocco could (and is) for example, step up efforts towards regional development through SMEs and entrepreneurship; and continue working on the framework conditions needed for enterprises and individuals to thrive (infrastructure, education, financial markets, etc.). In terms of the particular policy areas analysed in this chapter, key actions that could be taken are as follows:

- Adopting a more complete definition of SMEs, including employment criteria, and unifying the use of such definition across support policies and programmes.
- Moving on with the statistical agenda by completing the establishment of the MSME Observatory and joining the OECD Scoreboard on Financing SMEs and Entrepreneurs and the OECD-Eurostat Entrepreneurship Indicators Programme so that it can compare its conditions and performance with international peers.
- Continuing working towards the improvement of the business environment by not only targeting specific indicators in *Doing Business* but also establishing a formal system for regulatory impact analysis and, importantly, an SME test. The completion of the ICE and the project to enable business start-up procedures online would be important in this regard too.
- Consolidating the framework for the establishment of a registry of moveable assets and creating such an important mechanism for access to finance. At the same time, more work could be done to develop the market for alternative sources of finance, including equity.

- Developing and implementing a comprehensive system for the monitoring and evaluation of SME support measures, in particular those related to enterprise creation and growth, in the context of Morocco SME impact evaluation programmes.
- The National Commission on Public Procurement (*Commission Nationale de la Commande Publique*) could act as Public Procurement observatory and share data on public procurement and SMEs' access.
- Develop an action plan in order to implement the strategic vision to include entrepreneurial learning in upper secondary education. The plan should include monitoring and evaluation mechanisms and specific funding to ensure good conditions of implementation.
- Develop a mechanism to monitor and evaluate the impact of measures implemented to support women's entrepreneurship.
- Develop more innovative training methods, such as online modules to support SME internationalisation.

Notes

[1] Law 53-00, www.droit-afrique.com/upload/doc/maroc/Maroc-Loi-2000-53-charte-PME.pdf.

[2] Agreements have already been signed with the General Directorate for Taxes (DGI), the Social Security Agency (CNSS), BAM, and the National Office for Intellectual and Commercial Property (OMPIC).

[3] Ministry of Industry, Investment, Trade and Digital Economy, "Industrial Acceleration Plan 2014-2020", www.mcinet.gov.ma/fr/content/plan-d%E2%80%99acc%C3%A9l%C3%A9ration-industrielle-2014-2020.

[4] Morocco SME, http://candidature.marocpme.ma.

[5] Comité national de l'environnement des affaires, http://www.cnea.ma/.

[6] For example, in "Starting a business" Morocco has moved up 53 places; in "Paying taxes" 71; and in "Getting electricity" 50.

[7] Organic Law No. 065-13 on the organisation and conduct of the work of the Government and the status of its members.

[8] These efforts have benefited from the support of the project Enhancement of the Business Environment in the Southern Mediterranean (EBESM), which has helped MED partners to implement reforms identified in the SME Policy Index 2014.

[9] The negative company name certificate can now be obtained online. Registration costs were reduced first by the replacing the 1% fee to a flat fee of MAD 1000, and since January 2018 the fee was completely eliminated. It is no longer necessary to deposit a certificate at the Labour Ministry. The use of physical company seals has been replaced through the use of the Integrated Tax System.

[10] CNEA's Action Plan was published in July 2017 and lasts 18 months.

[11] Identifiant commun de l'Entreprise, www.ice.gov.ma/ICE/.

[12] Articles 146, 164 and 198 of C.G.I.

[13] El Hourri, A. (9 November 2017), “Difficultés des entreprises: ce que prévoit le projet de réforme”, Medias24, www.medias24.com/MAROC/DROIT/178074-Difficultes-des-entreprises-ce-que-prevoit-le-projet-de-reforme.html.

[14] Experian, www.experian.co.ma/maroc/navigationfdfa.html

[15] Creditinfo Maroc, https://ma.creditinfo.com/. In 2015, Credit Info bought Experian Maroc.

[16] According to *Doing Business*, the depth of credit information system measures rules and practices affecting the coverage, scope and accessibility of credit information available through either a public credit registry or a private credit bureau.

[17] Ministry of Economy and Finance, “Note de presentation du projet de loi portant réforme du droit des sûretés mobilières”, www.sgg.gov.ma/portals/0/AvantProjet/122/Avp_loi_18.15_Fr.pdf.

[18] The World Bank Enterprise Surveys (2013), “Morocco”, www.enterprisesurveys.org/data/exploreeconomies/2013/morocco#finance.

[19] Auto-entrepreneur, http://ae.gov.ma/qui-est-l-auto-entrepreneur/.

[20] Ministry of Economy and Finance, “Note de presentation du projet décret relative aux avances en matière de marchés publics”, http://www.sgg.gov.ma/Portals/0/lois/Projet_decret_2.14.272_Fr.pdf.

[22] Decree n°1675-15 du 30 rejeb 1436

[23] A youth-centered non-profit organisation established in Jordan in 1999 active in the European Union and worldwide, including in the Middle East, North-Africa and Pakistan.

Chapter 12. Palestinian Authority

The foundations of SME policy: definitions, statistics and institutions

The Palestinian Authority (PA)[1] has yet to put into place a full-fledged SME and entrepreneurship policy. PA has an official **SME definition** introduced by the Ministry of National Economy and approved by the cabinet in 2011 (see Table 12.1). However, the definition is not consistently used between different policy actors. The definition was already reported in the SME Policy Index 2014 and has not changed; although there are reports that the Ministry of National Economy, the Palestinian Investment Promotion Agency (PIPA), the Palestinian Monetary Authority (PMA), the Prime Minister Office, the Palestinian Central Bureau of Statistics, the banking association and private sector organisations are working on updating and adopting a definition accepted by all relevant parties.

Table 12.1. SME definition by the Cabinet

Criterion	Micro	Small	Medium
Employment criterion	1-4 employees	5-9 employees	10-19 employees
Financial criterion	Annual turnover ≤ USD 20 000	Annual turnover ≤ USD 200 000	Annual turnover ≤ USD 500 000
	Paid-up capital ≤ USD 5 000	Paid-up capital ≤ USD 50 000	Paid-up capital ≤ USD 100 000

Source: SME Definition by the Palestinian Authority.

PA has official sources of **enterprise statistics** from the Palestinian Central Bureau of Statistics; however, the data published is not broken down by size class.[2] PA is not covered by the *Enterprise Surveys* of the World Bank, which makes data availability scarce, except for the coverage by the *Global Entrepreneurship Monitor* (*GEM*).

The **wider economic development agenda** in PA is characterised by a difficult and volatile context, especially given regular instability, fragmented markets and high dependence on donor support. Following the 1993 Oslo Agreement, PA has direct and exclusive competence over a number of areas related to the broad business environment and enterprise development agenda, including SME policy, business regulations, access to finance, innovation, entrepreneurship education and training. But it has limits regarding trade, territorial development and other civilian functions.

The development agenda is framed by a number of policy documents such as the *National Policy Agenda 2017-2022*, which includes a series of priorities and objectives in terms of creating job opportunities, improving the business environment and promoting the Palestinian industry.[3] However, there are no **formal co-ordination mechanisms** and there is no SME strategy yet developed, although there have been recent discussions on this issue by the Ministry of National Economy and the Palestinian Federation of Industries. The Ministry of National Economy continues to be the main authority in charge of private sector development and the improvement of the business environment, although most enterprise support activities continue to be financed by donors and managed at the local level by business associations and non-governmental organisations (NGOs). Other important agencies with an economic portfolio are the PIPA, the Palestinian Industrial and Free Zone Authority, and the Metrology Institute.

Public-private dialogue (PPD) continues to be strong in PA. The main forum for public-private consultation cited by the SME Policy Index 2014 was the Private Sector Co-ordination Council which held regular consultations, although, the report noted, SMEs were often sidelined as SME associations did not play a significant role. This interim assessment's findings suggest that the Private Sector Co-ordination Council still operates and has expanded its membership, although it does not meet regularly with the public sector anymore.

There are other instances through which PPD takes place. For instance, the Palestinian Export Council (led by Ministry of National Economy) was created to implement the National Export Strategy and works as a PPD advisory council with the private sector. The Ministry of National Economy is also implementing a Clusters Development Project to promote five business agglomerations. This builds on a strong mechanism for public-private dialogue representing hundreds of SMEs (leather and shoe, palm and dates, stone and marble, tourism and furniture).

For further action: PA is still at the very early stages of developing a multidimensional, multipartite SME policy. Important elements such as an official SME definition and sufficient SME statistics are still missing. There is also a need to establish a multiannual SME strategy and an implementation unit. So far PA is the only MED economy lacking an SME agency, unit or department. Indeed, the strong culture of public-private dialogue in PA and the active role played by business associations in policy making could provide fertile ground for the strengthening of SME policy making.

Improving business environments for SMEs and entrepreneurs

The SME Policy Index 2014 reported that the introduction of **regulatory reform and simplification** was at a very early stage. PA had completed a first draft of a manual for primary and secondary legislation, and a Core Technical Team from public and private organisations was working on administrative simplification focusing on the areas covered by *Doing Business*. The technical team was being co-ordinated by the Ministry of National Economy.

This interim assessment finds no clear evidence on the continuation of the Core Technical Team although there have been some reforms registered by *Doing Business*, notably on getting credit, in which PA ranks a remarkably high 20th (see section on access to finance). Nonetheless, the implementation of regulatory impact analysis (RIA) and the SME test is not in practice.

In terms of the **operational environment for enterprise creation**, the SME Policy Index 2014 reported that the company registration process in PA was complex and lengthy. Reforms had helped simplify the process and reduce costs but there was still much room for improvement. PIPA was in the process of fully implementing a one-stop shop and there were ongoing projects to simplify registration processes and increase decentralisation, however, the absence of adequate infrastructure hindered the development of e-registration services.

According to *Doing Business,* the only reform over the past few years in terms of starting a business is the elimination of the paid-in minimum capital requirement (2014).[4] However, the multiple responses by private sector and incubators representatives to the consultations for this interim assessment noted that there is much to do to improve the registration process. For example, it is perceived that although minimum capital requirements have been supressed, there is still need to pass through a lawyer for registration. This cost is perceived as high. According to the consultations, this requirement has been removed in the latest draft of the Companies Law.

The consultations did not lead to a consensus on how well the one-stop shops work; some stakeholders consulted indicated that PIPA's One Stop Shop concerns itself mainly with approval of investment projects and investment promotion. Others noted that one of the services provided is addressing obstacles facing the registration of a business of any kind.

In terms of **bankruptcy procedures**, the SME Policy Index 2014 noted that the framework was based on two laws: the Jordanian Commercial Law Number 12 of 1966, valid in the West Bank, and the British Mandate Bankruptcy Ordinance Number 3 of 1936, valid in the Gaza Strip. A draft new debt resolution (bankruptcy) law was under review. There has been no concrete progress on this area, although a Companies Law that is under discussion in cabinet will have clauses addressing bankruptcy.

For further action: PA continues to have an important margin of action for the improvement of the regulatory environment for SMEs and entrepreneurs. None of the policy elements analysed in this area by this interim assessment is under development (i.e. introduction of regulatory impact analysis and SME test; single identification numbers; online registration; and one-stop shops for enterprise creation). Furthermore, according to *Doing Business*, PA is a "no practice economy" in terms of bankruptcy. In this view, PA could prioritise and sequence important actions such as the passing of the Companies Law, the elimination of unnecessary or redundant regulations, and the easing of procedures to start a business. Such actions could be undertaken following the importance and feasibility determined by public and private actors and considering the specific circumstances of the wider economic, social and political context; for example, the establishment of effective one-stop shops may have a greater impact than the introduction of online registration, but they may also be more costly and difficult to implement.

Fostering access to finance

PA continues to perform higher than the regional average in terms of the **legal and regulatory framework** for access to finance. The SME Policy Index 2014 noted that the Palestine Monetary Authority (PMA) had established one of the most effective credit registries in the region, involving all banks and other financial institutions, such as microfinance institutions. By law, individuals and firms could access their credit data. But the coverage of the bureau at the time was only 8.8% of the adult population. This coverage has expanded in recent years to 19%, which is slightly higher than the OECD average of 18.3%. Furthermore, according to *Doing Business* the credit registry began to distribute credit data from retailers and utility companies, increasing the wealth of information and therefore providing more complete reports.

Important progress has also been made through the introduction in June 2017 of an online collateral registry for moveable assets hosted by the Ministry of Economy. According to *Doing Business*, the collateral registry is operational, unified geographically, searchable by a debtor's unique identifier, modern, and notice-based. According to the consultations for this interim assessment, the difficulties of land registration and hence of having an operational cadastre or register of immoveable assets have worked as a drive for the establishment of the collateral registry for moveable assets.

In addition, a Secured Transactions Law was issued by the end of 2016 with the support of the World Bank. According to *Doing Business*, the new law implements a functional secured transactions system by allowing a general description of single categories of assets and a general description of debts and obligations. The new law gives priority to secured creditors outside insolvency procedures and allows out-of-court enforcement, hence addressing indirectly some of the shortcomings of the bankruptcy system.

The creation of the registry of moveable assets and the passing of the Secured Transactions Law contributed to a remarkable ascent of PA in *Doing Business* to 20th place, by far the highest among MED economies and the OECD average. It also placed PA at a distance to frontier of 80, also much higher than the regional and the OECD average.[5]

In terms of access to **sources of finance**, the SME Policy Index 2014 noted the existence of two credit guarantee schemes: the European-Palestinian Credit Guarantee Fund (EPCGF, supported by the European Union and KfW) and the Loan Guarantee Facility (supported by the Overseas Private Investment Corporation) which guaranteed about 60-70% of loans. It also noted the existence of several equity/venture capital funds operating and focusing on SMEs and start- ups.

This interim assessment finds that the EPCGF and the Loan Guarantee Facility continue to operate and that two new vehicles have entered the market: the Swedish International Development Cooperation Agency (SIDA) Guarantee Scheme Facility, launched in 2015 and managed by the Loan Guarantee Facility; and the Middle East Investment Initiative, focusing on SMEs and housing loans. New venture capital funds also have also been established since 2014. However, there are no facts and figures on the reach and effectiveness of these measures.

For further action: PA has made great strides on the legal and regulatory framework for access to finance and has introduced new financing sources. However, the specific impact on the financing of SMEs and entrepreneurs is unknown. An in-depth analysis of the financing conditions and the impact of ongoing measures would therefore be helpful to identify policy gaps and strengths. It could also be useful to know the financing conditions and access for different profiles of SMEs and entrepreneurs.

Nurturing start-ups and SME growth

PA continues to have a diversified market for **business development services** (BDS) provided by a network of public, private and donor-funded institutions. Some of the support services aim at a better economic inclusion of women and youth while other target activities such as export and information technology. Furthermore, 22 business incubators support new firms mostly in the area of information technology and also because of the lack of government control over trade policy. Yet, access to information on business development services is dispersed. The creation of an SME unit or agency under the Ministry of National Economy could help to facilitate access to information on the multitude of business development services and providers available.

In terms of **public procurement**, the SME Policy Index 2014 noted that there were measures to facilitate the access of SMEs to this important market. These measures included the possibility to split tenders into lots and the publication of free information on procurement opportunities online and in newspapers. E-procurement was not available though and penalties on late payments were reflected in the law but not enforced in practice.

This interim assessment notes nominal progress in this area through the approval of a Procurement Law of 2014, developed with the support of the World Bank. According to the consultations for this interim assessment, the Law is open and transparent and has a website with information (although no information was found whatsoever on this claim). There is no evidence of how this new law can benefit or has benefited SMEs.

Concerning **SME internationalisation**, the SME Policy Index 2014 noted an important number of initiatives from different actors, including the development of an export strategy to make the most from economic co-operation agreements (e.g. with the EU, United States, Canada, Turkey, Greater Arab Free Trade Agreement, Russia and Mercosur), the establishment of a specialised council to implement the strategy and specific support measures for enterprises. On the latter, one of the main actors was the private sector organisation as secretariat for named council, a public-private initiative to support international trade.

This interim assessment points to continued progress in this area, including the adoption of the National Export Strategy and the establishment of the Export Council composed of 26 members from the public and private sectors, as well as academia, and headed by the minister of National Economy. However, as it is the case of other policy areas, there is no evidence on the impact of these initiatives on the access of SMEs to international trade.

For further action: On paper there has been progress in terms of nurturing start-ups and SME growth in PA. Key initiatives are the introduction of new business development services, the adoption of the new Procurement Law and the establishment of the Export Council in charge of implementing the export strategy. However, there is no evidence on specific results of how this has helped SMEs.

Investing in entrepreneurial human capital

PA has committed to promote **entrepreneurship learning in upper secondary education** through the 2014-2019 Education Development Strategic Plan. There are plans to develop pupil-centred learning, curriculum modernisation and teacher training with more developed linkages between vocational education, training and businesses. The Ministry of Education has introduced entrepreneurship studies within secondary education but entrepreneurship as a key competence remains is not well understood. Nonetheless, aspects of entrepreneurship key competence are promoted by way of non-formal learning. For example, INJAZ Palestine[6] provides support to schools that includes aspects of entrepreneurship key competence e.g. financial literacy, leadership and critical thinking. Further, the Start-up Boot Camp efforts to build entrepreneurship understanding amongst young people through cooperation with schools is good practice and ensuring schools are connected into the wider entrepreneurship eco-system.

Future donor-supported initiatives to upgrade technical and vocational education and training (TVET) should include entrepreneurship key competence in addition to promoting business skills. Expertise and experience from non-governmental organisations working on labour market preparation and employability programmes, such as the Palestinian Education for Employment Initiative, are a good reference for improving TVET entrepreneurship capacity.

Important to next phase developments will be to ensure that all students have the opportunity to acquire entrepreneurial experience. This could build on the wider vocational in-company apprenticeships developed at TVET schools but include more business administration skills.

The policy environment supporting **women's entrepreneurship** is underdeveloped. However the National Policy Agenda 2017-2022 (NPA) and a multi-stakeholder task force on women's entrepreneurship led by the Business Women's Forum (BWF) both provide basis to carry forward the policy dialogue. Policy efforts to empower women economically should look both at women's entrepreneurship and the integration of women into the labour market. This will require interfacing core employment, economic and entrepreneurship policies to ensure mutual reinforcement. Similarly, access to finance and training should be combined as a package for women entrepreneurs, such as in the "Start-up Palestine" initiative.

Some successful initiatives can be replicated and scaled-up to provide additional training for women entrepreneurs. The "buddy" mentoring facility of the Bank of Palestine, which helps women grow their businesses, could be extended to early-phase start-ups. The Bank's online training offered to women entrepreneurs to address mobility constraints between Gaza and West Bank underlines how available technologies can be used to extend training opportunities.

Data on women entrepreneurship is weak and undermines policymaking and prioritising support. With tight public finances, ensuring that training for women's entrepreneurship, defined with an action plan, is addressed by the national budget may be difficult but options to combine national and donor finance could be considered to reinforce commitment and sustainability of action lines.

Regarding **training for SME internationalisation**, a national export strategy gives specific attention to the importance of occupational and management skills within SMEs. Similarly, sector-specific export strategies underline skills weaknesses as a constraint in building SME export potential, and include an action plan to bring forward skills development in these sectors.

The education-enterprise nexus, particularly in terms of skills to support businesses in the export drive, needs to be more strategically developed to meet standards along the manufacturing value chain. Owners and managers require more developed know-how in quality assurance, planning and management of the complete export cycle. In this regard, the co-operation between the Palestinian Shippers' Council and Birzeit University stands out for its export management training. A next step could be to upgrade this course for online learning purposes.

Across all sectors, it will be important to determine how low-value added production, particularly in manufacturing, can evolve towards higher value-added. This is important in developing innovation base to the economy, allowing access to new markets and generating new and higher-skilled jobs.

A cluster-based approach to training SME owners/managers on export management by the Federation of Palestinian Chambers, Industry and Agriculture is good practice. Training is available in a number of areas (e.g. export market mapping, e-commerce) and for a range of sectors. A new training in 2018 is focusing on quality assurance in the leather and shoe and furniture clusters, considered critical to export promotion. While the cluster members have access to training materials online, a next step could be to provide the online modules beyond geographical coverage of existing clusters.

Sector-skills partnerships involving vocational (secondary and higher) education as well as other training organisations, industry associations, chambers and national authorities (e.g. PALTRADE) could be considered to close the education-business gap. Alternatively, the skills development agenda could be integrated within the sector-specific strategies (e.g. the stone and marble sector). Sector skills partnerships or consortia could additionally build and share intelligence on available trainings. To ensure that the skills dimension of SME internationalisation is given strategic attention, sector skills strategies should be monitored by the National Export Council.

For future action: It is necessary to promote a better understanding of entrepreneurship as a key competence through awareness-raising measures and capacity building. Women's entrepreneurship can be supported by scaling up successful local initiatives, but developing accurate data will be necessary for evidence-based policy making. With good skills coverage in sector strategies, the vocational training community including universities must be engaged to accommodate the demands of businesses in sectors with export potential.

The way forward

This interim assessment notes continued improvement of SME policies in PA, particularly the significant reforms in terms of the legal and regulatory framework for access to finance. However, PA is still lagging behind the rest of the region in terms of laying down the building blocks for SME policy, notably the development of an SME strategy and the designation of an official SME body (SME unit or SME agency) in charge of co-ordinating the many initiatives already in place. In terms of the particular policy areas analysed in this chapter, key actions that could be taken are as follows:

- Building on the strong practice of public-private dialogue and, with the support of international partners, improving SME policy co-ordination by implementing a multi-year strategy.
- Significantly stepping up efforts to improve the business environment, including 1) by introducing an insolvency framework, a regulatory impact analysis and SME test mechanism and 2) by facilitating enterprise creation.
- Better tracking of the impact of specific measures on SME and entrepreneurship performance. For example, to what extent have access-to-finance reforms resulted in SME creation and growth? What has been the impact of the export strategy in SME internationalisation? What are the results of the many business development services available? The implementation of an SME strategy and the related monitoring and evaluation mechanism could be fundamental in this regard.
- Raise awareness and understanding of entrepreneurship as a key competence across the education and training community with strategic piloting as a basis for further developments.
- Develop data on women's entrepreneurship to ensure better focus within policy.
- Afford higher recognition of skills to economic development by operationalising the human capital dimensions of sector export strategies.

Notes

[1] For the OECD, "PA" is an abbreviation of Palestinian Authority and defines either the territories in the West Bank and Gaza under the administration of the Palestinian Authority, or the Palestinian Authority itself, according to the context. For the European Commission and the EU institutions contributing to the report, PA stands for Palestine and its institutions. This designation shall not be construed as recognition of a State of Palestine and is without prejudice to the individual positions of the EU Member States on this issue.

[2] See Preliminary Results of the Population, Housing and Establishment Census, 2017. www.pcbs.gov.ps/Downloads/book2364-1.pdf.

[3] State of Palestine (2016), *National Policy Agenda 2017-2022: Putting Citizens First*, https://eeas.europa.eu/sites/eeas/files/npa_english_final_approved_20_2_2017_printed.pdf.

[4] The World Bank Group Doing Business (2018), "Business Reforms in West Bank and Gaza", www.doingbusiness.org/Reforms/Overview/Economy/west-bank-and-gaza.

[5] An economy's distance to frontier is reflected on a scale from 0 to 100, where 0 represents the lowest performance and 100 represents the frontier. The distance to frontier score helps to assess the absolute level of regulatory performance over time. It measures the distance of each economy to the "frontier", which represents the best performance observed on each of the indicators across all economies in the *Doing Business* sample since 2005.

[6] A youth-centred non-profit organisation established in Jordan in 1999 active in the European Union and worldwide, including in the Middle East, North-Africa and Pakistan.

Chapter 13. Tunisia

The foundations of SME policy: definitions, statistics and institutions

Important progress and reforms have been achieved over the past few years in terms of the overall economic agenda. However, in terms of SME and entrepreneurship policy Tunisia is still putting in place the initial building blocks. First, since 2016 there is a new **SME definition** in the context of the new Investment Law; however, this definition is mainly based on financial criteria (an SME has to have total assets of less than TND 15 million, or roughly EUR 5 million), with no distinction made between micro, small and medium-sized firms (see Table 13.1). Furthermore, although the definition is used by the Agency for the Promotion of Industry and Innovation (APII – one of the institutions in charge of enterprise policy) to delimit its field of action, there are other definitions used by several other actors, such as the SME bank (BFPME) and the statistics office (INS).

Table 13.1. SME definition by the National Statistics Institute and the Investment Law

Type of enterprise	Employees	Total assets
Micro	< 6 employees	Paid-up capital
Small	< 49 employees	< TND 15 m
Medium	< 199 employees	(< EUR 5m)

Source: National Statistics Institute and Investment Law.

The National Statistics Institute publishes an annual report on **SME statistics** from the National Enterprise Repertory using a definition based on the number of employees.[1] The repertory is one of the most complete sources of information in the region with structural, demographic and business dynamics (firm entry and exit) indicators. According to the consultations, the Ministry of Industry is working to establish an SME Observatory in order to produce official statistics on SMEs.

The wider **economic policy framework** in Tunisia is given by the National Development Plan 2016-2020,[2] which targets a growth rate of 4% per year, a reduction in the poverty rate to 2% of the total population, the creation of 400 000 jobs, a reduction in informality to 20% of the economy, and reduction in unemployment to 12%. The plan expects to meet these objectives through the development of human capital and the improvement of infrastructure that better connects the inner regions. As noted before, the government also adopted a new Investment Law in 2016 that is designed to attract investment by increasing both freedom to invest and protection of investors.[3]

In terms of the **institutional SME policy framework**, as in 2014, co-ordination and implementation of SME support continue to be fragmented. The Ministry of Industry is the main authority responsible for SME and entrepreneurship promotion, notably through the General Directorate for SMEs (DGPME) and the Agency for the Promotion of Industry and Innovation (APII). As noted before, a new Investment Law was approved in September 2016 and includes some provisions affecting SMEs. Despite the fact that the

Investment Law has created a specific governance structure for the investment regime, it is not a specific instrument or strategy for SME development. From the information gathered in Tunisia, there is an unresolved issue with SME co-ordination. Each Ministry or institution has some mandate to work with SMEs, typically by sector. For example, the Ministry of Agriculture supports SMEs in the agribusiness sector, the APII focuses on the industrial sector, etc. Nonetheless, there is no strong co-ordination mechanism.

In terms of mechanisms to monitor and evaluate SME policies, the APII has launched a first version of a "barometer" to measure the impact of public policies and reforms according to the perception of SMEs. This work was conducted with SMEs in the industrial and industry-related sectors.

Public-private dialogue (PPD), on the other hand, has continued to be strong. This has built on the complex process of political and economic transition and dialogue among numerous actors over the past few years. This has also been reflected in important economic reforms such as the adoption of the new Investment Law. Concerning the specific case of enterprise development policy, in 2014 the National Business Agenda (NBA) was established in order to create a public-private dialogue platform to advance reforms that improve the business climate. The NBA includes the government, the Tunisian Union of Industry, Commerce and Crafts (UTICA), the Tunisian Union of Agriculture and Fisheries (UTAP) and the Arab Institute of Business Leaders (IACE). Additionally, the Regional Business Agenda was developed as a second phase to the NBA to assess challenges and obstacles at the regional level. This represents an important progress in the implementation of the reforms identified by the SME Policy Index in 2014.

For further action: As recommended by the SME Policy Index 2014, Tunisia could start putting into place a more coherent SME and entrepreneurship policy by developing and implementing a multi-annual SME strategy. Such a strategy could define the specific mechanism of co-ordination among the many actors involved in SME support. The strategy could also help to better target the different types and needs of SMEs (subsistence, low productivity or opportunity, high potential driven; micro, small or medium; in the services, manufacturing or agriculture sector, etc.). The SME strategy should also consider and be an integral part towards the achievements of the goals of the wider policy framework. The strategy could also build on the NBA and could serve to frame a formal SME public-private dialogue platform. Tunisia could also set up an effective SME agency which could be in charge of policy co-ordination and of monitoring and evaluating the impact of policies on the health of enterprises and to adapt policies to the needs of SMEs. The establishment of an SME strategy would also provide an important basis for a comprehensive monitoring and evaluation system of SME support.

Improving business environments for SMEs and entrepreneurs

The improvement of the **regulatory framework and administrative simplification** for businesses is under the responsibility of the General Directorate for Reform and Administrative Outlook (DGRA), within the Office of the Head of Government. A decree to implement regulatory impact analysis (RIA) through a regulatory guillotine exists since 2014 and the DGRA was then working on a pilot project for a strategy on regulatory reform. The DGRA had done an inventory of more than 1 000 business laws and regulations to establish afterwards the regulatory guillotine.

Since then, Tunisia has registered much progress in this area. According to DGRA the strategy was developed through a consultative process between the government (seven ministries), professional organisations and business and regional organisations. As a result, seven procedures were supressed, 147 simplified and 86 kept. The exercise was then extended to five other ministries (decree of September 2014). Furthermore, the Regulatory Guillotine project was accompanied by capacity building activities including trainings and awareness campaigns both at the national and local level. Several workshops were organised for government officials and regulators at the beginning of the project, as well as at the end to disseminate the results. Workshops were organised in three different regions (Tunis, Sousse, and Sfax) in order to raise awareness among regional government officials about the importance of the project and the simplification process.

One of the initiatives that have seen the light thanks to the NBA is a new hotline called "SOS Ijraat", created in 2016 to provide information on administrative procedures to companies which are encountering administrative obstacles. Through this hotline, businesses should be able to flag problems to the administration, and a mechanism to address it should be activated.

In terms of the **operational environment for enterprise creation**, the SME Policy Index 2014 noted that company registration was one of the most efficient in the region. The country had a single identification number for three administrations related to the Ministry of Finance; there were no minimum capital requirements for start-ups; it had a network of one-stop shops in 19 regions; and an online registration system but it only covered Tunis and was specific to declaration of investment projects.

More recently, a draft Start-up Act has been introduced (2018), focusing mostly on innovative start-ups (part of the wider strategy Digital Tunisia 2020). The Start-Up Act aims to simplify administrative procedures, but also to facilitate access to finance and international businesses.[4] The Act envisages the creation of a single point of contact for entrepreneurs to obtain information and conduct the required formalities for registration and operation.

In terms of **bankruptcy procedures**, a Collective Insolvency Proceedings Act (*loi 2016-36 du 29 avril 2016 relative aux procédures collectives*) was enacted in April 2016. The views on the effects of the Act, according to the consultations for this interim assessment, are contrasting. For example, some see it as more concerned with the liquidation of companies than their restructuring for an eventual redressing. Others pointed to its positive aspects such as alert systems for auditors of enterprises that could be in difficulty; or new rules of conduct to be observed by the courts and judicial experts, and the various partners of the company during the phase of amicable settlement, judicial settlement and eventually, bankruptcy.

For further action: The RIA mechanism could be strengthened to integrate not only a regulatory guillotine (inventory of existing regulations) but also a forward-looking system to assess the merit and effectiveness of new business regulations *vis-à-vis* other forms of intervention. An SME test could be implemented to look particularly at regulations and administrative requirements that can disproportionately impact SMEs. The National Business Agenda could become a powerful platform to drive the reform agenda in this field.

Fostering access to finance

Tunisia has registered progress in terms of the **legal and regulatory environment** for access to finance. Credit information mechanisms have improved in recent years and a number of legal reforms are ongoing. First, the credit registry improved its services making historical information available for individuals, while before it was limited to enterprises. The credit registry now covers almost 27% of adult population, which is higher than the OECD average of 18%.

Furthermore, a credit registry for microfinance (CRM) was also created in 2016 to facilitate credit assessments. Through this mechanism, microfinance institutions are expected to extend their credit operations, reduce losses and reinforce their institutional stability. There are no figures on the impact that this has had on the microfinance sector, although the number of users had increased from 280 in March 2016 to 478 by the end of that year.

Second, a new law on (private) credit bureaus has been developed by the government and presented to the National Assembly.[5] The law seeks to establish a legal framework to, among other things, authorise the sharing of negative and positive information on credit; establish the rights and obligations of all parties involved (credit bureau, users, consumers, etc.); and protect the right of users and enterprises to confidentiality in their information. It is expected that the approval of the law will pave the way for the establishment of the first (private) credit bureau in Tunisia: Mitigan Credit & Insurance Bureau (Mitigan CIB).

Additionally, a reform on the registry of moveable assets is ongoing in order to extend the array of assets that can be pledged as collateral, to allow the non-possessory security over moveable assets and rights, and to establish a general registry of moveable assets. The aim is to inform creditors of any pledges for a given asset, and to determine the beneficiaries of a right over a given asset. No information has been provided in terms of the expected results of the reform and when it would enter into force. There is no information on the improvement of registries of immovable assets (cadastres).

An administrative instruction has also been published by the Central Bank establishing the rules for the development of a credit rating scheme by financial institutions.[6]

In order to facilitate access to capital markets for SMEs, the Tunisian authorities launched a project in 2016 to overhaul regulations on private equity activities and approve a single code, the Collective Investment Code. The draft code is under review at the National Assembly. Other initiatives have been launched between 2016 and 2017 to facilitate access to finance for SMEs. The APII has launched an initiative to introduce crowdfunding by engaging public and private actors involved in SME financing. A bill on crowdfunding in Tunisia was finalised in February 2018 and is awaiting approval.[7] On the other hand, the Start-Up Act (new Law n ° 2018-20 of 17/04/2018) aims to create a Guarantee Fund for Start-ups and other funding sources were launched between 2016 and 2017 to facilitate access to finance for SMEs.

Finally, a draft code for collective investment bodies has been developed to improve the regulatory framework for venture capital and promote these sources of funding (this draft code is currently being examined by the parliament.

Concerning the availability of **sources of finance**, the SME Policy Index 2014 noted that the main actors in this area were public agencies such as the SME Bank (BFPME) for credit, the Guarantee Company (SOTUGAR) for credit guarantees, and the Solidarity Bank (BTS) for microcredit. Other public funds are still dedicated to strengthening the financial base of SMEs, such as the Industrial Promotion and Decentralisation Fund (FOPRODI), which is managed by APII. Under the new Investment Law, this Fund will be incorporated into a single fund called the Tunisian Investment Fund (FTI).

For this interim assessment there is no evidence of an increased role of the private sector in the provision of finance. What is more, the BFMPE has created new funds in co-operation with different international programmes and other ministries.[8] Nonetheless, the full implementation of the laws, reforms and administrative instructions mentioned above should provide a better environment for a greater participation of private actors in the provision of access to finance.

Tunisian authorities are developing a new programme, *Investir PME*, that aims to facilitate the introduction of SMEs to alternative markets through the stock market. As the cost of entering this market is normally high for SMEs, the new programme will focus on reducing entry barriers and helping SMEs diversify their sources of financing.

Finally, several websites have been created to provide information on financial support programmes for SMEs.[9] Nevertheless, they are limited to listing the different institutions that provide financing, so the information could be better organised to guide SMEs towards the adequate instruments for their needs.

For further action: Tunisia is undertaking a large number of initiatives to strengthen access to finance for SMEs, but most of the legal reforms are still pending final approval. Hence, a first priority would be for the government to pass and implement these reforms. The SME Policy Index 2014 also noted the need to create incentives for the expansion of the provision of finance by private sector actors. Many of the pending reforms and laws also point in that direction; nonetheless, to date there is not much evidence of an increased role of private sector providers over the past few years.

Nurturing entrepreneurship and SME growth

The provision of **business development services** (BDS) seems to continue increasing. The network of business centres and incubators in Tunisia has been expanding over the past few years.[10] The APII manages the Business Incubators Network, providing services in the 24 governorates. The Ministry of Industry manages the Business Centres regional network which is developing non-financial services in collaboration with financial institutions. The bank BIAT launched an incubator, B@labs, offering 4 to 16 months services for innovative start-ups.[11] International accelerators like Founder Institute,[12] Flat6Labs[13] and Boost have also opened offices in Tunisia, offering training and mentoring services.

Several websites provide information regarding existing entrepreneurship support and BDS facilities. For example, the platform *Wajjahni* was created to provide information to entrepreneurs while the Foundation BIAT has developed an interactive map to locate support services across the country.[14] Furthermore, each institution involved in SME support has its website with relevant information, but there is no single platform.

Several initiatives have been implemented in the last few years to encourage women's entrepreneurship. A National Plan for Women Entrepreneurship, called RAÏDA, was adopted in 2017 by the Ministry of Women of the Family and Children. The company HP, in partnership with the United Nations Industrial Development Organisation (UNIDO) and with the APII set up an Entrepreneurship Training and Support programme called "HP-LIFE" to support students, aspiring and established entrepreneurs to acquire ICT skills.[15] The *Ligue des Femmes d'Entreprises* was created to guide women entrepreneurs developing small projects, including in rural areas.

The regulations on **public procurement** provide for the obligation to set aside a percentage for small businesses[16] of up to 20% of the estimated amount of works, goods and services contracts and studies.[17] If it is impossible to reserve these contracts within the limit of the aforementioned percentage, the public purchaser must indicate the reasons in a report which is transmitted to the relevant Contracts Control Commission (in accordance with Article 169 of Decree 1039-2014) and which expresses its opinion on the reasons mentioned.

Information concerning annual purchase forecasts, texts governing public procurement, tender notices and results of calls for tenders are centralised and accessible to registered public purchasers and potential bidders. TUNEPS and the National Observatory of Public Procurement are two commissions that are part of the higher commission of control and audit of public contracts, which was created in the framework of establishing a system of good governance of public procurement.

Tunisia is one of the few economies in the region where procuring agencies have to pay interest in overdue payments to the contract holder in the event of delays on down payments or the payment of a balance. Bidders are not required to register on a government registry of suppliers and there is a legal period of minimum 30 days for bids submission from the date on which the contract notice was published. However, some cost-related aspects can be a barrier for SMEs facing resource constraints. For example, tender documents are not always accessible for free, and the cost is subject to the discretion of the procuring entity. Also, bidders are required to pay a provisional guarantee,[18] for which the public purchaser fixes the amount by applying a percentage between 0.5 % and 1.5 % of the estimated amount of orders by the contract. This sum is returned to the participants in the market whose offers are eliminated after publication of the results. The sum is replaced by a performance bond paid only by the contract holder after notification and signature of the contract (which will be returned after execution of the contract).

Decree 1039-2014 also includes specific provisions for e-procurement through TUNEPS, a platform that manages the online public purchasing system (in the context of markets or for off-market acquisitions). There are also training sessions for SMEs to use the platform and there is a practical guide for SME participation in procurement. UTICA, TUNEPS and public institutions provide training courses to familiarise SMEs on public procurement procedures to SMEs to facilitate their access to public procurement contracts. A decree of 2018 provides for the obligation to issue the public order only via TUNEPS as of 1 September 2018.[19]

Concerning the **internationalisation of SMEs**, in order to support SMEs linkages with foreign firms participating in global supply chains, the government and the European Bank for Reconstruction and Development (EBRD) signed a loan agreement for USD 50 million to increase and diversify SME exports. Several funds have been created, including the fund "Primo-Export" which has accompanied 30 newly created SMEs over the last two years to export their products and activities. The World Bank launched a series of projects to support global value chains.

Several reforms and initiatives have been undertaken to expand export services. In 2016, the APII launched a project in collaboration with five other institutions, including business associations to facilitate the internationalisation of enterprises in the technology sector through better access to market data. The APII has participated in several international conferences and events in order to connect Tunisian enterprises to international markets. Tunisia joined the Enterprise Europe Network (EEN) in 2016 through the creation of a Consortium "EEN Tunisia" formed of five national organisations: the APII as co-ordinator of the consortium, the Centre for the Promotion of Exports (CEPEX), the Chamber of Commerce and Industry of Tunis (CCI of Tunis), Technopark Elgazala and the Confederation of Tunisian Citizen Enterprises (CONECT).

The APII, through the services and activities of the EEN network, offers services to companies such as the identification of business partners, participation in business-to-business meetings, and dissemination of information on European legislation.

For further action: Tunisia has a very well-developed market of BDS from private and public actors. The establishment of a comprehensive information system to disseminate information among targeted enterprises could increase the coherence of all these efforts. This could take the form of a wider initiative such as the establishment of an SME Observatory (a useful tool for the dissemination of statistics, studies and SME information) along the lines of those being developed in many other economies. The information could also include the many initiatives being undertaken to promote SME internationalisation and participation in global value chains.

Investing in entrepreneurial human capital

Tunisia already had in the previous assessment a clear policy framework to promote **entrepreneurial learning in upper secondary education**, as reflected in Law 10/2008 on Vocational Training. Since then, the government has produced a new Charter to promote an entrepreneurial spirit, and a National Strategy on Entrepreneurship. In 2016, the Ministry of Vocational Training and Employment appointed a State Secretary for Entrepreneurship, reflecting the political commitment to this topic.

Several initiatives have recently been developed in co-operation between training centres and companies. Most of them rely on external support, such as the European Training Foundation (ETF, promotion of entrepreneurship as a key competence) and INJAZ[20] (simulation of the creation of companies "CP Company Program" and "EMC Entrepreneurship Master Class"). The new "soft skills" project (adaptability, sense of efficiency, creativity, collective work, initiative) with the Ministry of Vocational Training is an innovative approach and should be consolidated.

Tunisia has actively supported **women's entrepreneurship** in the past few years through the 2016-2020 National Programme for Women's Entrepreneurship (RAÏDA), which has provided many support initiatives focusing on start-ups and diversified geographically. These activities have taken place in the context of a dynamic social dialogue involving civil society, international donors and the government.

There is a rich offer of training programmes supporting women, which is well-tailored to their needs. Some examples are the training programmes delivered through the network "*Entrepreneuriat Pluri'elles*", as well as the initiatives undertaken by Women's Enterprise for Sustainability (WES) and the Tunisian Association for Management and Social Stability (TAMMS). The Center of Arab Women for Training and Research (CAWTAR) is also particularly active.

In the context of the 2016-2020 Programme to Develop Exports (PDE-3), the Skills Plan 2017-2020 recognises the importance of **training to support SME internationalisation**. Different institutions provide this type of training, such as the APII, which works with the EU EEN-Tunisie network, as well as the Center for Export Promotion (CEPEX), chambers of commerce, and other actors including UTICA. An Export Academy is planned to be created. On the other hand, there is little co-ordination between the different actors active in this field.

Tunisia has also adopted a sectorial approach, developing tailored training programmes through different channels. The project "Skills for trade and economic diversification"

(STED) is an interesting example in this regard. Other sectors that are particularly active are the textile industry, including lingerie and denim clothes, and ICT.

For future action: It is recommended that the government develops action plans for the implementation of the policy framework, which should include monitoring and evaluation mechanisms and adequate funding. These plans could be developed together with national institutions such as the "*Observatoire national de l'emploi et des qualifications*" (ONEQ). Also, it should be ensured that the training mechanism for teachers and trainers concerning the entrepreneurship as a key competence is well-structured, for which the European framework EntreComp could be a useful tool.

The government and local actors should develop better data and establish mechanisms to monitor and evaluate the implementation of initiatives that support women's entrepreneurship as well as SMEs' internationalization. Data collection initiatives could be developed together with relevant stakeholders from the private sector, such as UTICA, Co-ordination between different institutions providing training courses for SMEs to export could be improved. Also, the use of online trainings could be used to increase the offer and reach of training programmes.

The way forward

The assessment for the SME Policy Index 2014 was undertaken in a context in which Tunisia was undergoing an intense important political transition and was preparing the ground for economic changes. These changes are still ongoing and have focused on broad economic policy areas such as regaining macroeconomic stability, strengthening security and re-activating investment and economic activity. To maintain this progress, Tunisia could increase its efforts towards developing a better business environment and a more strategic SME policy. Key actions that could be taken are as follows:

- Developing and implementing a multi-annual SME strategy with institutional co-ordination and dialogue mechanisms and targeted to the different profiles and needs of SMEs and entrepreneurs.
- Adopting a full-fledged RIA mechanism and introducing the SME test.
- Encouraging and facilitating the creation of new firms through technical mechanisms (e.g. online procedures, one-stop shops, etc.) and well-designed incentives.
- Implementing reforms and initiatives for access to finance that are pending approval and assessing whether the existing financing sources are satisfying the needs of different firms and entrepreneurs.
- Better disseminating information about the myriad of BDS and the possibilities of access to public procurement opportunities for SMEs.
- Develop action plans for the implementation of the strategic policy framework to promote entrepreneurial learning, which should include monitoring and evaluation mechanisms and adequate funding.
- Develop better data and establish mechanisms to monitor and evaluate the implementation of initiatives that support women's entrepreneurship as well as SMEs' internationalisation. The private sector could lead these efforts through representative bodies such as UTICA.

- Co-ordination between different institutions providing training courses for SMEs to export could be improved.

Notes

[1] Statistiques Tunisie, www.ins.tn/en/themes/entreprises#sub-318.

[2] "Plan stratégique de développement économique 2016 -2020".

[3] Law n°71-2016 dated 30 September 2016, which entered into force on 1 January 2017.

[4] http://www.huffpostmaghreb.com/2017/04/13/startup-act-tunisie_n_15986206.html Consulted 24 Oct 2017. Also see Bouguerra, B. (25 April 2017), "Tunisia's #Startup Act catching the wave of Innovation", *Voices and Views: Middle East and North Africa Blog*, The World Bank, http://blogs.worldbank.org/arabvoices/tunisia-startup-wave-innovation.

[5] Loi sur le crédit bureau.

[6] Administrative instruction n° 2016-06.

[7] The bill has been developed in support of the Enhancement of the Business Environment in the Southern Mediterranean project. See http://www.ebesm.eu/posts/developing-a-legal-framework-for-crowdfunding-for-tunisia.

[8] For example the Swiss Fund, the Qatar Friendship Fund, Intilak Fund 2 (in co-operation with the Ministry of Development and International Cooperation), the BADER Fund (in co-operation with the Ministry of Finance), and the Corporate Social Responsibility Fund (in co-operation with the Tunisian Company of Petroleum Activities and the Company of the Phosphates of Gafsa).

[9] These include Wajjahni, http://wajjahni.com/fr/categories/financement; and Entrepreneurs of Tunisia, www.eot.tn.

[10] Agency for the Promotion of Industry and Innovation, Tunisian Industry Portal, www.tunisieindustrie.nat.tn/en/doc.asp?mcat=16&mrub=138.

[11] B@labs, www.biatlabs.com.

[12] The Founder Institute, https://fi.co/about?target=tunis.

[13] Flat6labs Tunis, www.flat6labs.com/location-offering/?l=2653#top.

[14] Wajjahni, http://wajjahni.com/fr.

[15] HP Inç, "HP Life creates hope and opportunity in Tunisia as Mashrou3i program expands", www.life-global.org/?q=node/112&language=en.

[16] Companies in activities or recently constituted and defined by paragraph 2 of article 20 of decree 1039 -2014.

[17] Article 20 of Decree 1039 -2014 in particular, which replaced Decree 3158-2002.

[18] For participation except for study contracts which do not require the payment of a provisional deposit to participate.

[19] Decree 416-2018 of 11-05-2018 amending Decree 1039-2014 on the regulation of public markets.

[20] A youth-centered non-profit organisation established in Jordan in 1999 active in the European Union and worldwide, including in the Middle East, North-Africa and Pakistan.

OECD PUBLISHING, 2, rue André-Pascal, 75775 PARIS CEDEX 16
(03 2018 21 1 P) ISBN 978-92-64-30415-4 – 2018

www.ingramcontent.com/pod-product-compliance
Ingram Content Group UK Ltd.
Pitfield, Milton Keynes, MK11 3LW, UK
UKHW051502290926
15471UKWH00008B/1374

9 789264 304154